ADVANCE PRAISE for *Badge of Color*

"In 1966 I was a hard core militant who was soon to become the leader of the Santa Ana, California branch of the Black Panther Party. During this same period Harlen Lambert became the first African American police officer in Santa Ana. Needless to say, we were not friends but enemies—nor would we become friends for many years.

Earlier this year (2019) at an event sponsored by the Heritage Museum of Orange County, Harlen and I came face-to-face for the first time in 50 years. It was there that we shook hands, hugged and expressed a new found love for each other.

It was also there that I learned details of Officer Lambert's experiences as Santa Ana's first Black police officer on its all-White police force in John Birch Orange County. This book gives us a peek into what it was like and the racism he experienced. I had no clue. Reading some of the things he endured moved my heart and gave me an even stronger love and a much higher level of respect for Harlen.

This is a history that must be read by all who have even the slightest interest in the truth of what it was like growing up Black in America—whether you were a Black Panther or the first Black man on an all –White police department. Highly recommended. This is a 10 stars read!"

DANIEL MICHAEL LYNEM, SR

Pastor and former Black Panther

"This book should come with a warning label. If you're not interested in being challenged or pondering your own courage and integrity, I highly recommend you skip Lamb Lambert's story. However, if you are ready for a powerful truth teller, then this is the book for you. Standing strong, doing the right thing, often the heroic thing, in the face of gross injustice and hate-filled stupidity was Lamb's daily bread—a meal most of us couldn't stomach once, much less daily.

Read it at your own risk."

GRETA BORIS

Author of *The Seven Deadly Sins* Series,
novels of psychological suspense

HARLEN "Lamb" LAMBERT

"This book took me on a real journey. Mr. Lambert came from humble means and a supportive family that gave him a good foundation. The era he grew up in was fraught with roadblocks, but he managed to persevere by becoming a man of incredible mental strength, resilience and courage. He was able to keep the faith while he experienced life as a black American man during the vexing times of Jim Crow and the Civil Rights movement.

Being a black man in law enforcement myself, I could not imagine the amount of restraint it took for him to endure the unlawful treatment he received. I want to whole-heartedly thank Mr. Lambert for helping to pave the way for the many black men and women in law enforcement that came after him. I hope that one day soon, the City of Santa Ana finds it in their heart to recognize his dedication to their city, in light of all that he had to endure by being the first.

I recommend this book to anyone who wants to understand what true courage, strength, and self-determination looks like while still being fascinated and entertained by Mr. Lambert's life story."

JASON O'BRIEN
Detective, Los Angeles Police Department
President, Fontana School Board

~~*~~

"As a confused teenager headed down the wrong path, I met the first African-American police officer that I ever recall seeing, Harlen 'Lamb' Lambert.

Little did I know, that police officer would have an immediate & lasting effect on my life.

Lamb's perseverance, tolerance, love, faith in man-kind and will to win, will affect every reader of this book."

MUSTAFA KHAN
Safe Community Initiative Leader;
Youth advocate and coach, SCJC Executive Development Director;
Criminology Major, Senior Investigator and Executive Protection Agent

"A wonderfully honest account…I'm certain will have a deep impact on everyone who reads it.

As someone once said: the two most important days in your life are the day you are born and the day you find out why. It seems Mr. Lambert has discovered those two most important days. I love his story and the way he told it."

JERRY SCHAFER
Author-Producer-Director, Silver Moon Pictures
North Las Vegas Deputy Constable Commander, Retired

~~*~~

"Lamb's story is very poignant, well-written, and really gives me a feel for what it was like for him growing up and taking on the challenges of being the first Black police officer in the Santa Ana Police Department, Orange County. Many will find it eye-opening as well, especially young adults in Santa Ana, and I am honored to have been able to be part of helping tell Lamb's story."

CHERYL A. EBERLY
Librarian
Santa Ana Public Library

~~*~~

"Lamb provides detailed visualization of breaking barriers and becoming the first black police officer in Orange County. Badge of Color – Breaking the Silence is a powerful story of navigating the obstacles with the utmost honor. A true man of the law."

KEVIN CABRERA
Executive Director
Heritage Museum of Orange County

~~*~~

"This book should be required reading in all universities, police academies, and even religious institutions. It teaches important history, the law, and values that are quickly disappearing from the American landscape."

SHARON SEKHON, PhD
Historian

HARLEN "Lamb" LAMBERT

"Harlen Lambert's book is a must-read. You will get acquainted with a remarkable man worth knowing.

In childhood he became an entrepreneur to earn money, informing you about how to be an excellent shoeshine boy and how he successfully sold snow cones from his wagon. He came from a large family blessed by a mother whose comforting and inspirational sayings often came to him at trying times. A fantastic basketball player, his scholarship to a Southern California college fell through.

Wanting to serve the public he became the first African American police officer for the Santa Ana, California PD, where his experiences were much like Jackie Robinson's. Subjected to abuse by the public on daily patrols and even fellow officers and supervisors, he could say nothing. But a wall in his home is crowded with commendations and awards – and two children owe their lives to him.

A fascinating book. Don't miss it."

BARBARA FRENCH

Author, *Radio Actress: Romping Through the 40s* and *Someday Street*

Ms. French teaches Creative Writing in Southern California

"Lambert's unique inside view of what goes on in a racist police precinct is a true story of his character as an officer of the law who provided protection of and for citizens amidst criticism and condemnation of himself.

A plain-spoken concise string of incidents links together giving readers a story of his life—a view little-known by the public yet blatant in its most telling forms, from headlines to hidden lines of lies and scorn. The reader will not be disappointed."

JOAN HORRIGAN

English Instructor (ret)

ISBN: 9781688074125

The following lyrics are excerpts from works in the public domain:

"Amazing Grace." John Newton, 1772
"There's a Great Camp Meeting." John W. Work, 1940
"All You Need is Love." The Beatles, 1967
"I'll Take You There." Staple Singers, 1972

Cover and Book Designers: Sharron Read-Lambert and Sharon Sekhon

Garamond is the font employed in this book.

10 9 8 7 6 5 4 3 2 1
FIRST EDITION

BADGE OF COLOR

Breaking the Silence

A Documented Memoir

Book One

Harlen "Lamb" Lambert

DEDICATION

To the memory of my Mother – Anner Day Lambert
April 1910 – July 1994

Her words of love and wisdom are forever etched in my heart:

*We're like flowers that God made in different colors. That's
why the world is so pretty! We're just like the flowers.
One day, son, all the flowers will be in one field, I promise.*

and

To all people of color who have pioneered as a "first" in
law enforcement and other protective services.

and

To my son Fernando,
who helped to plant the seeds of this book
while in the innocence of his youth.

Table of Contents

FOREWORD by Sharon Sekhon PhD

I first met Harlen Lambert in 2011 when I participated in the Raitt Street Chronicles with Cheryl Eberly and Kevin Cabrera at the Santa Ana Public Library. This summer program for kids living in the Raitt/Townsend district sought to have the teenagers document their neighborhoods alongside gathering the history of some of the elders who spent time in Santa Ana. Through this program, the young adults interviewed Gonzalo Mendez Jr and Harlen Lambert. Mendez is the son of Felicitas and Gonzalo Mendez who helped to desegregate Santa Ana schools. Harlen, as the first African American police officer to be hired in Santa Ana, Orange County, was a natural fit and perfect person for the students to interview. I was immediately taken by his accessibility, candor, and genuine love of his community.

I became reacquainted with Harlen and his wife Sharron, who is dynamo, in 2017. As I began to research his life, I learned Harlen Lambert is so much more than what this nation allows us to call him: he is a pioneer, a civil rights leader, a father, a friend, a husband, and a teacher. Knowing he and Sharron has been one of the highlights of my career as an historian. They both humble me in their commitment towards the overall good of Southern California and the United States. Moreover, the love they have for one another is a great American love story that should be documented in another book. Getting to know them better, I wanted Harlen Lambert recognized by different institutions in Orange County with a vested interest in democracy, multiculturalism, history, and the truth because of the healing his story provides our region.

Over the Spring semester of 2019, I asked Harlen Lambert to come to my Honors courses in American history at California State University, Fullerton. Lambert generously allowed my students to read an early copy of this book, and as part of the requirements of the class the students reacted to the book in a project. I know that Harlen Lambert is bigger than all of us due to their responses and how these eighteen year old and nineteen year old students recognized his achievements, courage under fire, and kindness. One of the lessons I try to impart to my college students is the importance of kindness and Harlen has it in spades and best manifested in his nickname "Lamb."

The students composed poetry, painted paintings, wrote essays, and expressed their respect for Harlen Lambert in beautiful ways that showed me the importance of his history to young people. But this is not anything new in his life. He has served as a mentor to young people throughout his career.

For example, Lamb showed me again the importance of play, competitive sports, open areas for green space, and open minded public servants in the building of a public trust. I learned that as a police officer in Santa Ana, Harlen Lambert was known to use his breaks to play basketball with local kids. Lamb served as a mentor and friend to many young people. One of those players, Mustafa Khan, recalled:

> I was in my late teens, well actually 16, when I met him. We were playing basketball at the park and this police officer gets out of his car. A black police officer, by the way, gets out of his car, comes over to the basketball court. Takes off his weapon and starts playing basketball. So we figured, he's a cop. We're gonna hurt him. This guy was better than everybody. We didn't know he was an Army All-American.

> But, I got to know Lambert, we became very close friends. We played ball a lot together, with each other, and against each other. We were always competitive. The thing that stood out to me was that he was a very good friend but if you crossed the line of the law, he was going to put you in your place.

Similarly, Jimmy Payne, one of his classmates at Southern California College in Costa Mesa, later re-named Vanguard University, remembered the joy that took over Lamb's being while playing basketball. Lamb's enthusiasm was infectious and he was an excellent athlete.

> I first met Lamb at the Southern California College gymnasium. And he had this huge, gargantuan smile. And he had these white teeth with a gap, I'll never forget the gap, and he was like so jovial. He was like a kid on Christmas morning. Talking about "shooting the rabbit," and jump off on one leg.

> He would lean back. He would fall back and he would say, "Let's go back." This was his words, "Let's go back." And he was nothing but pure net. I have never seen anybody shoot the ball so well and so effortlessly.

Like Harlen Lambert's classmates and the students in my classes at CSUF, I too wanted to articulate the ways Harlen made an influence on my life and in a manner that would be valued by Lambert and his wife.

Upon my suggestion, the University Honors Program Director Dr. Sandra Perez developed a leadership award for Harlen Lambert that will be given out every year. It is befitting that Harlen Lambert be the first person for the award and made me feel more connected to the Honors Program for respecting Harlen Lambert beyond a soundbyte for someone's career or a line on a CV, something I see too often in the local press and by university scholars. This award begins a great tradition.

As you read this book, you too will be subtly taken in by Lambert's straightforward accounting of his life and distraught at how he was treated, and arguably still treated, by those in power who know better. Harlen Lambert endured hell on earth and didn't turn to violence as a means to solve the violence wrought upon him. This is an American hero.

At the end of this book, Lambert has generously included one of my student's poems. "Rainbow Protector" by Isabella Beltran is a great example of how one may learn so much by understanding Harlen Lambert's life and his brave choices.

Harlen Lambert inspires people to be their best because of his sacrifice, which isn't a sacrifice to him; it is how we are supposed to behave in order to make our community the best it can possibly be. I know readers will enjoy this book, but what will probably surprise them is how much they will also learn.

I am personally grateful to Harlen Lambert for teaching me about my own community and serving as a lifeline to the past in his generous availability to our young people. I am equally thankful to Sharron for including me on this journey of discovery and love, for cheering on my own efforts in sharing history, and modeling who I would like to be when (if) I grow up.

Sharon Sekhon is the founder of the Studio for Southern California History. She is also an instructor in the Honors Program, American Studies, and Ethnic Studies at California State University, Fullerton. Her work may be explored online through the LA History Archive at lahistoryarchive.org.

A Word to the Reader

The stories and material contained in this book are true, factual, and documented. I saved documents, photos, news clippings, awards, commendation letters, and believe my memory serves, based on the personal depth of my feelings associated with the consequences of serving as a law enforcement officer in Santa Ana, CA. The encounters are genuine, though some names and details of events mentioned in this book have been altered to protect the privacy rights of those in my precinct as well as citizens involved. These changes in no way alter the substance of what happened.

These memoirs are not censored. Censorship would diminish the reality of what took place, and they can be told only in candid honesty—even to my embarrassment in some situations.

The memoir deals with my experiences as the first black police officer in the city of Santa Ana, Orange County, California during the turbulent 1960s. At that time Santa Ana was one of the most ideologically conservative cities in the United States. Within the department itself, a group of officers that became known as the "John Birch Conspiracy" tried to wrest departmental control from Chief Edward J. Allen. The crime control strategies in those days were simple, if not simplistic: "Kick ass and take names." At the same time, I want to be clear that most of my fellow officers were professional and honorable—but their supervisors were the same as mine, and I understood their conflict about supporting me and staying on the good side of our superiors.

Keep an open mind as you read these memoirs and accept the contrast in different people's life styles and thinking. Try not to judge as many officers tend to do from time to time. And to those who may read about themselves keep in mind that these accounts are from my recollection of them and often from written accounts, some of which will appear herein. You may recall incidents differently than I do, but then five people witnessing the same event may come up with five different versions of what happened.

These are my words, my story, my sorrows and successes, typically American, but unique to me.

Thank you for reading my book.

Harlen "Lamb" Lambert

BADGE OF COLOR: *Breaking the Silence*

PROLOGUE
March - April 1967

March 20, 1967 was my first night as a rookie on police patrol. Earlier I had extended my hand and introduced myself to Officer Verlyn Powers, my field training supervisor. His black hair and deep blue eyes stood out garishly against his pasty white skin. He ignored my hand. Embarrassed I felt my face and neck flush.

Officer Powers was from Mississippi and spoke with a slow Southern drawl. "Yo only job is to sit in the cahr. We get a call, you get out of the cahr, keep your mouth shut, and listen up!"

We rode in darkness and in silence. It didn't take long to figure out that I wasn't wanted and that Powers didn't like my company. The only sounds came from the dispatch radio.

We cruised silently through a rubber company complex. Nothing was visible but shadows from dim and distant lights. Officer Powers stopped the patrol car in the middle of a dark street. "Get out of the cahr, nigger, and close the door."

I stepped out. He gunned the engine and sped away, leaving me standing in the street.

Standing there, I looked towards the disappearing car and thought about another officer's words my first day. "Powers is hateful. He'll do everything he can to get you fired."

I clinched my fists in anger. Officer Powers' treatment wasn't part of police training. It boosted his self-esteem and gave him power over me, made him feel superior. I couldn't say or do anything—I was a rookie on twelve-months probation.

Finally, the police car reappeared. Powers stopped and said, "Okay, nigger, get in." As I grasped the door handle he accelerated. I had to let go or I'd fall.

We repeated this until he got bored. Each time he left me standing longer than the previous time. He finally allowed me back in.

I felt like a volcano ready to erupt. But I couldn't. I wanted to be a cop. A good cop, but this department was riddled with bigotry and hatred. It took all the willpower I could muster not to reach over, grab

Powers and beat the shit out of him.

One cool damp mid-April night, that fury turned into something else. I rode in silence next to field training supervisor Powers. The vehicle scraped against a hedge that hid the entrance to the endless geometric rows of citrus trees beyond.

Officer Powers suddenly stopped the patrol car in the orange grove. He yelled, "Get out of the cahr, nigger, and close the door."

What could I do? I did it. Powers slowly backed up the unit until his headlights were mere pinpoints of yellow.

The orange grove had a waiting, ominous feel. I knew rats and other small creatures were active at night, and that everyday noises were made sinister by the darkness. I stood there just waiting.

Minutes later, I saw the headlights of a second car stop and park beside Powers' patrol unit. Together, the officers turned their headlights off.

I stood there uncertain of what would happen next. About fifteen minutes later, the air was stolen from my lungs when suddenly the headlights snapped on, their bright beams lighting a path directly at me.

Side by side, the patrol units began coming forward. At the same time, I heard rustling behind me. My heart began to hammer. I backed up but the hedge stopped me.

This time I was gripped by desperate fear. The fear stuck like a chicken bone in my throat.

They didn't run me over. I was furious and afraid, but they weren't getting rid of me!

I was the first black officer in Santa Ana, California in 1967. Nobody cared, except me.

HARLEN "Lamb" LAMBERT

PART ONE
WARM FAMILY, COLD WORLD

We cannot escape our origins,
However hard we might try
Those origins contain the key
--could we but find it--
To all that we later become.

JAMES BALDWIN
Notes of a Native Son

CHAPTER ONE

1936 - 1942

That bone of fear first hung in my throat when I was five. I couldn't breathe. Only mama recognized my plight and pounded my back until I choked it up. I needed her now. She was my stable point. She taught me about God and how to pray for help, or calm, or courage. Feeling her presence sent me back to her reassuring stories of my life beyond my memories——back to the day I was born.

It was 1936, a year when Hitler was the thug and a threat to peace and calm. Hitler and his German armies continued to show the world he was not scared of anyone...until the 1936 Summer Olympics were held in Berlin. Hitler had hoped that his Aryan supermen would dominate the track and field events and therefore back up his claims of racial superiority. But he was humiliated when those events were dominated by the great Jesse Owens, an African-American man. Although Owens was hailed as a hero by the people when he returned home to the United States, he still faced prejudice and discrimination in our still racially segregated country.

In 1936 families across the southern states were recovering from a series of devastating tornadoes that had cost the lives of four hundred-fifty people, and an estimated 3,500 people injured. The depression lingered on with unemployment rising to 16.9%. Many of America's unemployed travelled to California hoping to get work, but the local police chief had posted guards at main entrance points blocking the "undesirables." That was illegal and later stopped.

July 1936 had a full moon then. I came into the world feeling a deep loss and later learned I was one of three, no longer a triplet since my brother and sister perished that day when my life began. Mama would often have watery eyes when she told me this story. Sometimes that took my breath away like that chicken bone did, like Hitler did, like those officers did.

Actually, I grew up never being lonely because I had so many siblings. I enjoyed being around a crowd of loved ones, since my mother and father had five children by previous marriages and would have six more together.

Fred, Clotel and Gladys are my half- brothers and sisters from my father's first marriage. Herman and Lula Mae are my half-brother and sister from my mother's first marriage. Lula Mae would become significant during my growing-up years.

Daddy was a long-time cotton and vegetable share-cropper for a wealthy family in the railroad flag village of Bonita. He received farming tools, seed, the use of mules and a one-third share of the crop yield designated to him from the land owner. With Daddy's share of the crop, he could sell it to a merchant who extended credit to the land owner. Or he could buy things like food and clothing on credit, normally at exorbitant rates, from a merchant—who in some cases, was also the landowner.

When the Great Depression hit, unemployment had already reached record levels. By 1937, when I was learning to sit and walk, farmers could not make a living selling cotton crops. The price of cotton, formerly 25 cents a pound, fell to 5 cents a pound. Neither the landowners nor the share-croppers could survive.

Supporting our family was Daddy's first priority. He moved our family of eight at that time from Louisiana to Pine Bluff, Arkansas, where he soon found work at a lumber mill. He had stepped into a pattern of an agricultural/industrial way of life that became common in the lumber industry. When work was slow at the mill, Daddy helped Mama in the garden, milked the goats, and collected eggs from the henhouse.

No matter what my father was doing, he either sang or hummed the same tune. I watched him and learned many skills. Once in a while, he would simply stop what he was doing and bow his head. I would learn he was singing the hymn Amazing Grace:

> *Through many dangers, toils and snares,*
> *I have already come;*
> *Tis grace hath brought me safe thus far,*
> *And grace will lead me home.*

I asked, "Daddy, who is grace?"

He crouched down. "God is Grace. Grace is love that finds you when you have nothing to give in return."

Daddy and Mama instilled in us the values of God, family and hard work – guiding values I've tried to live by throughout my life. Daddy walked two-miles each way between work and home. The mill owners provided houses for rent to their workers for $12 a month. Our 12-foot wide shotgun style rental home was a one story wood-frame structure with a front porch, meaning rooms were arranged one behind the other with doors at each end of the house. A brick fireplace connected the living room and kitchen with two tiny bedrooms at the rear.

I was a precocious two-year old. Mama would warn me, "Sunny, you move away from the fireplace, so you don't get burnt!"

She was in the kitchen cleaning vegetables. I didn't see a fire with the telltale shadows flickering up the walls – so I crawled right onto smoldering fragments. My cries brought Mama running. To this day I have a burned hand with two fused, bent fingers that on occasion bring discomfort. Mama never had to caution me again about fireplaces or fires.

She couldn't know that this fire episode was nothing compared with what was to come.

~~*~~

The front porch was a gathering place to play quietly or share one of the two rocking chairs always available for Mama to keep an eye on the children. Taking a few minutes break from working in the garden that she had planted on both sides of the house, she would say, "Sunny, go pull some carrots for the soup." Or Lula and I would laugh as Mama, waving a stick, ran after a goat rummaging in her garden, or a chicken racing away from the chicken-coop.

Mama's vegetable garden, goat's milk, and eggs provided the means for Daddy to barter for goods. His largest trade got us Fanny, a small beige mare that would become a welcome means of transportation. Soon after, Daddy bartered for a wagon for Fanny to pull. She pulled the family to town and to church. She pulled the wagon to market full of produce that Mama and the older kids had hoed, picked, cleaned and packed.

On rainy days, instead of taking the wagon, Daddy would ride Fanny to the lumber mill. Fanny watched for him to come out of the house. She neighed in pleasure when he picked up the headgear, and whistled for her. He quietly talked to her while attaching her bit and the reins. "Good girl, Fanny." Daddy stood on a block of wood and jumped up on her back. Then Mama came out with a cloth sack of food for his supper, and grain and cut carrots for Fanny. With a loving caress to Mama's face, he was off for a long day at the mill.

To this day I can see how devoted Mama and Daddy were, sitting side by side on the porch, chairs rocking, quietly, talking together after a long day.

The outdoor toilet at the rear of the house was close enough to be accessible, but far enough away to minimize odors. The half-moon-shaped carvings on either side of the plywood walls provided light and ventilation. Inside were newspapers and old catalogs. The corn cobs and leaves were in a can to protect them from mice and other rodents. The catalogs served a dual purpose by giving us something to read.

Over the next eleven years my mother gave birth to my younger five siblings: Dorethea, Samuel, Charles, Harvest and Joe.

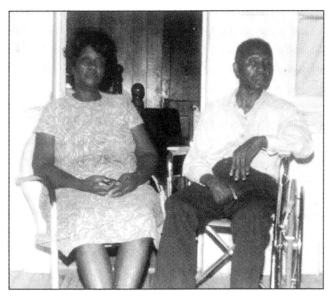

I was three when my sister, Dorethea was born. My parents told me that the stork brought a new baby girl. With each successive child, I got the same stork story. I came to believe that we were on that stork's regular route.

Our home was five miles outside Pine Bluff. Because of money and distance, hospitals were out of the question for childbirth. Midwives, like our Granny Portia, delivered the babies.

I came to know her well over the ensuing years. Granny Portia, a practicing West African midwife, came to America as a slave, along with her mother. Later separated from her mother, she was placed into personal service on a plantation in the antebellum South. She learned the skills of birthing informally. After being emancipated in the early 1930s, she began attending to both Black and White poor women in the rural South.

When Granny Portia came to the home, she would shoo the kids with, "You young'uns take yourselves outside to play or work in your mama's garden!"

We would pull weeds, carry water, or kick a ball. I watched for the stork to fly over and drop a baby. I was nine when Charles was born and Lula Mae laughingly told me the truth about the birds and bees.

~~*~~

Daddy was only 5'4" and weighed 150 pounds soaking wet. He spoke softly and on rare occasions. We children knew that when he did speak, we listened. Daddy was a no-nonsense, hard-working, faithful man. He cared deeply about providing for his family. He was not a demonstrative man, but we knew without being told that he loved us.

Mama, on the other hand, was 5'10", big-boned and elegant. She remained at home performing the unending chores of housewife and mother. Outgoing and friendly, she could talk about anything to anybody. She was also quick to discipline when it was needed.

Daddy wore the pants in the home, but Mama enforced his rules.

Our neighborhood was a segregated rural community with plenty of space to play without fear of being hit by a vehicle.

I was a happy, friendly boy. Hence, the nickname Sunny, with the letter U. At three, I began slipping off down the road to play with other kids in the neighborhood. We didn't have grass, but the towering shortleaf pine and cherry-bark oak trees provided shade for hide-and-seek. We younger children would stand with hands shading our eyes, as we watched the older kids play double-dare-you to see who could climb the highest. Here and there were plume-like clusters of the royal purple smoke tree, where we could lie still and scare the seeker.

Mama tied a small cowbell around my neck. I thought I was cool, because I was the only kid with a bell. Other kids wanted a bell, too, but I remained the only one making noise as I played – and the first one to be found. It was well after a year of wearing the cowbell that I found out Mama had placed it there so she would find me.

Another reason I was cool, was because of my puppy, Lee. At four years old, I was surprised with a three pound, six-week-old, white fuzzy wire-haired terrier puppy a neighbor had given to Dad. I named the puppy Lee, after my favorite neighborhood playmate, but I refused to let anyone, including him, touch my dog.

The puppy was my new and favorite buddy. I carried him everywhere, until he got too big at five pounds. We played, ate and slept together. I cried when Mama separated us, even if only long enough to change my clothes, brush my teeth, or take a bath. Lee slept with me and did everything with me unless Mama said he couldn't.

Since our growing family needed more room, Daddy, with the help of church members and neighbors, constructed a three-bedroom home just blocks from the shotgun house. Fred joined the Army. Herman became a bellboy at the Jefferson Hotel in town and kept a room there. The new house was larger, but I missed racing, with Lee, from the front door straight through the old house and skidding out the back.

At our new neighborhood I began to notice some people were a different color from me when Mama and I walked home from the local grocery, near the main highway. I stared at the occasional oncoming car. Inevitably, the passengers were light-skinned. They stared at us as I stared at them.

As we turned onto the dirt road leading home, I asked, "Mama, why are the people in the car a different color than me?" Mama set her groceries on the ground and looked into my eyes. "We're all the same, Sunny. "We're like flowers that God made in different colors. That's why the world is so pretty! We're just like the flowers."

Even so, there was an underlying tension as she spoke.

Some months later Lula Mae, Mama and I went to town. I had to go to the washroom so with both women on either side of me holding my hands, we crossed the street to the Greyhound bus station, where we waited in a line. I wailed, "Mama, I really have to go!"

Mama said there were two washrooms. One was for White people, and the line we stood in was for colored people. My sister chimed in, "Get used to it, Sunny. We can't eat at the same places or drink from the same water fountains. We can't even sit in the front when we ride the bus."

I looked up at Mom. "We never ride the bus, Mama, and you told me we were all the same!" With a sigh, she bent down. "We are the same, and don't ever forget it. Man makes the rules where we can go to the washroom, not God. One day, son, all the flowers will be in one field, I promise."

I heard what she said, but young as I was none of it sounded right to me, even as I watched my mother and sister look away from direct eye contact, or step off the sidewalk when a White person approached. It would be some time before I would have much contact with people outside my race.

My parents were Christian. Religion and faith in God were central to our family life. As a child, attending church didn't mean sitting on a hard, wooden bench listening to things I didn't understand, when I'd rather be outside playing.

As I became older, I tried to live as my parents taught me, and came to understand and believe in the basic tenets of Baptist teachings and in God and His goodness.

The time would come when I could make my own decisions about what was right or wrong for me, the way I chose to serve God, and the realization that He was the Master of my destiny and the paths I would walk.

There would come a time, too, when I would have conflicting emotions about organized religion, and even God himself.

~~*~~

Several times a week the family walked the mile in the Arkansas heat to attend the Baptist church, where Daddy was a deacon of the one-hundred-member congregation. The single story wooden A-frame, with a small upstairs balcony, had the appearance of a box with a room in each corner. The choir assembled in one room, the deacons counted collection money in another, a room lead to the upstairs balcony, and members hung hats, coats and sweaters on nails hammered in the walls in the coatroom.

Reverend Bob Given, at 5'1" and 140 pounds, baldheaded and with a dark complexion, wore an oversized suit jacket holding four ink pens in his outside lapel pocket. We knew the reverend was ready to stress a scripture, when he stopped speaking for a few moments and rolled up the sleeves of his jacket and the legs of his slacks.

The reverend pinched his pant legs, stood on tip-toes, and danced to music the choir sang. The volume increased as member after member made their voices heard, too.

My three sisters sang in the choir, while I normally fell asleep unless something unusual happened during the service.

One Revival Night I was nodding off on the seat next to Mama. An older, heavy woman sitting on the bench in front of us jumped to her feet, shouting and waving her hands. The strands of gold chain she wore moved rhythmically back and forth. She moved faster and faster and shouted louder and louder. She lost her balance. She pitched over the bench in front of her, catching herself before dropping into the lap of a gentleman with a cane across his lap.

Her hair came off - and landed right at my feet!

In my five years, I'd never seen a lady's hair fall off. I'd never seen a bald woman, either. I began laughing uncontrollably and clutched my stomach. As loud as I could, "Mama, look! The lady lost her hair!"

Mama rose to her feet and reached for my hand. I knew what that meant.

She quietly ushered me outside of the church. As she swatted me on the bottom, she said, "Son, you don't laugh at people for the way they express themselves in the House of God."

Sobbing, I said, "But Mama, I wasn't laughing at the lady for shouting. I never seen a person lose their hair."

Later Mama told me that the lady was wearing a wig and explained to me what a wig was.

~~*~~

When company came to visit, Mama had a plan in place if I made noise or was out of control. She looked at me once, long enough to get my attention. That was my cue to be quiet. If she had to get my attention again, she gave me her evil-eye look - one eye closed, eyebrow raised. That's when I knew it was too late. Even if I sat in my chair and never moved a muscle for the next twenty years I was going to get a spanking.

Sure enough, when company left, she would say to me, "Go outside and get a switch." I went to the cherry-bark oak tree in front of our house and brought to her the smallest branch I could find. As I stood in front of her, she would tell me, "Hold it for a few minutes." I thought, why am I holding my punishment?

So I asked her why.

"I want you to think about why you're going to get a spanking."

I believe that hurt me even more than the whack itself.

When Mama spanked me, she didn't hurt me, but she never missed a stroke. I would try escaping her hand by going between her legs, or around her any way I could. But she held me with one hand, while her other hand, with the switch, followed my behind whenever I squirmed. She just kept spanking until she thought it was enough.

Daddy did everything different from Mama. Whenever I did something bad, he didn't punish me then. He just looked at me, "I'm going to spank you for this."

Months later I finally did something wrong enough and he decided it was time.

After a few attention-getting strokes from Daddy's belt, he would remind me, "Sunny, I told you before that you would get a whipping."

My outgoing and easy disposition wasn't going to get me out of this situation.

I had hoped Daddy would forget, but he always remembered the offense – I didn't do a chore, acted up in church or I back-talked. He had a memory like an elephant.

With his belt, buckle in his hand, Daddy asked, "You know what you did? I told you I was going to spank you." And while he talked, he thrashed my bottom until he got tired or felt pity for me.

My father's remote, reserved nature and his absences during the week while he worked made him a strong, but intermittent, presence in my young life. I didn't have the time with him to develop the closeness I needed to confide in him, or to ask him the difficult questions about things like race or sex. Yet, his example was before me: a man who was good to my mother, didn't swear, or criticize, or argue, whose only vice that I knew about was chewing tobacco. As far as I could see, he walked his talk. He expected me to do the same.

Neither of my parents inflicted harsh, over-zealous spankings, but they made sure I knew I was responsible for my actions.

I never doubted that my parents were right about their demands for my behavior, or that they had the right to correct me. I also believed that they were fair, and if they punished me, I deserved it.

~~*~~

Christmas 1942 was different from previous years. The small brown paper bag with my name on it filled with peppermint candies, an apple and a handful of walnuts, was missing. Mama helped me count the bags to make sure they were all there. My older half-brother Herman, and sisters Clotel, Gladys, and Lula Mae had bags with their names on them. Oldest half-brother Fred had enlisted in the Army and was gone before Christmas, so he didn't count. Younger sister and brother, Dorethea and Samuel, had bags with their names printed on them. They didn't count either, because she was only three and he was a baby.

All things considered, there still should have been seven. Just as Mama pointed out the last bag and before I could protest, Daddy said, "Sunny, close your eyes and turn around." I turned, eyes wide open, to see Daddy kneeling down in front of me, hands behind his back and a twinkle in his eyes. I heard a soft bounce and saw my first basketball, with Daddy's help, roll towards me. "Lee, No!" Mama yelped, as my five-pound wire-haired terrier companion pawed the ball. Lee crouched down, looked at the ball, and growled, looked up at me hopefully, tail wagging.

I threw myself into Daddy's arms and thanked him for the surprise, before scooping up the weathered basketball and shouting, "Lee, come!" The two of us went outside into a pile of snow to inspect the ball closer. It wasn't perfectly round and the stitching on one end of the cloth panel was coming loose. I could feel the rubber bladder inside, adding to the weight of the ball. But it was mine and it would replace the game of rocks that we threw into the crude peach bucket attached to a shortleaf pine tree.

Tossing the basketball was different from tossing rocks: it was bigger, heavier, and had a different texture. I could throw fifty rocks into the bucket before climbing the ten feet up the tree to drop the rocks onto the ground and start over.

Snow, rain, or shine, every available moment a six-year old had, I practiced shooting the ball into the bucket. I stretched my small frame, arms extended, eyes on the bucket, and launched the ball. I practiced throwing with both hands, one hand, hand-over-hand. When I missed, I had to snatch it from Lee, who liked to roll it with his nose. When I made the bucket, I climbed the tree to retrieve it. The pine tree was on a dirt lot next to our house. The ball got muddy when it rained, but I would wipe it off and shoot it again. I was frequently tired from shooting the ball, chasing after Lee and climbing up and down the tree day after day.

One day I fell backwards and landed on my butt, Lee circling and barking. Lula Mae heard the commotion, and came running to my rescue. I wasn't hurt. I told her what I was trying to do, and she said, "Well, Sunny. I have a fix for that!" She raced to the barn, coming back moments later with a crude saw. She climbed the ladder leaning against the tree and sawed out the bottom of the peach bucket, which fell at our feet. Hands on her hips and with a satisfied smile, she said, "Now you don't have to climb up that tree for your ball!

CHAPTER TWO
1942 - 1946

When it was time to enter first grade, I was excited about joining the children who walked to the school house a mile away - until I learned I couldn't take Lee.

Mama tried to explain why my puppy couldn't go with me. My six-year-old mind couldn't grasp the reasoning, and I cried all the way to school the first couple of months. My joy came at the end of the day. I would run up the front porch and through the house to the back yard, where Lee waited for me. He would jump into my arms and lick my face. We would roll around, playing chase, until Mama called me in for the evening.

Lula Mae talked animatedly with her school chums, as we walked along the road to school. We would stop to stare at the bright orange bus, headed toward a different school, its seats filled with children whose white faces pressed to the windows, stared back at us.

Our large box-like school building sat back from the road on a dirt lot. Grades one through twelve were conducted in the crude, one-room schoolhouse by our teacher, Miss Findley.

The classes were set up around the walls by grade groups of three. Hats and coats hung on the nails. In the middle of the room was a huge, cast iron stove that provided heat, and separated the groups of students. The chimney reached up through the roof, belching crackling sounds that during quiet time was somehow comforting.

The youngest, grades one through three, clustered together on benches, giggling and unable to focus because of the novelty of being old enough to attend school. We were now "big boys" and "big girls." I began calling my parents Mom and Dad, parroting Lula Mae. After all, she was a big girl. And now I was a big boy!

Dad wore a gray hat with a black band around it. "Dad, I don't have a hat for school, and I'm a big boy now!" I admired his hat, and sometimes borrowed it. I wore it inside and outside and showed it off to my playmates. I fell asleep wearing it and squashed it.

"Time you have your own hat, Sunny." I prized my gray hat with the black band, because now I was just like Dad – and I had a hat to hang on the school wall.

Grades fourth through sixth and seventh through eighth shared wooden desks in a semi-circle around the stove. Lula Mae sometimes turned to check my behavior, motioning me to quiet down or stop wiggling around, or Miss Findley brought order with a sharp reminder of why we were there.

On the infrequent days when the book truck came to a grinding stop in front of the schoolhouse, Miss Findley asked the bigger boys for help. They each took a stack of books, piling them inside the entry door.

They were used books, hand-me-down textbooks in reading, writing and arithmetic. They were the only books we had.

I raised my hand, "Missus Findley, why don't we get new books?" She would look down at me with a smile, using my family nickname, "Sunny, the books are from another district." The tone of her voice told me that that was the end of the explanation.

~~*~~

Neighboring church families saved to purchase a used, rusted yellow bus for students who lived outside our neighborhood. Fathers took turns driving the bus. I learned that the walk to school for many colored students was an arduous and sometimes dangerous ten mile trek.

I would see the buses drop off some of my playmates. "Missus Findley, why is everybody here the same color as me?" She held the papers she had collected from us in her hands, "Because all the children are from the same neighborhood."

"Well, why don't the school busses bring white kids to school, too?"

She paused. "Because they are from their own neighborhood and have their own school."

Walking home from school, my wise fourth-grade sister did her best to answer my non-stop questions. Lula Mae took a deep breath and gushed an answer as long as my forearm: "Someday, little brother, we'll ride a bus and have new books and new clothes and a lunch other than a biscuit and we'll go to the big city and see a real film with Clark Gable, and I'll marry somebody wonderful like Daddy and we'll have our own car and we'll be famous!"

At that time I knew nothing about Black and White, or segregation. But intuitively, I knew something just wasn't right – that the colored community was somehow inferior. To what, or to whom, I would not know or understand until years later when I would be recruited into the army and took a memorable bus-ride south.

~~*~~

In 1941 the U.S. was beginning to come out of the Great Depression and families were looking forward to better times after a decade of scarcity. Then in December, Pearl Harbor was bombed.

The war meant that people had to put up with more hardships again. There were times we didn't have enough food to eat or enough clothes to wear. Early on, I learned the importance of being on time.

If I was late to the dinner table, I more than likely didn't eat. Daddy worked long hours and was rarely home for dinner with the family. Mom would set aside a dish for him, and when she said, "Time to eat," we stopped what we were doing and came in to dinner - or risked going to bed hungry.

The older pairs of hands snatched up the food ahead of me and would leave nothing but a few scraps for Lee, and we would sit together in the back yard while he ate.

I got the well-worn, patched older children's hand-me-downs to wear. In turn, the younger boys got my hand-me-downs. "Use it up, wear it out, make it do, or do without," was a saying heard throughout the neighborhood.

Mom spent hours sewing and patching shirts, pants, skivvies and socks for the boys, and thin dresses, undergarments and socks for the girls. My sisters helped Mom with sewing and washing our belongings.

Shallow wells were common to each rural household. We lifted the bucket of water to the surface by pulling the rope on a wheel with a grooved edge. The water was used for washing clothes, bathing, and gardening. We couldn't drink the well water because of saltwater contamination, high concentrations of nitrates, soil and animal pollution.

I helped my sisters pull up buckets of water to fill a tub for washing and a tub for rinsing. I liked the exertion of tugging on the rope, because it made me feel strong and I wanted muscles like my daddy.

Mom rested the flat board made of rough wood and chicken-wire across the wash tub and began scrubbing an article of clothing. When she was finished, one of the girls would rinse it in the second tub and hand it off to another sister for hanging on a clothesline to dry.

Mom showed me how to use her sadiron to press my clothes. I had to use both hands around the iron strap to plop the solid block of metal on the cast iron stove to heat. I would then wrap my hands around the strap once again to iron as fast as I could, before it got cold again.

~~*~~

I looked forward to the two times a month Dad hitched Fanny up to the wagon to make a trip to town for drinking water. "Sunny, Daddy needs help with the water. This is a job for big boys." The local grocer had a faucet with a lock on it. He unlocked it, hooked up a hose and stuck the end into the barrel resting in the back of our wagon. After paying the merchant, we made our way home, where Dad then transferred the water to yet another barrel on our back porch. We didn't have to worry about goat droppings or other contamination getting into this water. And Lee drank the same water I did.

This was the best my parents could do. And they did it lovingly, just like I did for Lee.

Lula Mae and I decided we needed to upgrade our meager wardrobes. And we knew just what to do.

School was out for the summer. Lula Mae and I rose and dressed before sunrise.

We heard the grinding gears of the truck coming to a stop. Lula Mae grabbed a blanket and bolted for the door. "Sunny, grab some biscuits and hurry!" We raced the two blocks to the highway to stand with a small group of people waiting to board.

Poor and/or illiterate White and Black day laborers, many of them migrants, filled the benches on both sides, and down the middle of the flat-bed truck. Our cluster of nine squeezed behind the outside benches, standing and holding on to the three foot panels for the seven mile ride that would take us to the fields to begin a grueling day of hard work. We were ready to work side-by-side to make money.

Lula Mae picked cotton, "Because I'm fast with my hands!" I carried water for the pickers, "Because I'm fast on my feet!"

~~*~~

My arms were tired from hoisting the bucket up the well for the fifth time. Damn! I felt more grown up using a cuss word I learned from the older boys in school.

It was a hot mid-afternoon in July. I stumbled, trying with all my might to hold the pail steady. Just another few yards. Cold water sloshed over the sides as I made my way toward the rows of men, women and children bent over from the waist, dragging their sacks behind them. Those who had weak backs crawled along the cotton rows on their knees.

The sack had a strap that went over the shoulder, so both hands would be free to pluck the cotton from the boll. No one wore gloves. When both hands were full of cotton, it went into the sack. When the sack became full, it was emptied onto the blanket the laborer had spread out before he started picking.

Children as young as three and four years old, sometimes without shoes, worked alongside the adults. Mothers had infants strapped on their backs. When the baby got hungry, the young mother stopped to nurse, then went right back to work.

I stopped to catch my breath and to give my arms a rest from the heavy bucket. Crap! The other cuss word I learned.

I thought about getting through a row of cotton without a saw briar cutting my legs, or a cockle burr sticking to my clothes. But to really ruin my day would be the painful experience of getting stung by a packsaddle worm. It's a worm pretty in color with a design on his back that looks like a saddle. The worm loves cotton leaves almost as much as the boll weevil loves the cotton boll.

I could hear the workers singing. The songs were usually spiritual. Music was a form of communication. Song leaders would improvise lines and, in return, other workers would respond with other lines to coordinate the rhythm, feeling, or situation of the moment.

I lifted my bucket, listening as I walked:

Walk together children
Don't you get weary
Oh, talk together children
Don't you get weary
There's a great camp meeting in the promised land

Sing together children
Don't you get weary
Oh, shout together children
Don't you get weary
There's a great camp meeting in the promised land
Goin' to mourn and never tire

Mourn and never tire
There's a great camp meeting in the promised land

I offered the water ladle first to the youngest in the row of cotton. I pulled the squashed biscuit from my pocket and offered it to the skeletal, barefoot three year old in the torn, soiled dress. Eyes downcast, she reached out a dirty hand, fingers torn and bleeding from the cotton burrs. Seeing her age and plight made me feel bad about cussing.

Each person, Negro and White, young and old, had the same eyes. Eyes that burned into my very being. At eight years old, I couldn't articulate my feelings, but I intuitively knew. Knew they had seen sorrow and meanness. Knew they endured hardships. Knew they had to be here working in the fields. Knew my sister and I were here by choice. We all were ready for whatever life might bring.

I couldn't know then that one day I would be challenged by what life might bring my way. Would I be ready?

~~*~~

I made a final water run at the end of the day. Pulling a few cotton bolls along the way to the edge of the field, I found my sister emptying her sack. I took my paltry amount and dumped it on her blanket. We got help pulling the corners together, knotting them before the sack was hoisted onto the scale to weigh.

The going rate was a penny a pound for the cotton picked. In twelve hours, Lula Mae had picked 100 pounds. "Look, Sunny! I have a dollar!"

I shot back, "I helped you make that dollar!"

If looks could kill, hers did. "You didn't pull enough cotton to make a Baby Gay!"

The Baby Gay was a cotton swab later relabeled Q-tips.

I earned sixty cents for the six water runs I made that day.

My sister and I worked through the end of August. She had $62.00 saved, and I had $37.20 saved. The money would go towards buying new school clothes. There was a pride in having money in our pockets and time on our hands. But the pleasure fled when we reached the White part of Pine Bluff to shop at Sears and Roebuck and Montgomery Ward.

Lula Mae and I worked in the cotton fields the following two years during the summer months. She got faster in pulling cotton, and I got quicker delivering water. Our savings grew.

~~*~~

You wouldn't think a cotton field was a romantic place to meet the opposite sex. But it happened. The boys would rush to get the cotton row by a pretty girl and the amount of cotton picked depended on how much the girl could pick. If she picked a lot, the boy had to work hard to keep up and stay beside her. If she was slow, very little cotton was picked by either one.

Thomas, a tall, lanky fifteen year old, tried hard to stay next to Lula Mae. He not only kept up with her, but carried her full sack of cotton and emptied it on her blanket. At the end of the day, he pulled the corners together and hoisted it onto the scale.

I didn't like Thomas. And he was fifteen! When he talked to Lula Mae, he leaned in close, mere inches from her face. I could see her lean away from him. She was friendly, but reserved.

He didn't live in our neighborhood, but Thomas rode the same truck with us at the end of the work day. He would walk us home and hang around until it was obvious Mom wasn't happy seeing him. "Thomas, you shoo on home now, you hear?" Mom admonished, "Lula Mae, you watch yourself around that boy."

Picking season was over. The school year was beginning.

Thomas was a pest. I thought of him like the cockle burr that stuck to my clothes – or in this case, to my sister. He would come by the house without invitation at odd hours, asking for Lula Mae. The day came when Mom had had enough of Thomas. "You shoo on home now, and don't come back around here!"

We would not be able to prove that his intentions were not honorable - or that he would be instrumental in our family losing our home and everything in it one Halloween night.

CHAPTER THREE
1946 - 1949

Lee lay quietly in the shade as I threw my basketball into the peach crate nailed to the shortleaf pine tree. I heard a loud thud. Turning toward the sound, I saw across the street a wheelchair upside down at the bottom of the ramp. I could see a head and an arm. I rushed over there. Lee yelped, circled, and began licking the man's face as I tried to lift the heavy wheel that wedged the man against the ramp.

I screamed at the top of my lungs, "Help! Help!"

Mom and Dad, hearing my cries, threw down their garden hoes, raced around the house and across the street. They could see the problem, and together struggled to upright the man strapped in the heavy wooden chair. The man looked small, sitting against the low back with his arms resting on the chest-high planks. The wheels, almost three feet tall, were just shy of rubbing the arm rests.

Both his legs were missing at mid-thigh.

"Thank you kindly, neighbors," he said. "I got a little too close to the edge and spilled right out."

Mr. Steve, as we came to know him, had been hurt while in the army. "I was a foot soldier with the 23rd Infantry Regiment. In November of '43 we were in the jungle on patrol in Japanese territory off the Numa-Numa Trail on Bougainville Island in Papua New Guinea. Heard the shots, but don't remember a thing after that. Been in the hospital for the past year or so and now here I am."

Mr. Steve had light skin, lank hair and slanted eyes. He said his father was African and his mother was Eurasian. He thought maybe some French ancestry was thrown in there somewhere, too. He lived alone, and said he needed some help of the private kind.

Mr. Steve gave me a job. Every day after school and about the same time on weekends, Lee and I walked to his house, where he waited at the top of the ramp with a wooden bucket sitting nearby on the porch. Lee jumped up into his lap, eager for attention. Mr. Steve ruffled Lee's wiry hair and talked to him as I picked up the bucket.

I walked carefully down the ramp and made my way around to

the outhouse, where I dumped the contents. I hoisted a bucket of water from the ground well near his back door, rinsed out the portable toilet, and replaced the lid.

Mom directed me to, "Clean the bucket and drop in some pine needles, Sunny. Make it smell good for Mr. Steve." Sometimes Mom sent vegetables with me for Mr. Steve. Sometimes my folks kept him company as I went about my work.

He paid me every week. I got at least fifteen cents, but once a month he handed over a dollar. My earnings went directly into the fruit jar with my name scratched in the rusted lid.

~~*~~

One day I complained about my meager savings to my maternal grandfather, Papa Day. "Papa, do you have any ideas for me?"

He did. He presented me with his old Craftsman push reel lawnmower. "Sunny, get yourself out there and see who needs their grass cut, or weeds knocked down!"

Pulling the heavy duty, three-and-a-half foot wooden handle was easy. Pushing was a different matter. The heavy blades against the roller were difficult for me to maneuver as a nine year old. I hadn't developed height or muscle yet, but I was determined to fill up my fruit jar with lots of money.

On weekends I pulled the mower in a two-mile radius, looking for grass that needed mowing, or weeds that needed cutting down. I knocked on doors, "Good morning, Missus. For seventy-five cents I can cut your grass." If the grass was too tall, I charged a dollar.

Tall weeds were the worst. I was short, making the mower even more difficult to push. I took a step back to propel the mower forward, thrusting with all my might. I repeated the motion until I tired, resting only when the job was done. Sometimes I was rewarded with a twenty-five cent tip!

I saw steady improvement in my fruit jar. The school year was winding down, and I didn't know my tenth year would be turned topsy-turvy.

I was ten-years-old! I was becoming more independent as Mom had Dorethea and Samuel, and was now pregnant with Charles.

I had already learned some cuss words, but found myself sinning in other ways, too. At intervals I told small lies, little inconsistencies to Miss Findley about homework, losing things, being nosy, and that sort of thing.

"Where is your homework?" Miss Findley asked.

"I lost it."

"You lost it yesterday. You lost it last week."

Hanging my head, trying to look sheepish, I mumbled, "I'm bad about losing things, but I'll try to do better, Miss Findley."

Dad bought me a beige straw hat, just like his, to wear to church. It was too large for my head, so Mom put paper inside the headband to keep it from falling down over my eyes. If I turned my head too fast one way, the hat rotated the opposite way.

Every time I wore the hat to church I would forget to retrieve it from one of the nails in the coatroom.

Dad would say, "Sunny, where is your hat?"

I looked at Dad for the third time and gave him the same fib. "Dad, I looked and looked, and it was gone!"

He replaced the lost hat for the final time. "Two things, Sunny. I know you fibbed to me about looking for your hat. You're old enough to know that when you tell the truth, you don't have to remember what you said. But when you lie you have to remember everything you said." He had one more thing to say. "The next time you lose your hat I'm going to spank you."

I didn't want to take a chance on testing his memory. I was very careful and never lost another hat, knowing he would remember what he had told me, no matter how much time might pass.

After church, Dad would carefully hang his suit jacket and pants in his bedroom closet. I wondered what he had in his pockets. I wanted to make sure that I had what he had.

Chewing tobacco. Yuck. Loose change. I have my own. Ink pen. I have pencils, thank you. Church flyer. No thanks.

What's this? A tiny silver package with a little balloon wrapped around it. I unraveled the wiggly thing, putting it over my finger like a mini-glove. I put it in my pants pocket.

The following Sunday, Dad hung up his suit, and asked me to meet him on the porch. He looked at me for several minutes, before speaking. "Sunny. You took something that doesn't belong to you. Bring it to me."

I knew what he wanted. I handed over the contraband. His stern demeanor prevented me from asking what the little wiggly thing was.

"I did not give you permission to go through my things, and it's not okay to take what doesn't belong to you. Ever! If you want something, you ask for it. If you're told no, you leave it."

Dad patted his leg, indicating I was to sit. "Did you like it when somebody took your hat without asking you?"

"No, Daddy." I was ashamed of myself as I promised Dad I would never go through his pockets again – or snatch things up without asking first.

I would soon learn the depths of his feelings about people taking that which didn't belong to them – and the internal battle my father suffered from that very thing.

~~*~~

One scary night, coughing as the smoke rose around me, I clutched Lee to my chest. I grabbed my fruit jar.

"Children! Get up and move out the door! Hurry!"

Mom picked up Samuel, tucking him beneath the front of her robe. Lula Mae, holding Dorethea's hand, hurried out the door in front of me. I could hear shouting and crying as Gladys ushered me away from the burning house in the early morning hours. Light was just breaking.

Neighboring women brought blankets and jackets from their homes to wrap around us, trying to soothe us with words of comfort. Neighbors helped Clotel round up Fanny, our goat, and the chickens, assuring Mom they would take care of them.

Elderly Mr. Jenkins said to Mom. "Thomas asked to borrow a horse to take to town and get the firemen! I told him it would be too late, being so far away and all."

Mom looked shocked. "Thomas was here? Thomas! Where are

you, Thomas!" We scanned the area around us, but did not see him.

Missus Maybre said, "That young man took out of here like lightning a few minutes ago, Anner."

My bare feet were cold. I moved from foot to foot trying to stay warm, holding my dog tight against me. I watched my father and men from the neighborhood run to the livestock well with buckets. I could see the frenzy of the rope being dropped, hear the slosh of water, my father's rushing the rope up, hand over hand, as he hauled the filled bucket to the surface. He quickly emptied the water into a bucket a neighbor held, and would start the process of releasing the rope once again.

Attempts were made to throw the small amount of water each bucket contained on our burning home. Finally, the men dropped in exhaustion. Fire had gutted the structure. There was nothing left to be saved.

The only sounds to be heard were mumbled prayers, thanks that no life had been lost, and the muffled sobbing of my sisters and mother. I started to hiccup.

As the family huddled together in the chill air, Mom and Dad wondered out loud what happened to cause the fire. Dad held Mom's hand, and quietly added, "Anner, it's one more cross we'll get through with the Lord's grace."

I shivered uncontrollably. Gladys knelt in front of me, tucking the blanket tighter around my shoulders, as I looked into her blue eyes. My half-sister rubbed my arms for warmth. I could only stare at her, at her tawny skin, and long dark brown hair.

I had a striking understanding that I was seeing her for the first time.

I tearfully blurted out, "Gladdy! You have pretty eyes!" Pinching my skin in distress, I continued, "An' you, an' Cloey an' Fred have dif'rent skin!" Clotel and Fred had black hair, brown eyes, and darker skin, like mine.

I didn't consider our differences beyond that moment – until, after several weeks of eavesdropping on conversations and prayers, a bare bones picture of my parents emerged.

~~*~~

My father, a sharecropper on a farm owned by Buck Jones in Bonita, Louisiana, had been married to a light-skinned, pretty woman and they had five children.

The third child, a girl with straight hair and blue eyes, had been the product of Jones raping Dad's wife. Jones told my father he was Gladys's pappy and that she would have first choice of any clothing or food sent to my father's home.

Negroes were considered property. A man in this situation could not avenge his wife's honor or the intrusions into his or his family's lives - he would have been beaten to death. It was with great resolve that my father maintained an inner dignity and the pride to provide for his family, no matter the adverse circumstances.

In 1931 my father's wife and their two youngest children died from the spread of typhoid fever.

My mother was also a resident of Bonita. She was married with two young children, but soon divorced. Then she moved to Tiller, Arkansas, to find employment.

Bonita was a small, close, sharecropper community. My parents did not know each other at the time, but knew of one another. After he lost his wife my father contacted my maternal grandparents, asking for Anners' whereabouts. Later Mom received a letter from my father asking for her hand in marriage.

Mom also received letters from her parents endorsing the idea, since she had two kids and he had three. They believed him to be an upright man, and he would be a good provider for the family.

She agreed, and returned to Bonita, where they married and became a blended family.

It started out a marriage of convenience.

I didn't understand the import of this bit of family history, until much later. It was from my father that I learned resolve, persistence and determination. I lived in the warmth and love of nurturing, caring parents.

~~*~~

After the fire while our home was being rebuilt, the family stayed in a vacant house near the highway. I went off to school. Coming home one afternoon soon after the fire, Lee raced across the dirt road to meet

30

me.

I didn't see the black car come around the corner, too fast to stop. I heard Lee yelp. I heard the squealing tires. I saw my dog rolling, as I raced toward him.

I dropped to my knees at the side of the road and cradled him. He looked at me and tried to give me a final lick. He died in my arms. The driver stopped to apologize and tried to help, but I was inconsolable.

I had lost my best friend.

Dad helped me bury Lee under the shortleaf pine tree where I had spent countless hours tossing my basketball into the crude peach bucket. Lee had spent those same hours crouching, growling and pawing at the ball hopefully each time it came back to ground.

~~*~~

I had just turned eleven, school was out for the summer, and some of the year would prove to be promising.

Some of the time was the same – working in the cotton field, attending to Mr. Steve, and mowing grass and cutting weeds. I was filling up my fruit jar, once again, for clothes.

Some days were exciting - like watching the new brick buildings that were being constructed at one end of the one-room school site. I heard that students would be separated into elementary, junior and senior high classes. The new school would be completed the following year, when I turned twelve and was ready to enter junior high school.

Some days presented challenges – like the weeks of strenuous raking and clearing of the burned remnants of our home. I felt sad, but determined to be like my Dad, and overcome the obstacles.

Once again, neighbors and church members took up their tools and pitched in to help the family rebuild. After school and work and over weekends, we sawed and hammered. The well was cleaned out, and dug deeper. A new outhouse was constructed, a barn built for Fanny and the goat, and a pen for the chickens.

A second small structure constructed from left-over planks, and other discarded materials would eventually go up a block away. The floor creaked when it was walked on.

This became a store where Mom sold eggs and milk. It had electricity and a refrigerator. The light came from a single bulb attached to lengths of extension cords dangling over a piece of wood hanging from the ceiling.

Mom sold vanilla, chocolate, and strawberry ice cream, local favorites. Once a week Mr. Leo delivered blocks of ice to Mom's store. He cut the ice into twenty-five-pound blocks, packing it into the wooden box insulated with sawdust. Non-corroding tin lined the box to store the ice cream. The drip pan under the box was emptied daily.

Mom also sold vegetables from her garden. Barrels of flour, sugar, and rice were measured out on the scale she was given. Baskets of breads and cookies were placed in a glass display case. Small shelves with containers held mysterious liquids in shades of yellow and amber. A white

curtain covered the door leading to the back room, where she could rest when it was quiet.

I took pride in Mom and in her store. I helped her sweep, clean vegetables, set up tables, pack ice, wait on customers, and count change.

I didn't know then that she was teaching me lessons that would one day help me become a successful entrepreneur.

~~*~~

Some events that summer were surprises - like when Dad rolled up to the house in a 1939 dark green, four-door Packard. It had a large, square body saddled with names like "bathtub" or "pregnant elephant." We surrounded the car to admire it. "C'mon! Get in and we'll go for a ride!" It was exhilarating. The family laughed and praised Dad for his driving skills.

Dad didn't drive his car to work. That perplexed me. He still walked or rode Fanny to and from the lumber mill. He never gave an explanation, but I overheard talk among church members about gas rationing. Whatever that was.

I took it on myself to wash the car while Dad was at work. Dang. This car had the longest nose of any car I'd seen. I doused it with water, and dried it with an old shirt. Not only did I pride myself on helping Dad, but his words of praise on a job well done, and thanks for thinking of him, were music to my ears.

One day I decided to back up the car. I got in. The gears were grinding, as I tried to see over the driver's seat behind me. My foot hit the gas pedal, and boom! That shortleaf pine tree usually didn't move, but the rear end of Dad's car was shoved inward about a foot.

Shit. That was the only cussword I could think of as I waited for Dad and Fanny to make their way into the yard. Dad's eyes got big as he neared the car. Fanny trotted past me toward her pen, where Dad released her. He then walked past me, onto the porch and into the house.

I was frozen to the spot, wash cloth in hand. I dissolved into tears as I waited for Dad to say something to me. To yell at me. To spank me. Anything but ignore me.

Within minutes Dad called me in to wash up for bedtime. He displayed no animosity or anything out of character.

My father never said a word to me about the damage to the car and I never cleaned it again. Dad later traded the car in for a Plymouth – and I did not attempt to wash it.

~~*~~

Birds sang in the American sycamore. Fanny neighed and

chickens scratched. Little Charles made sucking noises, as Dorethea and Samuel squabbled over a biscuit. The sounds of hammers and saws had ceased.

The house was complete and ready to move into. The two oldest boys were gone, and Clotel and Gladys went off to chase their dreams and no longer lived at home.

At fifteen and twelve, Lula Mae and I were now the oldest.

Our new schools welcomed their students. Lula Mae was my playmate and mentor from the time I was a toddler. She was in her first year at Coleman High while I was in my last at Jefferson County Elementary. Student classes were conducted in separate buildings, but play grounds were shared by all.

My sister played guard on the school basketball team, was an honor-roll student, and was touted as one of the prettiest girls on campus. At 5'6" Lula Mae was taller than most of her classmates—and fearless. Always protective of me, at home and now at school, there would come a time on the school grounds when I had never been so glad to see her.

I hadn't had my growth spurt yet. Going into high school I was short, small-boned and geeky-looking. I squinted to see, but the cost of glasses was out of the question. I was good in track, football, and basketball; my athletic abilities brought me a lot of positive attention. My size, however, gave the school bullies a fine target.

One day I was being beaten up by a mean spirited, obese, black tenth grader the size of a rhino, who didn't like me. A classmate screamed, "Hang in, Sunny!" and raced off to find Lula Mae. When she broke through the small group surrounding us, I was on the ground, pinned between his muscular legs. I could hear the dull roar of kids, "Get up, Sunny! Kick him in the shins! Bite him!" My lips were bleeding and my left eye began to swell. I hurt. It was difficult to see.

"You have two seconds to get off him!" She yelled. Seconds

passed as his fists pounded about my head. I heard a loud thud, a grunt, and suddenly he fell away from me.

As I looked up with one eye, it was evident Lula Mae hit my nemesis on his back with a huge wooden board she spied and brought on her way to my rescue. She stood over him, board raised, daring him to do something else. "Had enough?"

I got up from the ground, talking tough, standing next to her. I felt tall looking down on what now resembled more a whale than a rhino. I went toward the whale, ready to kick him, when I was grabbed from behind by a classmate.

"Let me go, let me go," I yelled even though I hoped they would keep me back and hold on. If the fight started again I knew I would win. Lula Mae was there.

~~*~~

Brrring! Brrring! The end-of-day school bell rang, echoing through the halls.

I raced out the door, anxious to hitch a ride to the Jefferson Hotel in downtown Pine Bluff.

Mom was busy with baby Charles, the latest drop from the stork. Lula Mae helped with toddlers Dorethea and Samuel, while Dad worked hard putting in long hours. Some days I only saw him for a few minutes.

My parents instilled good morals, strong sibling bonds, and family togetherness in everything we did. We learned to share and be sensitive to each other's needs, including sharing food, clothing, and words of encouragement.

The fire had left the family without furnishings and other things, such as beds, towels, tubs, kitchen utensils and flour sacks for diapers.

I was the oldest male child left in our home, and I felt the self-imposed pressure of helping my dad make ends meet. Replacing things that would ease my mother's daily routine and make our home comfortable once again, became important to me.

I knew I had to do something, so one day I went to town.

I knocked on Herman's hotel room door. He was surprised to see me. "Sunny! What brings you here?"

"I'm looking for a job. Can I be a bellman like you?"

"No, Sunny. You're too young and the hotel isn't hiring."

I left the Jefferson feeling rejected, but determined.

I made my way to the Greyhound Bus Station, where Clotel worked in the basement laundry room. She washed and ironed tablecloths and napkins for the restaurant on the first floor.

I had tried on several occasions to get a job with my sister.

On this day, I found her folding a pile of freshly-ironed napkins. She smiled when she saw me. She spoke before I could say anything. "Nothing has changed, Sunny! You're still too small and the work is too heavy for you."

For the umpteenth time I left the station, but that day even more dejected than before.

As I made my way toward home feeling sorry for myself, I saw a thin boy on a street corner, a stack of newspapers at his feet. He held up a paper, shouting, "Right here! The Grits News gives you all you need to know. Only ten cents. Get it right here!"

I asked the boy, not much older than me, how to get a job selling the weekly paper. He directed me to The Grits News office, where I was greeted by a kindly gentleman stooped over a noisy press. The chemical smell of the press ink was overwhelming, and my eyes started to tear.

"How can I help you, young feller?"

I wiped my eyes on my shirt sleeve. "I want to sell The Grits!"

Before leaving the newspaper office, I was assured a bundle would be delivered to our house every Saturday.

I went door-to-door in the neighborhood, sold the paper for ten cents each, collecting the money on the spot. I took the proceeds to the newspaper office on Mondays after school, where the owner gave me five cents per paper sold.

Since my twenty-five papers were heavy, I built a flat-bed wagon to haul The Grits around. Before long, I knew how and where to sell each and every paper, adding a dollar and twenty-five cents to my income.

I averaged three dollars and fifty-five cents a week between my three part-time jobs. Three dollars and tips were given to Mom. Fifty-five cents went into my fruit jar.

~~*~~

Work at the lumber mill had slowed down, becoming increasingly difficult for my father to spread around his wages. Although I was helping, I never felt it was enough.

Lula Mae helped Mom with the children and household chores after school and on weekends. To contribute to the family, she found odd jobs in the neighborhood and continued to work in the cotton fields during the summer.

I confided in her. "Lula Mae, sometimes I feel like running away. It would be one less mouth to feed and clothe."

"That's selfish, Sunny! If you ran away, who would help Daddy haul water? Or help Mr. Steve in his wheelchair? Who would chop down those ugly weeds for old Mr. Jenkins? How would The Grits get delivered? And where would the younger boys get pants to wear!"

I knew my sister was right. She always was. But sometimes she just pissed me off. Just because she was right didn't make me feel any better.

~~*~~

One day, sitting on the front porch of our home, I began to cry. I'd been wracking my brain, trying to think of something I could do to help support the growing family.

I heard Mom walk across the cracked wood floor of the front room. The door creaked as she shut it behind her. She fanned herself and slowly sat her swollen body in the rocker next to me. The stork would be dropping by soon with Harvey.

She patted me on the back. "Do we need to talk?"

I asked her to go for a walk, because I didn't want my sisters or brothers see me cry. We walked silently along the middle of the dirt road leading from our home towards an open field.

I wiped my eyes and blew my nose. I tried to explain to her how I felt, and why I thought I needed to help Dad support the family.

We stopped walking. She turned to me and took me into her arms. We stood in the middle of the road. Mom didn't say a word, just cried and listened.

Oh, God, I made my Mama cry.

I blurted out, "Mom, you can't have any more babies!"

It must have been a surprise to her. She said nothing, just kept holding me. After a short time, as our sobs subsided, we turned and began the walk back.

I felt better after talking to Mom. She began treating me more like an adult, and we were closer than before. She began asking me to help her do little things around the house, and made me feel I was contributing in a way that helped my father.

I never talked to Dad about my feelings. I believed that would have hurt him. No one told me, but I thought I needed to be an example for my brothers and sisters. I simply believed we, as a family, should always look out for each other, stay close and together, whatever that meant.

~~*~~

School was out, once again, for the summer. I would soon be thirteen, and looking for yet another way to add dollars to my fruit jar.

I was slurping on a cup of vanilla ice cream, when Mr. Leo's ice truck stopped in front of Mom's store to make his weekly delivery. Mom said he had recently lost his helper, and suggested I talk with him.

I dashed outside just as he emerged from behind the brown leather flap that covered the open back of his truck. He was carrying a heavy block with his ice tongs. "Mr. Leo, can I help you with that?"

He handed me an ice pick and said, "You can help me chip for the ice cream box."

He pulled another pick from his holster and showed me how to pick ice quickly into smaller chunks. As he chipped away, he said he could use some extra help twice a week, if I was willing to be paid a dollar fifty for the day.

"I have a regular route of customers to deliver to," he said. "We start early at the ice house getting orders ready."

On Saturday I walked the seven blocks to Mr. Leo's ice house, a structure that was simply a large bin, made of rough boards and roofed over. The ice that he had harvested during winter from surrounding lakes and streams kept perfectly with the sawdust snugly packed over, under, and around the massive floor of ice.

Mr. Leo was thin and sallow. I thought it was from lighting up a Lucky Strike cigarette every hour. He was busy cutting the ice into blocks of twenty-five pounds. Coughing and pointing to a chunk, he said, "Clamp that block and haul it to the truck, Sunny."

We filled up the truck with blocks of ice and began the delivery route. We carried the heavy chunks into an unlocked home and installed them in the ice box.

At the end of summer I had added another seventy-seven dollars to my fruit jar.

I couldn't know then that one day, what I learned from working with Mr. Leo, would become a lucrative business on the streets of Chicago.

~~*~~

Who's this soft spoken, bald-headed guy my sister is talking about non-stop? I'd never seen a girl all googly-eyed before.

I peeked around the corner, as Lula Mae and her beau talked quietly with my parents.

Taylor "Junior" Dunbar, a stocky, 230 pound weight lifter and construction worker, was a former heavyweight boxer living in Chicago. He regularly visited his parents, who lived in our neighborhood. During one of these visits after he and Lula Mae met, I learned they would eventually marry.

My sister soon invested most of her time being with Junior. I came to know and love that beefy man as one of the most thoughtful and caring persons I would ever, in my lifetime, meet.

CHAPTER FOUR
1950 - 1951

At fourteen I started my first job during school nights washing dishes, where I learned the only thing the Colored and Whites had in common were the dishes and utensils I diligently and carefully cleaned.

The bicycle sat at the edge of the neighbor's yard early Sunday morning, a sign posted on its handle bars. "Headed North. Hercules. Three dollars." I walked around it, kicked the tires, patted the saddle and pushed on the seat. I didn't know anything about bikes, but everything looked intact. I knocked on the door, held up the sign, handed over my three dollars, and wheeled the bike across the road to Mr. Steve's house.

He was the first person to see my acquisition. I explained I had a new part-time job that started at five o'clock the following day. "I'll be coming by a few minutes early, Mr. Steve, so I can get to work on time."

Mr. Steve told me I had used good judgement, that the bike was a practical solution for getting to and from work.

I practiced getting on and off my bike. After a few shaky starts, I got used to braking while scooting along, using my feet to push off and gain balance before learning how to pedal.

Lula Mae's words came to me: Just like basketball. Keep your eyes on the ball and follow through to the basket. I pushed off, keeping my eyes focused on where I wanted to go. As I practiced speed, pedaling in circles, and standing, to maintain balance, I mastered riding and maneuvering my two-wheeled wonder.

I was ready.

My school day was over, and I knew Mr. Steve would be waiting for me. I pedaled as fast as my legs allowed, the chain guard clacking noisily.

"I heard you coming, Sunny!" I flipped the kick-stand with my foot, forcing the rear tire up for support as I parked my second-hand brown bicycle at the bottom of Mr. Steve's porch. He had a wrench in hand, pointing, "It'll take you just a minute to tighten up that guard."

After tightening bolts and attending to Mr. Steve, I straddled the bike and pedaled home. I untied the rope to remove my basketball from the rear saddle, and called a hello to Mom as I loped into the house.

The stork had been busy – Mom was pregnant with Joe.

I placed the ball under my bed, and began changing from my school clothes when Mom called out from the kitchen, "Sunny, I talked with Mr. Gunnert. He's to bring you home the nights it's too late and dark to ride your bike."

Mr. Gunnert was the proprietor of the Ranch House, a combination restaurant and fast food drive-in. He frequented Mom's store to purchase eggs and fresh vegetables from her garden.

~~*~~

I poked my head in the kitchen door, waved goodbye, and straddled the Hercules. I pushed off once again, looking forward to my first night on the job. I rode on the path along the highway, cars passing me in both directions.

Pedaling easily, I was jolted at the booming voice behind me, "Darkie, get your ass off the pathway!" The police car sped away as I wobbled onto the highway.

My stomach churned uneasily as I continued cycling the second mile, staying off the path, not understanding why I suddenly felt nervous and self-conscious.

~~*~~

Approaching the restaurant, I took in the sights and sounds before me. The aged exterior, with alternating faded horizontal stripes of red, white, and metallic silver, extended to the five drive-in stalls. Identical windows framed the front entrance door.

A man opened the door and stood aside as he waited for his companion to enter. I had a brief glimpse of the red chrome dinettes scattered around the room on blue checkerboard tiles. The bright orange, green, red, and yellow trim of the Wurlitzer™ jukebox blinked furiously.

I knew of the "Chitlin Circuit," road houses or makeshift bars where my sister and her friends went to listen to music from a jukebox – and to Jook – a dance with a somewhat vague link between music and the art of seduction. They Jooked to the jazz and blues sounds of such artists as Louis Jordan, Cab Calloway, Count Basie and T-Bone Walker.

When I biked by there, music blared from speakers mounted on the walls. Strong sounds of trumpets, drums, saxophones, and bass surrounded me, inviting me to tap my feet, clap my hands, or snap my fingers. Straddling my bike, I remained motionless. I wanted so badly to do those things - to outwardly feel the music - but I still felt uneasy, and I didn't want to bring attention to myself.

I would learn later that the music was called Big Band, or Swing, and I would become familiar with names such as Artie Shaw, Glenn Miller, Jimmy Dorsey and Frank Sinatra. The sounds were far different from the gospel, blues, and jazz I was used to hearing.

The jukebox was color blind in a segregated world. Black patrons thought Bill Black, Carl Perkins, and Steve Cropper were Negroes singing. White patrons were exposed to, and accepted Black artist's work, never having seen the performer in person.

A young couple in a Ford Crestliner, called the "Shoebox Ford," lip-synced a song to one another. Close by, an older gentleman sat upright in his brand new "Woodie," a 1950 Ford Country Squire station wagon, and frowned at the couple's outward suggestiveness.

The two-tone burgundy-and-tan Chrysler Imperial parked in the third stall was a young boy's dream – a work of art in its design. I'm going to have one, one day! A two-tone yellow and brown!

The four men inside flirted with the women in the bright yellow, massive Plymouth Fastback next to them. Suddenly, one of the men jumped out of the Imperial, snapping his fingers. He beckoned to one of the ladies as he moved backwards to the empty stall. "Let's swing!"

Mesmerized, I watched the smiling couple energetically spin. My breath caught as the male lifted and flipped the redhead during the quick-paced dance. Their friends piled out of their cars, clapping and cheering the dancing duo for more.

I wondered if the Jook was the same kind of dance. I made a mental note to ask Lula Mae.

A hand pressed down on my shoulder. "Hey, kid! You the new dish washer?"

Alarmed, I turned to the thirty-something carhop, dressed in his military-style uniform of drab olive trousers, peaked cap, white shirt, and brown shoes.

I squeaked out a reply. "Yes, sir."

"Well then, get crackin'. Follow that sign 'round to the back, and Abraham will fill you in." Still startled, I didn't move. "I didn't mean to scare you, kid. Just go on 'round, now."

I looked at the "Colored Only" sign, with the black arrow pointing to the rear of the restaurant. I walked my bike around the corner. I felt as if a door had slammed shut, cutting off the colors, laughter, and vibrancy I left behind.

There were two sections to the restaurant - front and back.

Whites entered fom the front, or parked their cars at the stalls. White waiters served food prepared by white cooks. The customers ate on tables covered with a red-and-white checkered cloth, or at the white prefabricated counter with red stools attached to the clean checkerboard tiles. Their outside drinking fountain and inside bathrooms were kept spotless.

I maneuvered my way around the broken door of an outhouse attached to the main building. Another "Colored Only" sign was affixed to the filthy water fountain next to the toilet. I was sure neither had been used in months, maybe years.

I leaned my bike against the wall, before cautiously opening the bright green door where I stepped inside and collided with a dingy brown stool, unable to catch myself before pitching forward and over the second of three stools in the pint-sized room. I landed face down on the cracked linoleum floor, my legs haphazardly straddling the center stool.

Gingerly I pushed myself up on my knees, embarrassed, as my eyes connected with the cook's pair of size twelve shoes.

Looking up, I saw and met Abraham, who leaned on a cane as he extended a hand to me. "Well, don't know what to say 'cept welcome to the diner!" He laughed, as I grasped his hand. "You ain't the first, and you won't be the last young buck fallin' over them stools!"

Abraham was stocky, had a bulbous nose centered between two bushy brows, and frizzled gray hair. One leg was shorter than the other so he limped, but moved quickly with the use of his cane. Abraham wore a faded pea-green apron over coveralls and was the cook——only for the Colored patrons.

~~*~~

During the next weeks when business was slow, he told me that he was a former slave taken out of agriculture due to a serious leg and foot injury. "That was nigh on eight years now. I'm b'holdin' to Gunnie for this here job and the room out back."

He looked out the tiny window at the setting sun. "Next hour Jiggles comin' in. Lemme show you where you go'in be."

I followed Abraham behind the five-foot long counter, and through a miniscule galley kitchen with a refrigerator, stove, deep fryer, and grill top. A big pot of chili simmered on the stove, releasing the combined aroma of beans, garlic, onion, tomatoes, and green chilis. I lifted my nose to take a deep whiff as I passed through.

Abraham enjoyed cooking, and teaching. He taught me the basics of preparing pancakes and eggs, how to make coffee in the aluminum percolator, season soups full of vegetables and chicken or pork – beef was reserved for the White patrons. He taught me how to properly clean pig intestines and hog maws (pig stomach), and pair them with rice, collard greens and corn bread. Abraham took pride in keeping a scrubbed, clean kitchen.

~~*~~

My work room – the one area common to both sides of the restaurant - had two hoses and two large porcelain enamel iron sinks, a slotted drain sitting in the cold sink for rinsing. A shelf above held steel wool pads and tubs of cleaning and rinsing agents, along with Red Devil Lye™ in case the sinks plugged up.

Left-over food and soiled paper napkins were scraped into the large pail sitting under the windows at the end of the room. A strip of flypaper hung from each of the two small openings. In the corner was a wringer pail and a cotton mop.

On the opposite side of the galley, a ten-foot table was stacked with dishes, bowls, and baskets of forks, knives and spoons. Dirty dishes and utensils were piled in wood crates on the other end. A shelf above the table held glasses and cups, stacked five-high inside one another.

Scraping food into the pail, I said, "Gunnie and Jiggles. Those are funny names!"

Abraham screwed on the hose to the hot water tap and began filling the sink. "I been knowin' the boss man a lot of years, an' long as no White folk aroun' I calls him Gunnie. He a good man. He be in to say h'lo fore long."

As Abraham got the words out, Mr. Gunnert came into the work room. "Your mama said you're a good worker. Glad to have you here, boy."

He was as round as he was tall, and reminded me of Humpty Dumpty. Mr. Gunnert referred to himself as a 'gen-u-ine Southern boy,' and spoke with a slow, exaggerated drawl as he told inflated stories to his White customers. He leaned in close, to make sure they heard every word he had to say, and waited for their knee-slapping laughter.

He was kind to the Negroes he hired, although he conducted business as was expected in the segregated South, and according to the old Black Codes of regulating occupations of Negroes. The Codes dictated hours of labor, duties and the behaviors assigned to them.

A short, bow-legged and balding man of an indeterminate age, with a pink birthmark across his forehead, came bounding into the now crowded space. Abraham announced, "This here's Jiggles, our waiter."

I would learn from Jiggles what regulated behavior meant for the Negro worker.

The pink birthmark creased into rows as Jiggles grinned wide and addressed Mr. Gunnert. "Evenin' boss man! Hav'n a gran' day? Yes sir, I hope!"

He tapped the doorway three times and smoothed down the pea-green apron he wore, identical to Abraham's, before turning to me. "We'll have us a gran' time, too. Yes sir. I'll show you a right good way a-doin' them dishes. Yes sir!"

~~*~~

When the stools were empty, Jiggles tapped the countertop three times before pulling the string to the overhead light, which indicated the kitchen was now closed. He made his path through the galley-way, compulsively tapping the refrigerator, the stove and the open doorway three times each.

Abraham, cleaning the grill, grunted. "Jiggs, cain't you get yo'self

45

through here 'thout makin' that noise!"

Jiggles tapped the stacks of dishes, bowls, cups and glasses three times. "Got me a widder-gal waitin' at home. Yes sir, let's get these dishes done." Jiggles continued to talk while we scraped last bits of food, washed dishes, scrubbed pots and cleaned the floor.

Jiggles told me he was a two-time widower himself, and divorced once. He often told Abraham, "If you'd gotten married, you wouldn't be such a grouchy critter."

He went on to tell me he was from Smyrna, Georgia. He worked for a wealthy family in the kitchen and dining room from the time he was a small child. Jiggles was taught to boisterously recite the evening menu to the large groups of people the family regularly entertained. He sang, danced, and proclaimed the South would rise again. He, along with other Negros in bondage, were expected to portray a world of smiling slaves who loved serving the kindly White people who held them in bondage.

Jiggles was emancipated in 1943. His first wife had family in Pine Bluff, Arkansas, so they decided it would be a good place to start their new life together.

He learned freedom wasn't exactly as he had anticipated. "Din't know 'bout them rules, no sir." As Jiggles reached up to stack glasses, his voice softened. "We all knows we livin' diffurnt than the White folks. It's okay. Things okay, but I truly thought life be better here, yes sir."

Jiggles explained that since he was not a field worker or in domestic employment, it was the law that he carry written permission from Mr. Gunnert to work in the restaurant. He explained Negroes were subject to regulated civil and legal rights, from marriage to the right to hold and sell property, to growing vegetables for their personal use, to the freedom to roam. "Some places don' even lets you in town 'thout your boss-man's okay. Why, me and the widder can't even have a night out after ten o'clock, 'thout bein' arrested and charged as vagrants!"

Abraham chimed in. "Yep, an' I carry my own lettuh from Gunnie sayin' I kin stay in the shack out back. He responsible for me an' whut I do."

~~*~~

I listened to the many personal stories Abraham and Jiggles shared. I paid attention to Negro history as they understood it, and told it to me. Before the enactment of Jim Crow laws (originated from the Black Codes), Negros enjoyed some of the rights granted during Reconstruction (the period after the American Civil War when the South was in political, social, and economic turmoil, and eleven Confederate states had seceded).

Gains included the addition of the Thirteenth, Fourteenth, and Fifteenth Amendments and the Civil Rights Act of 1875. But rights dwindled after Reconstruction ended in 1877. By 1890, Whites in the North and South became less supportive of civil rights and racial tensions began to flare.

Jiggles tapped the galley door three times. "Yes, sir, we livin' them old Codes right-chere." Abraham locked the outer door behind us, with a final thought. "Jus' the way things are, young buck. Jus' the way things are."

Mr. Gunnert waited as I jumped in the back of his truck and lifted my bike up behind me. He drove me directly to our front door, as Mom had made him promise he would do.

~~*~~

There at home the old baby buggy was loaded with breads, fresh vegetables, eggs and goat milk. My Saturday morning job was to ferry groceries from Mom's market to homes of elderly people in our neighborhood.

Mom handed over the list of who got what. "Tell me about your job at the Ranch House, Sunny."

"Well, I like listening to the music coming in through the windows. It sure makes time go by fast. And I like Abe's cooking. It smells good in there all the time. And the stories Abe and Jiggs tell me make me happy that I live with you and Dad!"

When my mother had something to say and wanted me to listen closely, she would ask me to sit with her. "You have a few minutes before you start your deliveries, Sunny. Abraham and Jiggles are right when they say 'It's just the way things are' for us. But it's temporary – remember what I told you about the flowers in the field?" She looked me directly in the eyes before continuing.

"Daddy and I have sheltered you children the best we could from the dangers that you hear about. Look around you, son, and really see our people, person-by-person, and learn how to live happily with who you are and with what you have."

~~*~~

My personal experiences through these times were limited. I didn't know anything different from the way we lived, and I was for the most part a content and happy fourteen-year-old. I was looking forward to basketball practice after the last groceries were delivered.

Lula Mae's sudden appearance surprised me. "Sunny, wait up! Mom said you might want company this morning. Wanna know what "behind the veil" means?"

What I want is to be on the court throwing balls. But go for it, Sis.

My sister was serious about education and listened to every word her teacher spoke. In minutes I knew what her recent studies included. Lula Mae launched into an explanation of how Negros developed a social and political system to bear hardships of segregation and prejudice - behind which they remained largely invisible.

"This way, we're not a threat to the Whites." Lula Mae continued, "That's why you see more people like us building more churches, schools, and social clubs!"

Social club? My ears perked up and I interrupted her, "Is that the Jook club you're talking about? Can I go?"

She laughed and pinched my arm. "Yes and no, in that order. And I'm not done talking."

Lula Mae went on to say her teacher said, "They're vital to fighting segregation, improving conditions, and generally uplifting our race." *Pay attention, Sunny. I don't understand, but it's important to Lula Mae.*

"Do you remember when we went to town and had to go inside the grocery store? Mom had you and me wait just inside the entrance, almost invisible to others." Lula Mae's eyes suddenly teared as she explained, "Mom was protecting us, Sunny, from the white shopkeeper's insults to the 'Mammy' or the 'spook' in front of other customers."

She wiped away a tear. "Mama and Daddy have been exposed to humiliation and anxiety forever. But we've been taught subtle ways to combat these very things."

"Like what?" I was still thinking of the Jook club and what

happened in such a place. *Must be fun, since you and Junior go all the time!*

Lula Mae sighed, recognized my attention-span was short. "We combat Whites by refusing to answer to insults or name calling. We're responsible for the path we walk, Sunny. Mama said so. End of lesson. I have something else to tell you."

Her eyes sparkled. "Junior and I are getting married after graduation, and I'll be moving to Chicago!" That announcement took me by surprise. Lula Mae was my best friend, a second mother figure, my protector and basketball coach. What would I do without her?

~~*~~

All through high school I worked evenings during the week at the Ranch House.

I never again rode my bicycle on the path along the highway, but kept a watchful eye for the police car. But I felt the need to move almost without end; if my limbs were moving the anxiety was gone, or at least I could ignore it for a while.

I listened to a variety of music that pulsed from the Wurlitzer ™, caught on the slight breeze and drifted through the two small windows in my work room. The music helped me wash and clean in a rhythmic motion, while day-dreaming of becoming a basketball hero. I clapped and bowed over the cold water sink.

For three years Abraham taught me how to cook new recipes, and Jiggles continued his three-pats on everything within reach. Abraham never married. Jiggles "widder-gal" became his fourth wife.

Mr. Gunnert never failed to give me a ride home when I worked late. He always asked about my parents, and never neglected to say thank you for a job well done.

This is the first time that I remember a dream that kept recurring. *I'm flying from something. But I don't know what. I'm not fearful. I launch myself with a short run, arms spread wide, face down, head moving from side-to-side.*

I fly high in the air over fields, downtown areas, and tall buildings. Sometimes I stop on top of a building. Then I come to a body of water where my altitude drops to just above the water. I have to see. I have to get to the other side.

Then I wake up - always landing on my feet.

~~*~~

The year I turned fifteen my sister, Lula Mae, graduated from high school, got married and moved to Chicago. I never did find out about those Jook Joints.

The stork dropped my youngest brother, Joe, into our busy

household.

That summer was filled with my numerous part-time jobs, which added dollars to my fruit jar each week. Occasional weekend practice with school chums on the high school basketball court kept me in shape for my upcoming junior year athletics in track, football, and basketball.

My junior year in high school was similar to the last, but an invitation would reshape my future.

CHAPTER FIVE
Summer 1952

Lula Mae and her husband, Junior, invited me to spend the summer between my high school junior and senior years in the city. I was just off a 17-hour bus ride from Pine Bluff to Chicago.

My stomach growled and gurgled noisily as we walked the short distance from the bus station to the White Castle hamburger stand. The 6x6 "Buy 'em by the sack" slogan mounted over the entry beckoned me! On the way to the stand, Lula told me I was in for a tasty treat.

While chatting about family news in Arkansas, we enjoyed the ten-cent 100% beef patty with onions and a pickle. White Castle was credited with being the first fast food chain in America – and it was my first hamburger - ever. Licking catsup from my fingers, I took pleasure in the building itself, which was made to resemble The Chicago Water Tower with its white porcelain enamel on steel exterior. It was a lazy Sunday evening. I had never before been among so many strangers. All colors, all ages. All friendly. But then, I had never before been in the city.

While eating my seventh burger and discussing how to go about finding summer work, a gentleman introduced himself. "I couldn't help but overhear you're looking for a job, young man, and I happen to be looking for some help." He extended his hand to each of us in turn and introduced himself as Cyber. He was mature, well-spoken, tall and gangly, with salt-and-pepper dreadlocks secured behind his head with a thick string. He wore a beige apron tied in front, over khaki pants. His brown oxfords were spotless and shiny.

Cyber said he had a shoeshine stand at the Blackstone Hotel and had been looking for someone to learn the business and to relieve him on weekends. He explained, "I emigrated with my father from Jamaica during the depression of the 1930s. He worked banana cultivation and there was a disease that killed the crops. Tata (father) and I had only each other, and he decided, with the economic and social unrest, we would come to America!" Cyber grinned widely as he explained, "I'm a bachelor, and I like playing cards and dancing. Haven't had much time to do either for the past 20 years!"

With a sweeping gesture and a courtly half-bow, he asked, "So what do you think? This is the uniform. You work for tips. We can work out the hours." We asked questions and got answers. By the time the four of us had eaten two sacks full of small square burgers, I was not only going to learn how to shine shoes, but to learn the shoeshine business.

~~*~~

Lula and Junior lived in a two-bedroom rented apartment in Jackson Park, 22 blocks from the Blackstone Hotel. Mid-day on Tuesday, I stepped into the Chicago Transit bus that would take me to my destination. I paid the driver my ten cent fare up front, exited the bus and then boarded at the back. The bus was segregated – Whites in the front and Negroes in the back. Bus drivers had the "powers of a police officer while driving the bus." That meant any order had to be obeyed, or possibly face fines or even imprisonment. On some days, I was forced to stand the 30-45 minute ride when the bus was full. That way, no White passenger had to stand or sit next to me or another person of color.

But at 16, I was focused on getting to the Blackstone Hotel in Chicago's South Loop downtown and to Cyber. The bus line ended two blocks from the hotel. As I walked toward the turn-of-the-century "Hotel of Presidents," I could not help but be impressed. Cyber had told us some of its history, but I was not prepared for the ornate terra cotta covering and cast aluminum post lamps that outline and illuminate the roofline. Or when I walked into the two-story lobby with its gilded French walnut paneling, the fireplace and mantle, the decorative plaster ceiling, brilliant chandeliers and the basket-woven patterned marble floor, or the rich hues of reds and golds.

I had never seen anything so beautiful!

~~*~~

I found Cyber at his shoeshine stand, near the lobby check-in. His stand consisted of an upholstered chair mounted on top of a flat platform, with steps for the customer to put his feet on while getting his shoes shined. Cyber had a tray of tan, brown, black, and navy shoe polish along with multi-colored cloths for shining. I waited quietly as he helped a portly gentleman with a snap-brim hat, button down collar and suspenders down from the platform. The customer checked out his black and white vintage brogues, smiled and handed Cyber some change.

When Cyber saw me, with a flourish he presented me with a clean beige apron. "Let's do this, young Lambert! All you need is your smock (apron), a rag, a can of polish and a smile."

And so I began learning the shoeshine business with Cyber as my hands-on tutor. "You can make of this job what you want. I started shining shoes at 12 years, on the streets. Five cents a shine. We're in a good place here inside the hotel with plenty of foot traffic. Fifty cents a pair. With tips you'll do fine." He went on, "There are some folk who look down on us. Even our own. But I think of myself as an artist, a leather finisher. I make an honest living. And you can, too."

Over the next hours and days I would learn about the different shoe skins: rough leather, smooth leather, reptile-grained, fabric and leather, hounds'-tooth. The types: one and two-tone wingtips, saddle shoes, penny-loafers, Monks, Nubecks and Welts. The styles: plain toe, wing tip, apron, medallion, cap toe, bicycle and French. I learned that conservative men wore wingtip oxfords and brogues, while gangsters in their Zoot suits preferred the gator-grained, or fabric-and-leather wingtip. I knew to go to the shoe vendor or repair shop to purchase the polish I would need. Cyber told me, "Average the number of customers and colors used during the week, check what you have on hand, and that will give you what you need to buy."

Cyber taught me that every shoeshine man had his own secret techniques. It might be the way he attracted customers, or how he related to them. He emphasized that the Blackstone Hotel was a favorite retreat for U.S. Presidents, royalty, Hollywood stars and sports legends. I generally saw only the back end of the celebrities and dignitaries as they swept through the lobby to their suites. Cigar smoking business men and politicians were daily regulars in the historic Smoke Filled Room.

Cyber cautioned me. "When the big names come in, treat them like anyone else. They come to get away from the public. Respect them, no matter who they are - no matter how they treat you."

His special technique might be the way he massaged wax into the leather shoe, rubbing it in with his index and middle fingers. "This way you can get the feel of the leather, skin to skin. Then buff it with your rag into a shine you can see yourself in."

I was intrigued with the way Cyber achieved musical effects when sharply popping a shoeshine rag. "It's an art! Do it with pride!" I became skilled in the natural rhythm of rag popping. It became a gratifying form of personal expression. Added to my smile, an upbeat –dignified-

presentation of popping my rag often led to bigger tips.

On Friday afternoon, Cyber said, "You've done well this week, young Lambert! I'm off to play cards and go dancing."

I watched him leave and smoothed my beige smock. Smiling, I helped "Tough Guy" Glimco, a capo (mafia captain) in the Chicago Outfit, an organized crime syndicate, step up onto the platform and into the chair. As he snapped open his newspaper, I picked up a can of black polish and a rag – ready to make music as an independent shoeshine boy.

~~*~~

A block from Lula Mae and Junior's apartment I found a place to play basketball.

The court was an abandoned tenement lot, complete with a hoopless rim loosely nailed to a piece of plywood on the top of a discarded rail tie. Ball tucked under my arm, I approached the four teens on the court. "Hey, guys, need a forward on your team?" Willie, Ira, Shorty and Canyon were two to three inches taller than I was, and at first hesitant about letting me play.

"Show us what you got, Lamb," Ira said.

I placed myself 15 feet from the basket, turned and dropped in a long shot. I ran for the ball, retrieving and dribbling before passing it to Ira.

With high-fives all around, Willie said, "Hey, man, those are some good moves. Ready to start?" The five of us spent hours together on the court competing with one another in a variety of drills during the summer.

I shined shoes on weekends and spent hours during the week on the basketball court competing with my new friends in a variety of drills.

~~*~~

It would be another two months before returning to Pine Bluff to enter my senior year in high school. Until then, I had a good amount of free time.

Think! Look for another way to add money to the fruit jar at home!

We lived in a two-story public housing building, surrounded by city blocks of other cinder-block buildings. A large group of African Americans, a growing arrival of Mexican-Americans and a smaller influx of Puerto Ricans lived together in the impoverished Jackson Park community.

The street was a microenvironment of socialization and economic endeavor for all ages: street peddlers pushed carts with a variety of goods and services; shoeshine boys waved their rags, news vendors shouted, "Get your latest news here," and fakirs who performed magic tricks and sold useless trinkets, positioning themselves amid the flow of likely customers; teamsters maintained street stands near retailers of furniture, while hacks cruised near the depots and hotels.

Youngsters dodged cars as they played ball, chase, tag, or jump rope. The low, warm blues sound of a harmonica caught the gentle afternoon breeze, and wafted through the laughter of the children and the honking horns.

I didn't know at that moment that the music would soon lead me to yet another activity.

The stationary snow-cone vendor with his large white ice crushing machine, giant yellow umbrella pitched precariously behind him, caught my eye. Ah hah! Wagon. Mr. Leo. Ice.

~~*~~

I had an idea - and enough money from shining shoes to get started. A real ice crushing machine was out of the question, but I knew what I could do on a small scale – and be mobile, too!

My work with Mr. Leo chipping and hauling ice would serve me well. Building a flat-bed wagon would be easy, since I had already built one back home to haul The Grits newspaper.

I laid out the wood, four buggy wheels, nails, red paint, a saw and a hammer on the narrow sidewalk between apartment buildings. The metal peddler haggled with me over the price of the non-corroding tin to line the wooden box that would store the 25-pound ice, and a drip pan that would be emptied daily.

After a long day, the wagon was finished. The following morning I made a trip to the local A&P economy store to buy a metal ice scraper, paper cups, ice, and three flavored syrups.

But wait! If I buy a carton of assorted flavors of Kool-Aid™ (raspberry, cherry, grape, orange, lemon-lime, and strawberry) for five-cents a package, I can make enough syrups for better profit. I returned the ice block and the syrups, and replaced them with large plastic containers, a bag of sugar and a carton of Kool-Aid.™ I would return for the ice the next day.

Pleased with myself and my purchases, I gave a nod to the "Kool-Aid Kid", wearing an alpine hat and lederhosen, posed on the billboard outside the grocery. My plan was to boil the sugar in water, then add the powder flavoring to make the syrups for what were commonly known as the Hard Times Sundae and Penny Sunday.

I prepped the kitchen to make the syrups and slowly stirred the mixture. I recalled Mr. Leo telling me how the snowballs got their nicknames. "Durin' the Great Depression and Worl' War II, snowballs 'came available outsid-a Balt'more. They so cheap, they one-a few treats people could 'ford. People in need-a job could sell them snowballs, cuz there's little to none ov'head, boy."

He went on to tell me the difference between a "Snowball" and a "Snow Cone." Snow Cones consisted of hard, crunchy, shaved ice and limited amounts of syrup. The Snowballs were made from very fine powdered ice about the consistency of actual snow, and were drowned in syrup. Snow Cone, it is!

I made a mental note to thank Mr. Leo when I returned to Pine Bluff for my senior year in high school. If not for him, I would not have the quick and efficient ice shaving techniques to apply to my new venture.

Past midnight I completed the syrups, planned out a route and work hours, counted out pocket change, and looked forward to the following day.

I created a route for myself on three streets in the neighborhood –always on the lookout for shade- where I sold snow cones to children and adults for ten cents each. I quickly shaved the ice, scooped it up in a paper cup, and asked, "And what flavor would you like on your cone?"

I waited. "I want the red one. No! The orange! Can I have both?"

On a good day I made $25.00. It took me only two weeks to realize it was time to expand. I approached my basketball buddies with the idea, and Ira immediately said he could use the job.

Together, Ira and I made another wagon and set up a second route. I paid him five cents for every cone he sold. Business was good!

Willie wanted to sell snow cones. We constructed a third snow cone wagon. I set up a third route and paid Willie five cents for every cone he sold. Business was outstanding!

After paying expenses, I cleared $50.00 to $60.00 a day, a lot of money at that time. Not bad for three to four hours a day!

When I wasn't working as a shoeshine boy or hawking my snow-cones, I was on the court practicing ball handling, passing, cutting and finishing. We had competitive shooting drills from different spots on the court to build confidence and rhythm, and just for fun.

I placed myself 15 feet from the basket, turned and dropped in a long shot. I ran for the ball, retrieving and dribbling before passing it to Ira. Willie boasted to Shorty and Canyon about the money he made from selling snow cones.

Ball tucked under his arm, Ira asked, "Y'all be leaving back South in a month, Sunny. Interested in selling the wagons?"

I hadn't thought about what I would do with them in the next month, but it took only a few seconds to respond. "Let's make a deal in two weeks!" I did not have the foresight to think that one day the snow cone business would become a multi-million dollar enterprise.

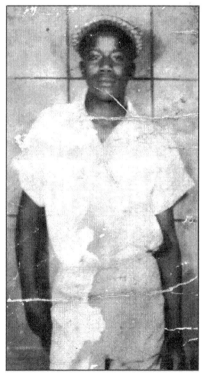

~~*~~

When we weren't competing on the abandoned tenement lot throwing balls into the hoopless rim, or selling snow cones, the five us: Willie, Ira, Shorty, Canyon and I, formed a singing group. We harmonized as best we could as we stood on a street corner ready to sing for anyone who might listen.

We became recognizable because of the colorful crocheted caps on our heads. We didn't sing without them, like it gave us an edge on our opposition on the corner across the same street. We did not have songs of our own, but copied the doo-wop sounds of the times, such as "Little Darlin" and "Earth Angel." I had a high, tinny voice that faded into the background as we snapped our fingers and moved our hips, stepping front, side and back. We thought we were "cool."

~~*~~

Before I knew it, the summer was over. I said my goodbyes to Cyber and thanked him for teaching me how to make music with a shoeshine rag. Willie, Ira, Shorty, Canyon and I assured each other we would be back on court the following year. I sold the three snow cone wagons to my singing basketball buddies.

I headed back to Pine Bluff for my senior year in high school.

~~*~~

I had earned enough money to purchase a black and white television set for the family back home – our first!

The blonde wooden cabinet with the RCA 12" screen was placed in the front room. An extra set of twenty-one tubes was stored to replace weak and burned out tubes.

As the TV warmed up, adjustments had to be made: the TV stations would go on air about mid-afternoon with a feathered Indian head test pattern so we could adjust the set's gray values; the picture would roll up and down at times, or pull horizontally; white streaks would cross the picture when a car drove by.

The picture was fuzzy at times, but it didn't matter to the younger boys there watching Amos & Andy, Bozo the Clown, Cisco Kid or Howdy Doody. Their laughter and shrieks of delight made everyone around them smile.

Neighbors sat with Mom and Dad in the evening to watch Meet the Press, The Ed Sullivan Show, and Truth or Consequences. Discussions about news and entertainment followed their favorite programs.

From the porch I heard the hum of the television. My mind

drifted to how quickly I had adapted to life in Chicago. I daydreamed I was in the city. My mother's laughter broke into my thoughts—and with it a hangover of guilt.

CHAPTER SIX
1953 - 1957

My senior year in high school was similar to my last. I lettered in football, track, and basketball. I attended to Mr. Steve before leaving for work at the Ranch House after school. On week-ends, I ferried groceries, mowed grass, cut weeds, delivered The Grits, and hauled ice with Mr. Leo.

After graduating I returned to Chicago, at Lula Mae's invitation. I couldn't know then I had left Pine Bluff for the last time.

I found work as a porter on the Super Chief, flagship of the Santa Fe railroad. A round trip between Chicago and Los Angeles took six days, twice a month. For the next two years I learned a grueling job, acquired a girlfriend, and kept loving basketball.

~~*~~

One day I got home to the apartment before Lula Mae returned from work. Without a key I perched on the steps to wait for my sister and openly stared at the attractive young Black woman, sitting on the porch next door. *On a scale from one to ten, this girl is a ten plus.* While I'm waiting I should make good use of my time, and there's no time like the present.

As I approached the porch, she smiled, and we both said hello at the same time. Her name was Marie. She had just finished high school and had just arrived in Chicago from Louisiana. She, too, was staying with an older sister, and would begin work the following day as a secretary. Marie was shy and soft spoken, and rarely made eye contact with me as she spoke, but when I was talking she looked directly into my eyes and listened attentively. Within a week Marie and I began to share an ice cream, eat popcorn at the movies, walk in the park, or window shop. She would become my cheerleader on the basketball court.

~~*~~

I found my friends Willie Tate, Ira Jackson, James "Shorty" Dickson, and Steve "Canyon" Kelly shooting ball on the court. We took up competing with each other as though I had never left, and confidently signed up for the Chicago Parks and Recreation summer league for the next two years. Fortunately, major tournaments were played during my free time from the railroad. Twice I switched trips with another porter so I could play.

Our team of five played other teams throughout the city. Our drills paid off, as we took the championship time after time. College scouts were seen at the tournaments, assessing individual players and teams as a whole. The five of us received, and accepted, full scholarship offers to go to Savannah State College, Georgia.

~~*~~

The others accepted, but I hesitated, and after considerable thought, I felt it was best to work a bit and then go to college. Lula Mae and Junior had spoken with me at length about limited work opportunities for the Negro in an era of significant racial prejudice and segregation.

"The railroads are hiring, Sunny. They're the biggest employer of Negros around." They believed the railroads held the promise of employment and opportunity and encouraged me to seek work as a porter.

~~*~~

The city bus came to a stop. I stepped onto the sidewalk and looked up at the pink granite, and red pressed brick-clock of the Dearborn Railway Station (also known as Polk Street Station) in downtown Chicago.

Me? At eighteen a porter for the Santa Fe Railway flagship, the Super Chief? Anticipation gripped me. The luxury passenger train known as "The Train of the Stars," carried celebrities between Chicago, Illinois, and Los Angeles, California.

Inside the passenger terminal, people lined up at the ticket counters, while others rushed away checking their tickets. Tearful goodbyes and excited hellos echoed throughout the terminal. Business men smoked cigars and read papers while women chatted together and attempted to calm noisy children in the waiting room.

I stopped at the Colored Only bathroom before weaving my way around the baggage area, and out onto the railway platform. The giant, diesel-electric Super Chief locomotive, in classic war-bonnet livery of red, gold and silver, hummed noisily as it warmed up in preparation for its 36-hour and 49 minute run to Los Angeles.

Since the station porters, sleeping porters, dining room porters, cooks, and Red Caps (railway station porters) lined up there, it was easy to find the boarding staff car. We were expected to arrive two hours prior to departure and on our own time, to dress and prepare the car we were responsible for. The railroad supplied our all-white uniforms, a club car with dormitory bunks for sleeping, and two meals a day. We only had to bring our shoes. We would be paid $80.00 a month for three round-trips between Chicago and Los Angeles.

Apprehension now gripped me. I was completely on my own for the first time – no family to come home to at the end of the day. Stop it, Sunny! This is one of the best jobs available for Negros. Mom and Lula Mae both would be sayin' to be thankful for what you have and do your job with dignity. And I don't doubt they're prayin' it, too!

I shook myself out of my reverie, as introductions were made. The new hires were separated into groups by porter designation. We listened attentively to the instructions of becoming "properly humble" dining room servers in uniform. We would greet passengers, serve food and drinks, keep the cars tidy, and always be expected to smile. Thus, the porters often called the job, ironically, "miles of smiles."

Departure time came and we heard the final call of "Board!" The locomotive shuddered into motion. The wheels rolled jerkily, then smoothed out, as the train moved slowly out of the ferry terminal. The rocking didn't affect the dining car – glasses didn't fall off the tables. The train would roll and lean slightly when going around a curve – glasses remained upright.

The dining car had ceiling lights running its length. Table lamps on top of the crisp white linens that covered the tables on either side of the center aisle leant an elegant ambiance to the dining experience.

Passengers began filling up the dining car, and the crew became busy with seating, filling water glasses, giving out menus and recommending the day's special, taking meal orders to the pantry and shouting them out to the chef.

Fresh food was prepared to order and served on china, in crystal and eaten with silver. Some of the dishes prepared by the chefs were: Braised Duck Cumberland, Hungarian Beef Goulash with Potato Dumplings, Lobster Americaine, Mountain Trout Au Bleu, Curry of Lamb Madras, Scalloped Brussels Sprouts, Pecan and Orange Sticks and Pennepicture Pie (a cream pie with toasted meringue).

We checked and double-checked orders before bringing them to the table – a happy passenger meant a tip. Tips were important to us, as the pay alone was barely a livable wage.

Green padded chairs swiveled, so passengers had the added unique visual entertainment of the ever-changing view through large windows.

At the end of the 14 to 16 hour day, we cleaned up the dining car and prepped it for the 5:30 morning call.

~~*~~

I made my way to the club car, tips in my pocket. At one end of the dormitory style room was a small area with a table and chairs. Porters would gather to talk about the day's activities, the various passengers we tended to, or what we saw from the observation car. The first night of the route we slept on board - or stayed up to play poker.

By convention, Negro porters were often addressed as "George" by passengers, but at the poker table we went by our given names. We played five-card stud for $5.00 a pot on our downtime.

Poker, in its most basic form, is a zero-sum game. When one player loses, another gains. How tough can this be?

"Harlen, empty those pockets and give yourself a sit!"

Thomas, a 44-year-old dining room porter from Georgia, was the heavyweight. He spent each night of the run between cities playing poker. His eyes continually flipped between the cards and the four men at the table.

I quickly learned that each of us (four to eight, depending on passenger needs) had a "tell." Some subconscious twitch or unnatural move that gave away what cards we held.

"Have a little ear itch, Harlen?" Laughter erupted as I blushed and removed my hand from the back of my ear.

I wanted to play all the time. It was a thrill to win. And when I lost, I just knew I would be a winner the next time. My motivation for playing changed from being fun to finding ways to play more skillfully.

"Got the last passenger tucked up. Deal me in."

Uriah, a sleeping porter, joined our game. He was a handsome fiftyish man and one of the best players at the table. I thought about leaving the game, but I was up $45. It was still early and, well, this was the only game in town.

Poker pits player against player. It took a mere four minutes of being dealt a new round of cards when Uriah called the first bet – and took the pot. I went from hero to zero in one hand.

~~*~~

The train sped through the night toward Union Station in Los Angeles. Shortly before arrival, we had finished removing the table covers, the cooks had the kitchen cleaned, and the sleeping porters had the beds stripped and remade. The crew gathered together in the dining room, and looked through the windows.

"Well, once we pull in, things'll be back to street-normal until we get back on in the morning, gents!"

Uriah was tired. His final job of the evening was to babysit, so the young married parents could have a few moments sans a crying four-year-old before departing the train.

We chatted about the street-normal: separate water fountains, the back-of-the-bus rule, separate hotels and eating facilities, and countless other injustices of a country with racial problems.

I couldn't understand how Black and White existed within a mutual relationship of trust and respect aboard the intimate confines of the railroad car. Well, other than being called George! Why did White people out in the community refuse to drink from the same fountain of water as a black man, and yet boarded a train and had black porters dress them and put them to bed and if they'd had one drink too many, press their clothes, babysit their children and a myriad of other personal details far more intimate than using the same drinking fountain?

Thomas said, "Think a bit. It's a struggle every day, but we interact up close and personal, and it's a step toward us being seen as real people instead of a stereotype. Bottom line, we're goodwill ambassadors!"

Uriah laughed and pointed a finger at me.

"Harlen, you keep working hard, you can be promoted to sleeping porter!"

Not only no, but hell no!

Some of the porters had changed to street clothes and talked about a woman to see, or a nightclub to go to. The train came to a stop at the huge depot across the street from the Los Angeles Plaza in Chinatown. The crew got off as quickly as did the passengers.

Where do I go – what am I expected to do in Los Angeles?

Thomas saw the panicked look on my face. "C'mon, kid. Come with me." As the redcaps swarmed alongside the train, Thomas pointed toward Aliso Street.

"Back in '48 the Super Chief lost its brakes coming into the station. It smashed through a steel bumper and concrete wall, and stopped with one third of the front of the "hog" (locomotive) dangling over Aliso. Nobody was killed or injured, but we never saw the "hoghead" (engineer) after that."

The railroad had a contract with the black owner of a run-down hotel for the dining car crew to sleep, directly across from the depot. Our rooms and meals would be paid for. The hotel catered mainly to black rail workers who came into town on trains operated by the Santa Fe, Southern Pacific and Union Pacific railways.

"This is where we'll eat, sleep and play, Harlen. We're not welcome in other hotels. But don't let it bother you none, it's only for a night."

We walked across Alameda Street and entered the ground floor, which had a pool hall, fast food place, and recreation center. All three of the upper floors were bedrooms. The owner had some prostitutes on the upstairs floors, and he supplied bad booze for those who suffered from a great thirst.

Despite the noise and boozy smells creeping under the door into my room, I was up and back on the train at 4:30 in the morning. I helped the crew prepare the dining car for our 6:30 departure back to Chicago – and thought about the upcoming evening and playing cards.

It became a constant thought – the next poker game. It took me five round trips between Chicago and Los Angeles to realize that it was a game I was becoming addicted to.

I made a decision to not play the game again. The decision had nothing to do with my family, religion, or my upbringing - I just couldn't stand to lose my money.

PART TWO
COLLEGE, MARRIAGE, DRAFTED

I was leaving the South
To fling myself into the unknown.
I was taking a part of the South
To transplant in alien soil,
To see if it could grow differently,
If it could drink of new and cool rains,
Bend in strange winds,
Respond to the warmth of other suns

And, perhaps, to bloom.

RICHARD WRIGHT

CHAPTER SEVEN
1958 - 1959

In August, 19 58, I took a 19-hour uneventful bus ride to Savannah State College. Again, I would have a grueling schedule: playing basketball, attending classes, studying nights, and working in the cafeteria as a food server. During lunch and dinner I served food from the steam table. The job gave me access to nighttime snacks for my study, and for my team buddies. Ham sandwiches, fruit, and a variety of drinks were sneaked into the dorm on a regular basis during the next year.

The Savannah State Tigers were the only undefeated team in the Southeast Athletic Conference (S.E.A.C.). I didn't know at the time how big a part basketball would play in my life, or how sweet would be the taste of recognition. Years later, I realized recognition could also be cruel.

I also didn't know that I would soon be taking a bus ride to Fort Leonard Wood, Missouri that would be a far different experience from college, and would set in motion future events that would change me forever.

In early November I learned that Marie was pregnant. The letter she sent me telling me the news was tearful. She told me she felt very alone and didn't feel I cared about her. During Thanksgiving break I returned to Chicago and married her in front of a Justice of the Peace. I assured her that I did care and that I looked forward to the child we would have. Marie remained in Chicago with her sister and continued working as a secretary. I returned to college and worried a lot about what I ought to do – quit school? Find a job to help support my family?

My son Fernando was born April 2, 1959. To fulfill the athletic contract I was bound to, I was not able to return to Chicago for his birth. At the end of the May semester, I boarded the overnight bus, anxious to see my new son: a beautiful, smooth-skinned boy with big eyes and sparse, but very curly hair. His tiny hand curled around my index finger gave me a deep pleasure I had never before experienced.

I noodled about continuing school or staying in Chicago to find work. Mid-June I received a letter from the U.S. Army Selective Service, stating they had tried several times to locate me. Through public records, they sent a letter to Marie. I was drafted into the army and was to report to the Addison Street recruiting station the following week. The college deferment I requested was not accepted.

~~*~~

The army provided bus tickets to leave for Fort Leonard Wood, Missouri, on July 1st I held Marie in one arm and Fernando in the other.

Looking away from me, she said, "I should be used to this now – you always leaving."

Over her head, I could see a group of 30 recruits saying tearful goodbyes to loved ones. I made a feeble attempt to assure her. "I don't know what to expect, Marie, but I'll do my best to make sure we're together soon." Before boarding the bus for the ten-hour ride, I kissed her and baby Fernando, my stomach in knots – part apprehension, part anticipation.

The trip was uneventful as we made our way into the rugged Ozark foothills to the training center. Black recruits sat in the back of the bus, a few humming quietly - Whites sat in the front half. We were all young. For many it was the first time away from home – and we didn't know what to expect.

The bus pulled to the front of the mess hall, where a line of soldiers waited for their dinner. We were hungry, and after a short wait in line we had our first army meal before being guided to the barracks for a night's rest.

I made my way up the stairs to the latrine on the second floor, stopping to look out a window. My heart raced when I saw a group of men walking towards a building 200 feet away. They were laughing and one of them, walking backwards, was bouncing a basketball on the walk. I watched until they disappeared into the building. I walked into the latrine, where the five toilets were all out in the open, against the wall. There would be no shame and no secrets here!

Back down to the first floor, I opened my military issued duffel bag. After pulling on civilian shorts and lacing up my high-top tennis shoes, I sprinted to the gymnasium. The men were playing three-on-three at one end of the court while other soldiers sat on bleachers against the wall, observing. The other end of the court was vacant. Not knowing how to approach them, I picked up a ball from the adjoining supply room and started shooting baskets by myself.

I dribbled, made long-shots, practiced handling the ball behind and around my body, and dunked the ball, aiming for quick repetitions. Within the half-hour, I was answering questions, "Where you from, man? Where have you played basketball? Are you stationed here? What's your assignment?" The questions kept coming, so fast I didn't know where to begin or to end.

The following day, I learned the men in the gym were new recruits, too. Fort Leonard Wood was merely a stop-over before we would board a bus to Fort Benning, Georgia, for boot camp. The next three days, between sleeping and eating, 12-15 recruits were on the court. I became close with three of the men that would be sharing the trip with me the following day.

On the fourth day, we lined up with our duffel bags, ready for the 16-hour trip to Georgia. Of the thirty-five recruits, I was the only person of color – and grateful for the new friendships between Ernie, Gary, Vincent and me.

This bus ride would prove to be like no other, and exposed me to a world from which I had, up to this time, been somewhat protected.

~~*~~

The bus driver pulled onto the dirt lot at a roadside diner in Gentryville, Missouri, so the troops could eat lunch and use the restrooms. One by one we stretched as we slipped out of our cramped seats to leave the bus. As I stepped out of the bus, the driver said, "You can't use the can – it's for Whites only." He turned away from me, following the Whites Only sign, arrow pointing to the east side of the building. I hadn't had anything to eat or drink since breakfast at sunrise, so I didn't have the need then, but I wondered what I was to do if the urge hit me.

The four of us entered the buffet line together, Ernie in front of me and Gary and Vincent behind me. I was the 14th person in line. The pimple-scarred server slammed the vegetable ladle on the countertop, and with a loud clipped accent, said, "Boy, you can't eat here. Go 'round to the back door for a plate. Can't you read the sign - Whites Only?" The buzz of conversation and quiet laughter quickly died as the recruits heard this exchange. I froze.

Entering the front door, meal tickets in hand, the 6'5" tall, pot-bellied, graying sergeant, walked directly to me. "Don't tell me I'm going to have to babysit you, boy. Get your behind around to the back door!"

Seconds passed, and with great restraint, I said, "With all due respect, sir, I will not go to the back door. I believe I'm in the same army as everyone around me."

He shrugged and said, "Suit yourself. Then you won't eat."

Maintaining as much dignity as I could, I walked through the front door to the closest rear tire of the bus - thinking along the way, we all had received the same kind of draft notices, were required to leave school, or careers, and families to serve under the same Uncle Sam. I could feel burning behind my eyelids – I had the sensation of being in this position before, but unable to make sense of it, or put a name to it.

~~*~~

In a show of support, Ernie, Gary and Vincent followed me. As I unzipped to relieve myself, my three friends did the same – all of us aiming at the bus tire.

As we stood in a semi-circle around the tire, Vincent, the quiet, serious one we called the professor, paused for a few seconds before saying in a pained voice, "Guys, we make a pact right now. These idiots will never know by our actions or expressions how much they've hurt one of us. It's a known fact what happens to one, happens to all. Karma can be a bitch, you know!" Smiling, we stacked our hands one on top of the other, sealing the pact.

Together, we went without food as we travelled through Jackson, Pocahontas, and Memphis, Tennessee; then through Union County, Mississippi. In Tupelo, I experienced my first For Colored Only water fountain attached, by a common pipe, to the For White's Only fountain. The White water fountain was on an upright stand, while the Black one was simply attached on a wall.

The bus continued through Birmingham, Alabama, on down through Montgomery and into Columbia, Georgia. We talked among ourselves, waging bets on if, and when, one of the recruits would sneak us some little bit of food or drink from a diner - it never happened. The worst among them were a handful of boys from the South. They would climb into the bus, never making eye contact with any one of the four of us, burping and talking about their latest meal - loud enough to make sure we heard every word.

We only left the bus to use bathroom facilities; if a For Colored Only sign was not posted, we made a semi-circle and peed on the bus tire.

~~*~~

Outside Tuskegee, Alabama, I overheard a soldier comment, "I don't think the colored boy knows about Jim Crow around here!" Laughing and back-slapping, they stepped away from their seats to disembark for yet another diner along the highway.

"What's a Jim Crow?" I asked Gary, sitting in the seat next to me.

He motioned to Vincent, "Hey, professor, we need you over here!"

We left the bus to stretch our limbs and get some fresh air while the rest of the troops, meal tickets in hand, went inside, ignoring us. I learned that Vincent, a history major, was in his second year at Dartmouth College in Hanover, New Hampshire, when he received his draft notice. His deferment request had also been denied.

For the next hour Vincent explained to me that Jim Crow was not a real person, but a characterization originated in 1828 by white New York comedian, Thomas Dartmouth "Daddy" Rice. He performed in blackface his song and dance that he called Jump Jim Crow. Rice's performance was supposedly inspired by the song and dance of a physically disabled colored man he had seen in Cincinnati, Ohio, named Jim Cuff or Jim Crow.

Rice performed across the country as "Daddy Jim Crow," a caricature of a shabbily dressed colored man. Jump Jim Crow initiated a new form of music and theatrical performances that focused their attention on the mockery of Negros. This new genre was called the minstrel show, and spread rapidly across the United States and eventually around the world.

An example of this influence came when the United States' special ambassador to Central America, John Lloyd Stephens, arrived in Merida on Mexico's Yucatan Peninsula in 1841. On his arrival a local brass band played Jump Jim Crow mistakenly thinking it was the national anthem of the United States. The popularity of Jump Jim Crow and the blackface form of entertainment prompted many Whites to refer to most Colored males routinely as Jim Crow.

Eventually the term Jim Crow was applied to the body of racial segregation laws and practices throughout the nation. White people had to make free slaves more equal, but soon feared that they would lose their status as being superior to Negros. So these laws were made out of fear that the Negros would become better than the White people.

As early as 1837 the term Jim Crow was used to describe racial segregation in Vermont; most of these practices, however, emerged in the southern and border states of the United States by 1876. The first Jim Crow Law was passed in 1888 in Louisiana. The laws were examples of social control legislation. In theory, the law was supposed to create separate but equal status treatment, but in practice Jim Crow Laws condemned Negro citizens to inferior treatment and facilities. The laws reinforced poverty and political exclusion.

The most important Jim Crow Laws required that public schools, public facilities, water fountains, toilets, and public transportation, like trains and buses, have separate facilities for Whites and for Negros. These laws meant that Black people were legally required to attend separate schools and churches, use public bathrooms marked "For Colored Only," eat in a separate section of a restaurant, and sit in the rear of a bus.

I tried to digest the significance of what Vincent was saying. Before he finished explaining Jim Crow to me, it was no longer an invisible prejudice, but in-my-face and real. I was beginning to understand things I had taken for granted up until now.

I didn't know then that I would experience these same prejudices in a variety of ways for the next 50 years.

~~*~~

Finally we arrived in Fort Benning, hungry, weary and disheveled. Minutes before arriving at the base, the aged, white recruiting lieutenant stood in the aisle, and said, "Listen up, all of you. You've had your fun. From here on out, Colored or White, you will live together, work together, eat together and crap together. The U.S. Army was ordered to integrate in 1948 – respect it!"

The bus stopped in front of a row of long, wooden barracks. He walked to the rear of the bus and in a no-nonsense voice said, "I want all of you to line up outside the bus – get moving."

Men poured out of the bus and as Ernie, Gary, Vincent and I started to get up, he motioned with his hand to wait. We looked at each other, eyes wide, brows raised. "Come along, gentlemen." We followed the lieutenant off the bus, where he said, "Next to me – two and two." Ernie and Vincent stood to his left, as Gary and I stepped to his right.

The lieutenant paced up and down the line of recruits before speaking, "Take a good look at the men standing in front of you. They're an example of teamwork and substance. They exhibited the highest standards of conduct under vile conditions."

He began pacing again, eyes sweeping over the men as he walked. He spoke with purpose, "They had each other's back. They're the kind of men this Army wants and needs – and the kind of men I want at my back!" He ordered the men to fall out, get their belongings and report to the Barracks 15 sergeant.

He turned to us once again, "Welcome, privates! Your conduct will not go unnoticed." Smiling, he dismissed us with a final, "And when you're done getting settled in, ask the sergeant for a brush and detergent. I want that tire cleaned before nightfall."

CHAPTER EIGHT
1959-1961

Within two hours of stowing my duffel bag in the barracks, eating a chicken dinner in the mess hall, and cleaning the bus tire, I found the gymnasium. My mind was made up. I was going to play basketball for the U.S Army team. We had a rigorous daily schedule during the next six weeks; free time was 8:00-9:00 p.m. I raced to the gym to shoot balls for thirty minutes before dashing back to the barracks to shower, write a quick letter, or organize my wall locker before lights out was called.

At 0430 hours the following morning, we began initial preparations for U.S. Army basic training. The day was spent getting a close haircut, physical exam, inoculations, and distribution of uniforms and personal gear, such as a mouth guard and groin protector. In the afternoon we were instructed in upkeep of the barracks, standing and basic marching.

The next five weeks were spent in daily fitness training, diet monitoring, and basic combat procedures to assure we could properly work together and defend ourselves – as well as our fellow soldiers, if necessary. Gary, in hand-to-hand combat with one of the back-slapping recruits on the bus, gleefully asked, "Got the concept, buddy?" We were given classroom instruction in army core values, day-to-day personal life in the army and race relations.

We progressed from unarmed to armed combat training, map reading, land navigation, and compass use. We learned marksmanship techniques and maintenance tasks, including field stripping: quickly disassembling, cleaning, and reassembling the standard issue rifle. Squads teamed up to negotiate a series of obstacles with emphasis on working as a team. We trained in evaluating and properly treating casualties. We were sent to the gas chamber, a large, sealed room where we were subjected to CS gas, a riot control agent. We removed our protective mask, gasping as we recited our Social Security number before exiting the chamber. We received a pugil stick, a heavily padded pole-like training weapon used for rifle and bayonet combat. Panting from exertion, I protested, "Darn, Ernie, take it easy with that thing!" I now knew why recruits were given groin protectors.

The final week was continual, intense physical training, as well as drill and ceremony training. The drill sergeants and platoon leaders were tough, but fair, encouraging success in each phase of the training. The final three days were considered recovery, where we ensured the barracks were in good order to receive the next platoon of trainees. We had a final fitting of our dress uniform and then practiced for our graduation ceremony.

Gary, Vincent, Ernie and I were given military assignments that would separate us. At graduation we shook hands and told each other we would keep in touch. We would miss talking together in the mess hall, playing one-on-one basketball in the evenings, and coaching each other through our exercises. One final time we stacked our hands one on top of the other, and proclaimed ourselves brothers forever.

~~*~~

In September, 1959, I received orders to depart in two days. I was to report to the 3rd Armored Battalion, 36th Infantry – at Ayers Kaserne, Kirch-Goens, Germany. The armored division, unofficially nicknamed the Third Herd, was stationed in West Germany for much of the Cold War, which was in a state of political and military tension after World War II between the United States and its allies, and powers in the Soviet Union.

As I held those orders in my hand, my mind raced and my heart pounded. How am I going to give Marie the news I'm leaving - this time for another country? I picked up the barracks telephone and waited for the switchboard operator. Marie answered. I listened as she breathlessly told me about Fernando loving his bath time, kicking and splashing. He would giggle when passing gas. He was sleeping less during the day. As she talked about her discontent at work and wishing we were together, my anguish was growing.

"Marie, I don't know how to say this, except to just say it. I'm being sent to Germany. I'm leaving day after tomorrow."

The silence was deafening.

I continued talking, "I love you. I promise we will be together soon."

I heard her sigh. I heard the dial tone. She had hung up.

I thought about Marie, as the military plane took off, noisy with the chatter of 100 army and navy personnel. Men who were returning provided us a few details about why the units were stationed in one of six bases in Germany. Just last year in 1951, U.S. major combat forces returned to Europe, becoming the public face of the army to Europeans and Americans as well as the rest of the world. The army sergeant said, "We directed almost all our training, equipment, and force development toward that potential day when our troops would face Soviet divisions coming through the Fulda Gap into Germany."

The words armored, battalion and infantry were becoming crystal clear to me, as the sergeant continued, "The establishment of a credible conventional deterrent in Germany, backed up with our nuclear forces, is one of the central linchpins of the U.S. strategy of containment of Soviet power." Those actions were a visible symbol to the world that America had placed its flag and its soldiers in harm's way to reinforce its commitment to peace and freedom in Europe.

Twenty-seven hours later, after a stop in Canada, we landed at the Ayers Kaserne Army base, one of the U.S. military installations on German soil. We were directed to our barracks, stowed our gear, and walked to the mess hall. The server, a fresh-faced blond, shouted out as he placed the bowls on our food tray, "Here you go, gents, rags and fleas for everybody!" It was the nickname for the steaming bowl of traditional German stew of broth, vegetables, potatoes and a meat. Sometimes the cooks would change it up with kale and smoked meat, or beans and pork.

We had been given a free flight recovery day from duty. I asked where I would find the gym before returning to the barracks for a shower and change into shorts and tee shirt.

Within the hour I was in the gym shooting baskets. Other soldiers playing three-on-three stopped to watch me. A couple of hours later a short, slender white man with a crew cut and dressed in street clothes entered the gym. He stood in the doorway watching for 15 minutes, before calling out to me, "Soldier, come over here." He introduced himself as Lieutenant Griffith, the basketball coach for the HQ 3rd Armory Battalion, 36th Infantry. "I believe you're Specialist 4th Class Harlen Lambert."

"Yes sir."

He said my reputation had preceded me, and that I was assigned to play on the 3rd Army Division basketball team. From that day forward I practiced four hours alone in the gym, followed by two hours team practice.

Two weeks later I played my first formal U.S. Army basketball game. Top brass, their families, and soldiers of all ranks filled the gymnasium. I could hear the shouts and clapping as I scored 43 points and pulled down 13 rebounds. Three nights later, the crowd broke out into an uproar, when I set an all-time individual scoring record for the Kirch-Goens Waynewright Gym record with 47 points and 17 rebounds. Seven days later I broke records again.

The Stars and Stripes Newspaper reporters covered the games: "Lambert collected 58 points – equal to the opposition's total score – to shatter a 49-point game record he set earlier in the week against the 3d Army. The 27 field goals, four free throw efforts lifted Lambert's game average to 37.2 – the best in the 3d Army Division."

~~*~~

In mid-October, I received orders to report to 3rd Army Commander General Abrams' office. I was nervous about meeting him. The desk sergeant announced me before I entered his office. The tall and slim general, in his early 60s, had an aristocratic air. He stood and welcomed me to the 3rd Army Infantry Division. "Congratulations, Specialist. You've been selected to play on the All Army Basketball Team."

The general indicated I was to sit and relax, "I've seen your personnel packet and I'm very impressed with all I've read and heard about you." The general immediately put me at ease with his warmth and friendly manner. We talked sports — basketball, baseball and football.

We then talked about family. He told me if I wanted to bring my family to Germany I had his permission, and he would assist in finding us off-base living quarters. He explained that sergeants and above were given military housing; therefore, recruits like me either lived in the barracks or had to find off-base living.

Obviously, I couldn't bring a family to live in the barracks. I left his office feeling on top of the world.

I went directly to the barracks telephone, and this time I wasn't apprehensive about talking with my wife. "Marie, it's time to plan a trip to Germany!" I explained I would search for an apartment in the small military community of Kirch-Goens, 25 miles out of Frankfurt. Over the next week we talked each day and finalized plans for her move.

Since my son was less than a year old, it would have been stressful to disrupt his established routines, so Marie and I, along with her family, made the decision to leave Fernando in the care of Marie's mother during our time out of the country.

In mid-November I picked up a tired, wan Marie from the Frankfurt airport. As the taxi transported us to Kirch-Goens, I told her about the apartment and what to expect. Off base housing was difficult to find, but I found a one-bedroom kitchenette. "It's small, Marie, with a wood-burning stove for heating and cooking. It's near the base, so it'll be easy to use the PX for grocery shopping and other items we'll need." I went on to tell her the base had a laundromat, cleaners, a movie theater and other entertainments to enjoy. We could also depend on base accommodations for use of a telephone and medical care.

~~*~~

When Marie arrived looking apprehensive, I reported, "I've met other military families living off base who look forward to meeting you, Marie. Some of the wives are already planning a shopping trip to Frankfurt. They want you to come! They've also offered transportation when we want to go from our apartment to the base."

Before long, Marie made friends with other service wives and became somewhat comfortable with her new surroundings. Using the wood-burning stove for cooking was a challenging experience for both of us, but we managed. We missed our young son, but took comfort in the monthly phone calls and letters we received from home, telling us of Fernando's first tooth, his first steps, his increasing appetite, and his easy smile.

Over the next 20 months, Marie attended all sporting events in which I played, except when the team traveled behind the Iron Curtain to Poland and Czechoslovakia.

When we were scheduled to play the Ray Barracks team at the Friedberg Armored Division. Marie and a group of wives came to the gymnasium earlier than usual. They also came gussied up more than usual, chattering excitedly.

Elvis Presley, now attached to the Friedberg Unit, walked to the center of the floor to sing the Star Spangled Banner before the game was to start. The crowd, along with the wives, erupted, standing and clapping. For years to come, Marie would tell anyone who would listen, that that night was the highlight of her time in Germany.

General Abrams took Marie and me under his wing. "Not only are you a soldier and a basketball player, Lambert, but now you're both friends and family." Mrs. Abrams, like her husband, was warm and welcoming.

General Abrams never missed an exhibition game. It didn't matter where, or in what country we played, he was there. He always made it a point to come into the locker room and congratulate the team.

~~*~~

During the off-season I was the trainer for the baseball and football teams. General Abrams' driver, Sergeant Dexter Fleming, would pick me up and take me to the practice fields. He would wait until practice was over and return me to our apartment near Kirch-Goens. One day he said, "We're coming up to the gate, Lamb. You gonna mess with Min today?"

Private Benjamin Dunn and his wife, Karen, lived in the same apartment complex. Benjamin had flaming red hair and a mass of freckles that jumped around as he mimicked Lucille Ball, Frank Sinatra or John

Wayne. We called him "Min," because of his lean, 5'5" frame. His quick wit and happy-go-lucky attitude drew people to him. We quickly became friends, and developed a question and answer game when I came through the gate, riding in the general's car.

On the way into the post, I would ask, "Hey, Min, how are you?" – on the way out, the question was "Hey, Min, what's up?" Private Dunn always had an answer that provided Sergeant Fleming, my driver, and me with a good laugh.

The Generals' car came to a stop at the post gate for its customary identification protocol. Private Dunn stood at attention, and saluted. I rolled down the rear window, smiled and asked, "Hey, Min, how are you?"

"I'm so happy! I finally got rid of the toe fungus!" Fleming and I erupted in laughter, as Min dropped his hand across his chest, indicating we could enter.

Team practice was over. "Great practice today, Lambert!" I heard as I walked off the field with the football squad toward the waiting car. As trainer for the team, and because I lived off base, the soldiers accepted that a car was provided for me.

On our return home, Sergeant Fleming stopped the car. Min stood at attention, and saluted. Through the open car window, I asked, "Hey, Min, what's up?"

He replied, "My middle finger." Fleming and I howled as Min indicated we could leave.

~~*~~

Entering my second year in the army, I was introduced to, and became friends with, Lieutenant Bradley, a former graduate and basketball player from the University of Wyoming. Meeting Lieutenant Bradley would prove instrumental to my professional future.

Bradley, a tall, lean blond with a crew haircut, his face scarred from teenage acne, became my self-appointed agent. "You have enormous talent, Lamb. When you're discharged and back in the States, I would like to see you pursue your education and basketball professionally."

He made contact with, and supplied numerous stateside universities with newspaper clippings, videos and action shot photos of me playing basketball. Before the end of the next season, Bradley had received scholarship offers for me to continue my education and to play basketball from no less than seven universities. One was the University of Southern California (USC). I looked forward to attending USC because of its academics, the reputation of the sports program, and the quality of its players. The fact it was located in Paradise, as the brochures claimed—— the California sunsets, Hollywood and Vine, movie stars, pearl beaches, and palm trees made my final decision a snap.

~~*~~

The day in June, 1961, came for me to rotate back to the States for discharge. I suddenly realized it was a sad day for me to leave good and close friends. General Abrams asked, "Will you consider re-enlisting for another two years? We want to keep The 36th Rangers at champion status!" He understood that I wanted to be with my son, whom I had seen only once since his birth - but I felt as though I had let the general down.

Lt. Colonel Fred Allen, Infantry Commander, placed a letter of commendation in my 201 file that laid out my contributions, services, and qualities needed to be a winner. He elaborated on my accomplishments as an outstanding basketball player, football trainer, and Little League coach. He stated my conduct manifested itself by "deeds not words." Lt. Colonel Allen stated I was a valuable asset and believed that as I returned to civilian life, my performance would continue to be outstanding.

General Abrams was a great friend and leader, and Lt. Colonel Allen, too, were great supporters. I was also thankful to have the friendship of Lieutenant Bradley, who worked diligently to make sure I continued my education.

Neither the Lieutenant nor I could know the roadblocks to education and playing professional basketball that lay ahead.

~~*~~

My wife flew back to Chicago on Lufthansa Airlines. As a civilian, she could not come home with me. As military personnel, I was required to cross the Atlantic on a gigantic military ship.

The ten day trip to New York was horrible. Troop accommodations consisted of sleeping compartments four-bunks high. The ship rocked and rolled crossing the ocean.

The first three days went reasonably well until the ship began listing to and fro. I became seasick the fourth day and spent the remainder of the trip in sickbay puking my guts out. I lost about a pound a day before reaching New York where I was honorably discharged.

I immediately boarded a United Caravelle twin-engine aircraft for Chicago to meet my wife and to see my son. I was looking forward to holding him for the second time since his birth, and getting to know him.

I dropped to my knees, arms outstretched. Fernando screeched and wobbled to me. Our connection was immediate. His arms tightened around my neck. My heart melted from Fernando's instant acceptance of his absent father.

CHAPTER NINE
1961 - 1964

Soon after, I left for Los Angeles to talk to the USC basketball coach, Forrest Twogood. He had salt and pepper hair and laugh lines around his eyes that crinkled with each frequent smile. "Let's take a tour, young man!" Within half a day, I knew the layout of the campus, what curriculum to explore, and details about the basketball team. I was impressed and looked forward to meeting with Coach Twogood again – this time as a student and team member.

I returned to Chicago and moved my family to an apartment in Los Angeles, fifteen minutes from the USC campus. Since it would be another three weeks before I was to meet with Coach Twogood for the second time, I searched out a local park with a basketball court and soon found new friends to practice with.

~~*~~

During rest periods, the players shared information. I listened intently to two of my new court buddies, who were black police officers. Bennie Wilkey, who we sometimes called "Hoagie," because we always saw him take one from his brown paper bag after games, became the first to share some of the trials he and others had gone through. He'd joined the Los Angeles police force in 1954 when it was totally segregated.

Bennie said, "We weren't allowed at any time to work with white partners or in White neighborhoods - couldn't even 'stand up' to a white man, even a white criminal." He went on to describe working only at night in the worst of areas. "Was a time, too, that if we didn't have a black partner to work with, we had to stay off the streets. A few years back, we had a station commander using his office as a distribution center for anti-black literature. And forget trying to advance! Bastards knock us back a hundred years if they can. Think about it, man. Word is Chief Parker's thinking about integrating LAPD. Even so, it'll still be slow for us to go forward."

After the basketball game, Tooey Loflun sat down next to us, wiped sweat from his brow, and chimed in, "Things are just as bad in Long Beach, man. Here it is 1962, and it hasn't been that long since restaurants down town wouldn't serve Blacks, so we had to sit in the car outside while our white partners ate inside. But let me back up. We started coming in,

84

and the white cops started quitting to join the LAPD. They were going to show everybody how they disliked integration." At this, he laughed and smacked his knee. Tooey had joined the Long Beach Police Department in 1952 and soon realized he would be disciplined for petty infractions that were routinely overlooked in white officers. He talked about whites receiving preferential treatment, promotions, and choice assignments.

Tooey and Bennie had more to say, but I finally had to ask, "So why, with that kind of environment, have you stayed?"

Opening his root beer, Tooey said, "There are times our two ounces of tin can be mighty heavy, but we have to believe in the system. The only way we can make a better world, not only for us but for everyone, is in the role of an officer within our communities."

Bennie, ever wise, said, "We have three basic choices, Lamb. One, you can resist and become branded as a troublemaker, which means you won't go anywhere in the department but out. Two, you can try to become 'one of the boys,' which isn't going to happen because you are chocolate, my brother. Or three, you can be like me and Tooey here, and don't say much, but carry yourself and do your job in such a way that you communicate to the worst of the Whites that you are an officer above reproach."

Tooey stood up, shifted the basketball back and forth between his hands, "And now, gentlemen, I challenge you to a twenty-point game. Losers buy the next root beer!"

I couldn't know then, that five years in the future, Bennie's number three would become a mantra for me.

~~*~~

Mid-morning I met with Coach Twogood for the second time. We walked to the gym, where he asked me to sit down.

"Harlen, the National Collegiate Association just passed the rule that an athlete who played for a four-year college prior, would have to sit out for one year to be eligible to participate in team sports."

Sitting there quietly, I tried to absorb this. Coach turned to me, "Why don't you attend Santa Ana College and play on their team? That would be better than just sitting out the one year."

I felt deflated, like the air had been sucked out of me. "Coach, at this point I'm not willing to follow up on other scholarship promises and changing rules. I would have to uproot my family once again, or leave them in an unfamiliar state – and I just can't do it again."

We parted with handshakes, and agreed that I'd enroll at Santa Ana College, and we'd meet here next year.

~~*~~

During enrollment at Santa Ana College I was told I was not eligible to play on the basketball team because of my age and because I had completed too many college units on the junior level. Another disappointment!

With great effort I recalled my mother's sage words, long ago explaining to me about all the different colored flowers one day being in one field. "Each of us is guided by a power larger than ourselves. Take one step at a time, Son, and let Him guide you. You'll be where you're supposed to be."

So I decided to put my energy in my studies.

~~*~~

After making a few trips into Santa Ana to seek a place to live, we quickly learned our only options were inside a specific area. Bristol Street was a solid invisible border that hemmed the Black population into an area known as "Little Texas" or "the Rock." Marie and I packed up our few belongings, most of them Fernando's, and moved into a rental house near First and Bristol Streets.

To support my family, I worked the night shift for Uniroyal, Inc., formerly United States Rubber Company, as a lab technician.

During a shift change, Austin, a co-worker, asked to speak with me. I followed his tall, lanky frame out to the parking lot. "Lamb, are you interested in a part-time weekend job as a motorcycle funeral escort?"

I was always looking for another way to make more money to provide for my family. "Sure. I'm very interested, but I've never operated a motorcycle."

Austin assured me that the two week training program provided by a private motor escort company would give me the certification and license needed – along with an escort uniform and a shiny, compact BMW motorcycle. The leather saddle-seat and the clear bug shield made the rides comfortable.

For the next twelve months I averaged three days a week and six processions, as well as taking refresher training courses to maintain the high standards of the profession.

~~*~~

One day when the funeral procession to Fairhaven Memorial Park was complete, I approached 17th and Tustin Avenue. A motorcycle police officer rode up beside me and asked me to pull over. We approached the curb, motorcycles side-by-side, hit the kickstands, killed the engines, and pulled our helmets off at the same time.

I thrust out my hand, "Hello, officer, I go by the name of Lamb."

"I'm Frank Rocha, with the Santa Ana Police Department. "I've observed you riding procession a couple times, and would like to get to know you."

Frank was medium height, slim build, partially bald with a fringe of dark hair. His easy-going manner and soft speaking voice belied the tough professional I would come to know.

After fifteen minutes of talk, he straddled his Harley Davidson and pulled on his helmet, "So, Lamb, think you'd want to be a cop?"

I straddled my BMW, helmet in hand, "Nope. Haven't thought about it."

Over the next months we spoke several more times. Frank always asked the same question, "Thought about it yet? Maybe one day we'll ride together!" We laughed and waved as he revved his engine, and pulled away to pursue the car speeding through the stop sign.

~~*~~

My shift at Uniroyal ended at 7 a.m. I would rush home to shower, have breakfast with Marie, play with Fernando, pick up my books and go to my political science class at 9 a.m.

The instructor, John Schmitz, made it clear to attending students that he was an outspoken conservative and staunch defender of the family. Schmitz was born in Wisconsin and studied philosophy at Marquette University. "My hero," he said, "is Senator Joseph McCarthy, who spent years trying in vain to expose communists and other left-wing loyalty risks in the U.S. government." Schmitz invited students to attend his class called 'Communist Propaganda Techniques' at the Marine Corps Air Station at El Toro, located near Irvine.

He lectured on the politics of the John Birch Society, of which he was a proud and outspoken member. According to Schmitz, (and later documented and titled "Orange County Civil Rights: A History of an Enduring Struggle for Equality" by OC Human Relations) following the killing of Captain John Birch by Chinese communists on August 23, 1945, Robert Welch started the John Birch Society in December, 1958, to fight communism in America. In its early days the group focused its efforts on opposing issues such as the Civil Rights Movement.

Welch argued that the average African American "has complete freedom of religion, freedom of movement, and freedom to run his own life as he pleases." So no movement was needed.

Schmitz was vocal, "Jews are like everybody else, only more so." He was anti-immigrant, anti-women's lib, anti-communist, anti-black, and anti-homosexual. Word on the campus was that he named his dog Kaiser and thought giving a Hitler salute a good joke.

In the early 1960s, Orange County residents joined the John Birch Society in droves. According to Lisa McGirr, author of "Suburban Warriors: the Origins of the New American Right," Princeton University Press, "The strength of the movement gained Orange County the reputation as the national home of the John Birch Society."

The actual headquarters were in Massachusetts. Orange County, in effect, gave birth in the early 1960s to a movement that would help shape the national political landscape and influence conservativism in the following years.

I was pleased when the semester ended, and I did not have to listen to more of, to my mind, John Schmitz's outrageous ramblings. My studies now consisted of community social services and small business elements. I attended two classes three mornings a week, and volunteered time assisting Coach Bob Boyd with their Santa Ana Dons basketball team.

HARLEN "Lamb" LAMBERT

PART THREE
LIVING LAW ENFORCEMENT

You may encounter many defeats,
but you must not be defeated.
In fact, it may be necessary
to encounter the defeats,
so you can know who you are,
what you can rise from,
how you can still come out of it.

MAYA ANGELOU

CHAPTER TEN
1964 - 1966

To stay in shape, I played basketball in the Santa Ana industrial league, a casual affiliation which would shape the next fifty-plus years of my life.

The Santa Ana police teams also played in that same industrial league.

Our three-man teams played sandlot ball. A game was twenty points and whoever made twenty points first met a new set of challengers. After defeating eight tough opponents, the Uniroyal team faced the Santa Ana Police - beating them decisively.

The teams came together with handshakes and shouts of "Great jump shot! Good shooting, man!"

I became friends with Andy Kahan, one of the players on the police team. Andy was a friendly, solid 210-pound motorcycle officer with a perpetual smile. After kicking some butt, and cooling down after a game, he suggested that I think about police work.

"You know, Lamb, the police department can use some good men. Don't know if you're aware, but the city's been criticized for not hiring Negro cops."

My first reaction was that he was joking, but I heard him and was intrigued. The subject came up again, increasing my interest even more when Andy's two partners on the team made similar suggestions: "The department is actively seeking qualified Negro applicants as police officers, Lamb. You might try the civilian ride-along program to get a feel for what we're about."

I was even more curious and told them I would give it serious thought.

~~*~~

I endured my year of attending classes at Santa Ana College that would allow me to enroll and play basketball at USC. At the end of that year, I contacted their sports department and was informed Coach Twogood was no longer the head coach and that I no longer had a scholarship.

"What happened to my scholarship?" I asked.

"Mr. Lambert, the National Collegiate Basketball Association (NCBA) has revised rules for the game, from scholarship requirements to on-court play rules."

The loss of my scholarship and dreams of playing basketball for USC was a major setback for me. I was stunned—with USC and the system itself. The childhood ambitions I once treasured were now a memory, a shadow lingering in the depths of my mind.

Soon after the telephone conversation ended, I sank into my easy chair remembering other disappointments. With each one, I was beginning to realize a pattern to my setbacks. Even at this moment, I'm losing my anger by rethinking things. I have allowed myself to mature and change, to grow into new perspectives. I have become comfortable enough in my own skin to use my creativity, to allow chaos and look it in the face. I can overcome, like King said. I am stronger from enduring setbacks. I can focus as needed to move in positive and perhaps new directions.

I decided to put my education on hold. I promised myself that I would one day return to college and complete my degree, no matter which school I ended up at.

I didn't want to talk to Mom about my latest upset with USC. In her desire to help, she would pull a quote from the Bible, thinking it would make me feel better, "Be humble and faithful to the Spirit in you. You're being burnished as gold."

And I didn't want to hear it. However, I realized I could quote my own verse. Mom taught me pretty well. Now, I can give her a call and reassure her that I can handle problems so she won't worry so much.

~~*~~

Now that we knew we would remain in Santa Ana, within two weeks of my conversation with USC, Marie and I purchased a trim bungalow with blooming rose bushes at 2301 West Cubbon Street, off Raitt Street. We were still within the West-side area, affectionately referred to as "Little Texas." Although segregated, it was a comfortable community, bound together by churches, clubs, barbershops, beauty salons, and the smoky tang from Shaw's barbecue wafting through the air.

I was entrenched in my full-time lab technician job, part-time motorcycle funeral procession escort, attending classes at Santa Ana

College, coaching the Dons basketball team, and playing basketball with the guys on the industrial league.

As I was putting on my uniform and buttoning my shirt to begin another motorcycle escort service, I remembered those police officers, Frank Rocha and Andy Kahan. The two men had repeatedly suggested I apply to become an officer of the law. "The department is actively seeking qualified Negro applicants, Lamb, and we think you'll fit right in. Why not try the ride-along program and get a feel for it?"

Initially I thought they were joking, but over a period of time, and with the loss of my scholarship, I thought why not?

~~*~~

Weeks later, I was in the front seat of a squad car as a civilian observer. Officer Katiz, an urbane, affable man of middle build and height, had a kind, deeply-lined face. "I've been on the department for eleven years, and still prefer to be on patrol. We have four districts and rotate between them.

"Santa Ana is 27 square miles and we only have 48 vehicles 'round the clock to patrol. Depending on what's going on, we can have five to nine units out at a time. In an emergency call, all or most of the patrol units would be on hand for backup."

Officer Katiz asked me gentle questions and made informing comments that reminded me of my kindly uncle Simon. "One of the first things you want to do, Harlen, is know where you are at all times. Look at street signs, neighborhoods, know what unit you're riding in, and get familiar with the districts if you decide to become a cop."

As a civilian observer, I could do only that – observe. And almost immediately, I realized that was not only a lack, but an absence of communication between the police and our communities. The police and the Black and Hispanic communities simply didn't know how to talk to each other, except through vulgar and hurtful name-calling.

Lack of communication is a commonly used phrase but difficult to imagine in its specifics. In this case, it meant that an officer responding to a call was often unable to find out what the problem was, much less solve it or resolve it peacefully.

Officer Massey, a burly, former Marine in his early thirties commented, "Those Black kids won't talk to us." He and other officers, by virtue of being White and from a different background, would often over-react, resulting in an arrest where the right question early in the situation would have quelled the disturbance.

I was affected as I watched this. For three months I rode as an observer with different patrol officers. I was concerned because I felt when groups don't know how to interact with each other, their knowledge of the other is more likely to be informed by hearsay, media portrayals, and cultural stereotypes, rather than personal experience.

My opinion was that racial equity was a priority objective to anyone committed to justice – and certainly to anyone wearing the blue uniform. Could I help bridge the communication gap?

With that thought, I was soon discussing with my wife the possibility of joining the reserves. Neither of us anticipated the problems that would come later. The issue was more the two hundred dollars a month cut in pay from my job as a lab technician.

Heroically – neither of us guessing at the time how heroically – she said to go ahead … "if that's what you really want."

~~*~~

Three days later, I went to the Santa Ana City Hall and filled out an application for the Police Reserves. The clerk, short and wide-hipped, looked at me through rose-rimmed glasses. She flipped through the application, pushed her graying hair behind one ear and shook her head. She chuckled, "You'll be called if you pass the background check."

It would be weeks before I learned that in the history of Orange County, now a population of 1,175,770, no Negro applicants had passed the background check or qualified for the position of police officer.

Later at the basketball court Andy jammed the ball into the net, "Harlen, we (the police officers I played basketball with) have no proof of whether that was deliberate discrimination." I suspected the climate of the late Sixties, and the Civil Rights Act signed into law by President Johnson the previous year (July 1964) suddenly made a more honest background check possible.

Within three weeks, I was informed I passed the background check and would now be interviewed by three different senior police officers. Once more, I felt grateful that sports and the loving concern of my family had kept me out of trouble earlier.

The questions were predictable. The most important question seemed to be "Why?" and I answered honestly. I repeated what I had noticed as an observer. I wanted to help.

~~*~~

I was accepted into the reserves and scheduled my time to ride with the officers four hours on week nights before dashing off to my regular job. On weekends I worked full eight-hour shifts. As a more in-depth background check was conducted, I would spend 186 hours with either a sergeant or senior officer. I would complete written and oral examinations, physical agility, psychological and polygraph tests.

There were no formal training officers. I wore a badge and uniform, showed up at roll call, and would be assigned to an available ranking officer. My role was mostly as an observer and backup support, and I was not to deal directly with the public unless asked to by the training officer I was with.

The seasoned officers I rode with were polite, but had little to say and other than the cursory questions of Why do you want to be a cop? Why Santa Ana? or Are you married? we rode in silence. The younger, more inexperienced officers had difficulty communicating with any person of color. In fairness, a few of them were awkward with everyone.

These were long, silent shifts, but I paid attention to how the lead officer performed as we patrolled the streets. During a coffee stop, I overheard two officers talking between themselves. "How do you like that nigger?" The second officer responded, "Niggers are good for only one thing, and that's to pick cotton." Before walking away to his patrol car, he added, "And I don't wanna be close to 'em, either."

At that time, neither that second officer nor I knew we would spend significant time together.

~~*~~

Within the department it was difficult to tell whether I was being scrutinized as a Black or just as a new member. I instinctively knew I had to stand up to the indignities of being a Black in White-controlled conditions. Reflecting on our basketball court discussion months before, Bennie Wilkey's words bounced around my mind in the quiet of the patrol car. "Carry yourself and do your job in such a way that you communicate to the worst of the Whites that you are an officer above reproach."

The more I thought about it, this job offered a chance to contribute to forming a badly needed bridge between minority citizens of Santa Ana and law enforcement – hopefully to the ultimate benefit of both sides.

Surely this would somehow be proof of the rightness of my being a police officer.

CHAPTER ELEVEN
December 1966 - February 1967

I passed my on-the-job training evaluation and all qualifying exams. December 8, 1966, *The Santa Ana Register* headline read "Santa Ana Police Hire First Negro." Out of 114 applicants, I was one of seven qualifying candidates. My official duties began on January 5, 1967.

~~*~~

On January 26, 1967 I entered the barracks-like Police Sciences building, on the 164-acre Costa Mesa campus of Orange Coast College to begin a seven-week police training program.

David, an athletic, straightforward family man in his mid-twenties and I were SAPD rookies; the balance of 36 cadets were from neighboring Orange County communities.

The instruction was both academic (learning police codes) and physical. In addition to several hours a day of classes, we had training sessions at night. Cadets were required to purchase a .38 caliber pistol and bullets at their own expense. We practiced weekly at the Orange County shooting range. We partnered to learn and perform suspect searches, handcuffing, arrest procedures, and baton use.

I spent eight hours a day with men who viewed me with feelings ranging from curiosity to derision. In an atmosphere of extreme discipline any response on my part might be interpreted as dissident or insubordinate. For example, classroom discipline required that at the end of each day the chairs and desks be arranged in almost military precision. Those who forgot had to run laps around the building or write essays.

No matter how tired I was, after days of strenuous physical exercise, or how much attention I paid to my chair arrangement, someone disarranged them. Consequently I ran lap after lap.

These were schoolboy pranks by cadets being groomed to solve murders, relate to different ethnic groups, and perhaps lessen crime. Or could it be the instructors? I tried to take the mischief with humor, but I took the sly 'mash' notes left on my desk ("Nigger – go home", or "Bye-bye blackie") seriously.

My peers thought leaving their notes and pranks were funny. It hurt me, but I laughed, hoping things would change. They didn't.

Sometimes I thought of dropping out, but I refused to allow fellow officers, inconsiderate asses as they might be, to make me quit. Perhaps it was my pride.

The only way I could get through some frustrating days was to say as little as possible to anybody. As I graduated and proved myself, I expected the harassment to fade – like some disease.

Little did I know that within a week after my graduation from the academy, things would change: not only my whole life, but the lives of my family.

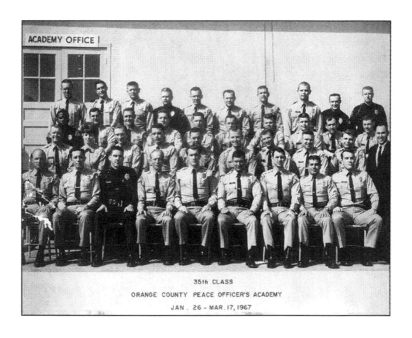

35th CLASS
ORANGE COUNTY PEACE OFFICER'S ACADEMY
JAN. 26 - MAR. 17, 1967

CHAPTER TWELVE
March - June 1967

In his wood-paneled formal office, I shook hands with Santa Ana Chief of Police Edward J. Allen, and smiled for a photographer and three or four reporters. The *Los Angeles Times* and *L.A. Herald Examiner* were not represented but would run a couple of sentences, I was told. *The Orange County Register*, and other suburban newspapers, however, would include my address. Were they really going to print my home address? I didn't remember ever seeing a newly hired officer's home address in the paper.

On December 8, 1966, my address was printed.[1] While reading about myself in *The Register*, I was interested to read City Manager Carl Thornton's comment that my appointment was welcomed by city officials. The article went on to say "The National Association for the Advancement of Colored People and the Congress of Racial Equality in August 1965, criticized the City for not hiring Negro policemen."

"We have actively sought qualified Negro applicants," Thornton said, "just as we have been actively seeking other qualified men for the police department. 'Personnel Director Don Bott said the City has had several Negro applicants in the past, but none previously was able to qualify.'"

I placed the newspaper on the table, and made a mental note to find out one day some statistics on the Police Applicant Success Scale.[2]

On Monday, March 20, 1967 I closed the door to my locker and did a last minute uniform check. I entered the briefing room for my first assignment as a rookie police officer for the Santa Ana Police Department.

Sergeant Brandon Webb briefed the officers and made assignments. I was assigned to the graveyard shift. My first field training officer would oversee my training and supervise me in the field. Immediately after finishing the academy, new officers were given specific districts to patrol as a one-man unit. I was the exception to this practice.

As I closed the door to my locker and did a last minute uniform check, I wondered if what I had heard about Officer Powers, Sergeant Webb, and Captain Tracey was true, or just an exaggeration. The rumor mill had it that the three were off-duty cronies with "anti-attitude." They were members of the John Birch Society and openly stated their negative feelings about immigrants, women's lib, communists, homosexuals, and Blacks.

The only thing I knew about the John Birchers, other than through hearsay, came from the offhand comments made by John Schmitz, my political science teacher at Santa Ana College. Outside the classroom during breaks or over lunch, Schmitz would talk about his experiences and beliefs as a John Birch Society member.

Officer Andy Kahan stuck his head around the lockers. "Hey, Lamb, meet me outside for a quick chat, will ya?" Checking my Timex, I had twenty minutes before reporting for roll call and meeting my field training officer.

When I caught up with Andy, he said, "Man, I heard Powers is going to be your FTO (field training officer)."

I was used to seeing Andy with a smile, and instinctively knew that his frown meant serious stuff.

"A quick rundown," he went on, "Watch your back and don't trust the jerk. Powers is hateful and will do everything he can think of to get you fired."

"Jesus, I haven't even met the guy yet. I've heard rumors, but don't know anything about him."

Andy said, "He's one of the Birch members and known in the department as a troublemaker. He was demoted from sergeant supervisor to patrol duty because of his less than stellar activities in the Society. Watch yourself and don't let him trip you up."

As Andy and I went our separate ways, I wondered if my assignment with Officer Powers was to be a road map for failure.

Outside the briefing room, I waited as two men spoke quietly. Sergeant Webb, who faced me, glanced my way and audibly cleared his throat. His full dark mustache, slightly hooked nose, receding hairline on a high forehead, and small eyes gave him a three dimensional look. He smiled and gave an over the shoulder nod to Officer Powers. His smile became a smirk as he stepped around me and left the area.

I extended my arm for a handshake and introduced myself to

Officer Verlyn Powers, my field training supervisor. He stood two inches shorter than me, and thin but with a slight potbelly. His black hair and deep blue eyes stood out garishly against his pasty skin. He smelled of tobacco. He ignored my outstretched hand. I felt my face and neck flush as I dropped my hand in embarrassment.

Powers was from Mississippi and spoke with a slow Southern drawl. "Your only job is to sit in the cahr, keep your mouth shut and listen up. We get a call, you get out of the cahr, keep your mouth shut, look, and listen up."

The first night we rode in darkness and in silence. It didn't take long for the genius in me to figure out that I wasn't wanted and that Powers didn't care for my company. The only sounds from inside the car were from the dispatch radio. I rode with my window down and could hear a mix of music, talking, traffic noises, and dogs barking as we patrolled through residential areas. The open window helped me breathe something other than the smell of stale smoke.

This was going to be a long two weeks.

I had been a committed civilian ride-along and observer under Officer Katiz's guidance some months previously. As Powers drove through the streets, I recalled Officer Katiz's admonition to become familiar with the streets, the neighborhoods, and the importance of knowing where I was at all times.

Maybe Powers's silence was a blessing in disguise. I was able to observe the area without distraction.

Santa Ana, with an estimated population in early 1967 of 125,000, was Orange County's second oldest city, dating back to 1886, and was the County Seat. We drove through pockets of charm and affluence and into areas of poverty and shabbiness. Single-family, ranch-style dwellings dominated the residential landscape. Most streets were modest but reasonably well kept, with trees, flowers, and wrought-iron fences.

Even the city's worst "slum" areas were blessed with sunshine and spaciousness in contrast to the slums of Chicago that I remembered. There was the same atmosphere of crime and violence, but the pastel streets did not convey the mean intensity of those in Chicago.

My first night on the streets was over. When we pulled up to the station, Powers unceremoniously told me to get out of the patrol car in front of the station.

"I don't mind walking with you, sir," I said.

"If I wanted you walking with me, I wouldn't a told you to get out." He drove off, parked the car, and entered the station from the rear with a key provided to him. I entered through the front entrance puzzled, but determined, as I made my way to the locker room.

~~*~~

The incidents started the second night and became habitual.

We patrolled in isolated areas housing closed industrial businesses, some of which were located in orange groves in south Santa Ana.

We cruised silently through the rubber company complex near Dyer Road. We could see nothing but shadows from dim and distant lights. Officer Powers stopped the patrol car in the middle of a dark street and turned to me. "Get out of the cahr, nigger, and close the door."

I stepped out, and before I could close the door, he gunned the gas pedal and sped away, leaving me standing in the street. Is this man crazy? I watched him drive the distance of a block, saw the brake lights as he applied them to turn the car around to face me. He stopped the police cruiser and switched off its headlights, leaving the parking lights on.

For an instant the interior light outlined Powers as he emerged and loudly slammed the car door. I could faintly see the flicker of his lighter as he lit another cigarette.

Standing there, looking towards the car, I thought about Andy's words in the basement. "Powers is hateful and will do everything he can think of to get you fired."

I clinched my fists in anger. The way Officer Powers was treating me wasn't part of police training, but I knew it boosted his self-esteem and gave him a certain power over me, promoting his feelings of control and superiority. Common sense told me that I couldn't say or do anything outwardly to antagonize him——I was a Rookie on twelve-months probation and it was smart for me to walk softly.

~~*~~

The sound of the engine was abrupt and the car came toward me. Powers stopped the car and said, "Nigger, get in the cahr." As I reached for the door handle he accelerated, causing me to lose my balance. I had to let go or I'd fall.

We danced this dance until he got bored and stopped the car, finally allowing me to get back in. The length of time he would leave me standing became longer and longer.

I had been intimidated to the point where I felt like a volcano ready to erupt. But I had to keep myself in check and weigh the value of time, uncertainty and experiences I had encountered in becoming a police officer in a department embedded with bigotry and hatred. It took all the restraint and willpower I could muster not to reach over, grab him around the neck and beat the shit out of him. As he drove, he did not say anything to me for over an hour.

Finally I couldn't take the silent treatment any longer. "What exactly is it you want me to do, Powers?"

He checked his watch, "It's Officer Powers, and it's time for you to buy me some food. Where I'm from, niggers buy for their masters."

I sat in stunned silence. Self-control, Harlen. We drove to a 24-hour diner a couple miles away, and sat at the first table inside the door. We ate in continued silence. The meal check was given to me to pay. We left to finish our shift in more silence.

This became a ritual: Drive to an isolated area, leave me standing in the street, play with me as I try to get back in the car, buy his meal, ignore me. As I stood pacing back and forth in the street, my mantra became what LAPD Officer Bennie Wilkey had said to me, "Carry yourself and do your job in such a way that you communicate to the worst of the Whites you are an officer above reproach." I repeated this to myself, eventually becoming calm as I waited for Powers to return.

One mid-April night the dance became different. The night air was cool and damp from a rain shower earlier in the day. It was the first night of the full moon, its buttermilk glow keeping me company as I rode in silence next to my field training supervisor. Officer Powers stopped the patrol car at an orange grove north of Grand Avenue on East Dyer Road. I heard the vehicle scrape against the hedge that hid any entrance to the endless geometric rows of citrus trees.

"Get out of the cahr, nigger, and close the door." I opened the door, stepping away and slamming behind me. I watched Powers slowly back up the unit until his headlights were mere pinpoints of yellow. This time he left his headlights on.

The shadows from a full moon in that orange grove had a waiting, expectant look—dark. Glossy leaves twinkled in the moonlight and disclosed their golden fruit and the silhouette of a ladder leaning against a tree from the day's pick. I knew from my childhood that rats and other small creatures were active at night, and that everyday noises, when robbed of the positive veneer of daylight, were made sinister by the cover of darkness. That line of thinking assured me as I waited.

Minutes later I saw the headlights of a second car stop and park beside Powers' patrol unit. Together, the officers turned their headlights off.

I mentally counted the passage of time with a "one-and" as my chest rose, and "two-and" as my chest fell. My breathing took on a sedative quality. Fifteen minutes later, the air was stolen from my lungs when suddenly the headlights snapped on, and their bright beams lit a path directly to where I stood.

Side by side, the patrol units began inching forward. At the same time, I heard rustling behind me. My heart began to hammer. With a knee-jerk reaction, I backed into the hedge, reaching out to steady myself.

For the first time I felt the hard lump of fear wedged in my throat like a chicken bone.

I repeated my mantra as the two vehicles slowly made their way toward me. Several feet away from me, the second car abruptly turned around and disappeared into the night. Powers gunned the engine of his unit, slid to a stop within inches of where I stood, and bellowed out, "Nigger, get in the cahr."

And our dance began once again, ending up at the 24-hour diner. This time, I finished eating, paid the bill at the counter and left the diner to sit in the patrol car until he finished eating.

Powers grunted contentedly as he positioned himself behind the wheel. I made an effort to keep myself calm, and set my face to casual indifference. "Officer Powers, two things. This is the last time I buy your food, because I can't afford it. Second, what is it you want me to do when you leave me standing in the street for an hour?"

He looked at me for a full minute, then with a smirk, "Listen, you coon ass, I have two things to say to you. First, you don't talk to me without permission, and second, you just stand where I put you until I tell you otherwise." His voice had gotten loud and his face was red as he finished. He started the car, and pulled into the street to bring to an end another night on patrol.

As we rode I made a silent vow. When I become a field training officer, I will dedicate myself to being the best training officer possible. One who will be respected and looked up to.

~~*~~

My ten days to ride with Powers were nearly over. Maybe this was the ultimate stress test to see if I could handle myself on the streets. I knew there would be some animosity simply because I was a black man in a position of authority, and that was something the community was not used to seeing.

We stopped at the Winchell's Donut Shop at McFadden and Bristol. As I reached for my hot chocolate from the server behind the counter, Powers called out to officers coming through the door, "Hey, boys, whaddya think of my nigger ride-a-long? Coon does tricks. Just ask him."

Turning, drink in hand, I acknowledged their presence with a nod and found a stool to sit on. Powers continued, "What do you call a barn full of Blacks?" He waited a few seconds, and answered his own question, "Antique farm equipment!"

I finished my drink and returned to the patrol car alone, hearing the laughter behind me.

My pride smarted as I tried to make logical sense of my feelings. Powers's mean spirit confounded me. He was my training officer, so I bit my lip and choked back my anger and hurt each time he chose to say or do something to degrade me. It was even more hurtful that Powers chose to be respectful and courteous to his fellow white officers in front of me.

There were times we were assigned to follow-up and assist other officers. When we arrived on the scene, officers huddled in discussion about the incident or the crime. The talk stopped when they saw me walking toward them. The officers strode toward their patrol cars, out of earshot, Powers tagging along behind them with comments about his coon ride-a-long.

The sergeants present said and did nothing to dissuade Powers from his behavior. I couldn't figure out why officers in charge would allow this conduct unless they socialized together off duty or, perhaps, belonged to the same "club."

I was aware of the prevailing blue code of silence and I knew that to make a complaint against a fellow officer could be far worse for me. But surely, if I requested a private audience with my commander to discuss the situation--without filing a formal complaint--my predicament would be resolved when my assignment with Powers was over.

~~*~~

At the end of the first week riding with Powers, our shift had ended. We changed out of our uniforms into street clothes in our 40 x 80 foot locker room. Lockers and benches lined the walls and a double row of lockers and benches stretched down the middle of the room. Officers noisily opened lockers, jostled one another and laughed as they tried to position themselves on one foot while changing shoes and telling stories of their day. Forty feet separated Powers's locker from mine.

"Lambert," Powers yelled out, "I'd invite you to breakfast, but I need to check with my neighbors first to make sure it's okay to have a nigger in the neighborhood."

Suddenly it became quiet. Movement appeared to be in slow motion as some officers, half dressed, stared at me openly. Others, supervisory officers as well, quietly but rapidly pulled on their clothes or just wadded them up in their arms in an effort to get the hell out of the locker room. They didn't want to be witness to what might happen as I removed my 38. I said nothing and continued to remove my boots and uniform, making every effort to appear nonchalant. I finished dressing and quietly but firmly closed the locker door and left the room without looking to my left or right. The only sound to be heard was my footsteps.

~~*~~

Again, leadership had nothing to say to Powers, and again, my self-control was tested.

The day my field training ended, I stood at Lieutenant Chrockran's open office door. "Sir, my field training is complete, and I believe I'm ready to go out as a one-man unit. May I have a word with you in private?"

He motioned me to sit, closed the door behind me, and as he

moved to his chair behind the wooden desk littered with papers, he asked with a slight lisp, "What's on your mind, Lambert?" His speech involving an 's' sounded like the voiceless 'th.' Interesting that it only happened at the end of a word.

I briefly outlined being put out of the patrol car in the orange groves, the name calling, and overall humiliation directed toward me. "Sir, I'm not asking that Officer Powers be fired, but rather that he receive some kind of counselling to address his behavior before someone is hurt."

"You've been on the job what—two weeks—and you have the balls to walk in here with this crap? How can you prove this claim, Lambert?" The Lieutenant stood and leaned over his desk, inches from my face.

He continued, his voice getting louder with each word, "I'll tell you how. You can't."

The Lieutenant dropped his tall, lean frame into his chair once again, and was silent. His straight brown hair was wet with perspiration. He fiddled with papers on his desk and flipped a paper clip end-to-end. He stared at a silver-framed photo of a woman standing with two young boys on either side of her. The photo accessory sat precariously at the corner of his desk.

Time stood still for what felt like hours, but could only be minutes, before he shook his head, "I want to be sure you know how to handle yourself, especially with White people on the street."

I'm 6'2," 216 pounds (220-225 pounds with my equipment on). "After the knowledge and training I've received I feel I can definitely handle myself."

Before turning away, Chrockran said, "Continue with Powers. I'll think about it."

After another two days with my Mississippi training officer, the lieutenant gave me permission to go out on my own. Overjoyed, suddenly free of Powers's harassment, I thought things would go better.

~~*~~

SAPD resources were limited. Our assigned, high-performance Plymouth Fury might be new or a hand-me-down three to five years. It had heavy-duty suspension, but no air conditioning and no power anything. No vehicles had mounted spotlights. Our accordion, hand-held spotlights were kept on the right front seat for quick access. We were required to wear our helmets at all times when we were out of our vehicle, so we kept them on the passenger seat, too.

We had a big chrome "growler" siren, a steady burning red light on the driver's side of the siren, a flashing red light on the passenger's side, and a flashing amber light in the back of the siren – referred to as "the triangle."

The siren was controlled by manually activating the horn ring when the red lights were on. I had to be careful not to wind-up the siren motor too much or else all the lights would dim from power drain to the car's generator and battery.

The patrol cars were equipped with a very simple Motorola radio with two channels, which could easily be changed by a toggle-switch. Channel one was a frequency shared by Santa Ana, Orange and Tustin police departments, and channel two was a car-to-car frequency. In case of emergency, we had to return to the unit to communicate with the dispatcher. And if the dispatcher wanted to relay information to an officer that could not be given over the air, the officer would have to use a landline. This meant we would either go to a public telephone or to a designated call box with a blue light on it in the downtown area.

We didn't have body armor for protection or portable radios to use outside of our patrol car. There were no shotguns in the cars, except in the sergeant's cars. If there were a major incident requiring more firepower, additional shotguns would have to be transported from the station.

~~*~~

The geographic district I was assigned to was residential and predominantly Black. Not quite a ghetto, but the parks and reasonably clean streets could be misleading. The crime rate there was high. FxTroop, Westside, and 5th Street gangs roamed the parks. Domestic fights were common, and behind modest storefronts were back rooms filled with bookies and gamblers. Topless bars and prostitutes lined Harbor Boulevard. As I patrolled, there were the usual number of stares, some normally curious and some outright surprised at seeing a black officer.

At Raitt and Willis streets, I observed an older model blue

compact speeding past the stop sign and through the intersection. The slight brunette, hunched over the steering wheel, appeared to be focused, eyes straight ahead, looking neither left nor right. I toggled my siren to get her attention. She coasted to a stop a couple blocks past the intersection. Her brake lights came on as she came to a complete stop.

She rolled the driver's side window down as I approached. "Miss, I stopped you because I observed you going through the stop sign behind us."

Before I could say another word, she explained, "Officer, I didn't want to wear my brakes down. I just had them repaired. They were expensive, and I'm in a bad part of town."

I hadn't heard that one before, but I had to issue a citation anyway.

As I walked back to the patrol car, another car sped by me. This too, was an older model compact, but bright green. I pulled around the blue compact, in pursuit of the green one. I again toggled the siren. The matronly, fleshy woman looked at me over the top of her glasses. "You're Black."

"Yes, ma'am, and I'm a police officer. You were exceeding the speed limit in a residential area."

Once again, before I could say another word or ask for identification, the female explained, "I'm on my way to a friend's house. She told me this is a scary part of town and that bad people live here, and I wanted to get through here as fast as I could."

Not bad. I issued two citations within a ten minute period.

I was finally assigned to day shift; our morning roll call had gone swiftly. The briefing at the station reminded me of a bad theater review: a litany of license plate numbers belonging to recently stolen cars, of all-night topless bars with drug dealing and the selling of stolen property, of new porno shops along Harbor and Tustin Avenues, and burglaries and activities of the watch before me.

As I drove, I was aware that sometimes one day on the street, with or without a training officer, seemed to approximate a year in the academy, or a day might be the opposite, maybe listless and ordinary, or a day spent watching citizens simply obeying the laws.

This day appeared to be neither. It seemed to be a day of small lessons, the first being that the non-communication I had observed as a civilian ride-a-long between Black citizens and White police officers had not automatically disappeared just because I was now on the force.

At 10:00 a.m. I observed a youth in a Chevy running a stop sign. At the sight of my flashing lights, he pulled over and stopped. Methodically, I switched off the light and opened the door to walk to his window. As I approached, he started his engine and sped forward.

Without the benefit of hand-held radios, precious moments were lost as I ran back to the car, radioed my position, requested assistance and began pursuit. Blocks later, with the help of two black-and-white squad cars, the youth was boxed in. I wasn't aware at that time that I should be thankful for the backup units.

Once again, but with more caution, I approached the window and recognized the young man, known as 'Pépé' on the streets.

"Man, I ran cuz there's no black cops!" He didn't believe I was for real. He'd never seen me in uniform before now. Whether or not this was true, I realized that he still didn't recognize me.

"Don't you remember me?" I asked. "You used to live next door to me with your family. You used to throw rocks at my Shepherd through the fence."

Of course, Pépé now recognized me. "I didn't know you were a cop." I gave him a citation for speeding and cautioned him to slow down.

I thought of Zeus, the sixty-pound, seven-month-old German Shepherd given to me earlier in the year by a family who couldn't keep him. He was a happy dog, running along the fence when people walked or drove by, tail wagging, looking for a "Good boy!" from all. Zeus would raise his head slightly, pricked ears forward, hairs bristling along his neck and back, only when this one kid came near the fence.

Rounding the corner of the house one day, I had heard Zeus barking, then saw Pépé throwing rocks at the dog through the fence. When he saw me, Pépé turned to run—right into the arms of his father. Mr. Arriola had heard the commotion and had rushed to the front of the house. He was a taller, weathered version of Pépé.

Frowning, Mr. Arriola collared his son and quickly marched him to stand in front of me. In broken English, he ordered, "You will apologize to our neighbor right this minute for your bad behavior, Jusepe!" Chin

111

resting on his collarbone, Pépé mumbled an apology, which I readily accepted. "My son will not be a problem again, I assure you." And he was not, although Zeus continued to bark when Pépé was near the fence. Not long after, the family moved to another neighborhood.

It would be some months after issuing his speeding citation that I would arrest a little older, larger, but not smarter Pépé for shoplifting at K-Mart.

Pépé throwing rocks at my dog was the least of the problems my family and I faced. Trouble had found us on the home front.

~~*~~

One Friday before leaving to report to roll call, as my wife and I were finishing breakfast in our comfortable ranch-style stucco home, and discussing the need to cut the grass and weed the roses, we heard a noise at the front of the house. Thinking it might be Fernando playing in the hallway and not finding him there, I opened the front door to find a knife stuck in the center of the door with a KKK business card attached.

Zeus lay at the bottom of the steps. Our friendly Shepherd had undoubtedly welcomed the stranger with tail wagging bravado. Disappointed the visitor hadn't come to play fetch, or chase, or hide-and-seek. At that moment I knew Zeus was at risk as he roamed freely in the front yard.

Hopeful, he looked up at me as I said, "Zeus, very soon you're going to learn new games to protect the home-front!" With pricked ears, he watched me for a moment, and snorted happily as I entered the house.

Shaken, but knowing I had to keep my composure when Marie asked me, "Who was at the door?" I responded with the truth. She jumped up from her chair and ran into my arms shaking and crying, "What are we going to do?" I assured her everything would be all right. Would it be all right? What kind of person would be so hateful?

~~*~~

As I drove back to the station to file my report, I realized that as a rookie in a one-man unit, my problems were really just beginning. I was responsible for all calls in an area of the city measuring several square miles. Watching me I had three sergeants, five supervisors, and seven senior officers who would then critique me to make sure I could handle myself.

I arrived at the station and pulled into a stall to park. I hit an oil slick and slid into a pole, causing minor scratches to the front bumper, and breaking the headlight lamp. Shit. I went to the sergeant on duty to report the damage and get a black mark for it.

That night, the telephone calls began. I wondered, could I handle emotional vandalism at home, at work, and crime on the streets?

~~*~~

The long, shrill ring of the rotary phone continued. Night after night into the wee hours the calls came, telephone calls that should have been directed to the city dump for disposal. But nothing like that happened. My wife had taken each phone call right smack in her ear and in her guts.

The phone began its nightly ritual. Marie picked up the receiver – for the ninth time. I looked at her small boned features and saw that she was trying to cover up, to conceal the frowns of worry that went past what we called the Primary Frown, the one that creased her forehead when I became a policeman.

"When you or your wife don't wonder why you became a cop, then you know something is wrong," Los Angeles Officer Bennie Wilkey, a black police veteran since 1954, had told me during one of our many talks about Blacks and law enforcement. I was in my fourth week as a rookie, and now I understood much better what his statement was all about.

"Honey, tell me. What did his voice sound like? The one that called five times."

Her voice trembling, eyes lowered, she said, "It was a woman's voice."

"What did she say?" I pressed gently, "C'mon now, tell me." My probing was to try to get a lead on one of the poisoned minds behind the calls.

She struggled to finish, to control herself, "She said she was going to cut Fernando's throat the next time she saw him."

As I pulled her into my arms, questions raced through my mind. Who the hell could it be? The 'nice' little old lady down the street? The wife or girlfriend of someone I arrested? A crackpot? Fernando's schoolteacher? Who?

The best I could do was to reassure Marie that the threat shouldn't be taken seriously, but underneath, neither one of us was fooled.

I call threats to your family "emotional vandalism." Then there is the other, more direct kind: the kind that spills garbage all over your front lawn in the middle of the night, smears the doors of your home with feces, and mysteriously causes damage to the paint job of your car and boat. My 1965 Pontiac suffered the most damage at that time, with broken windows and antennas, deep scratches on the hood and doors made by keys, and then smeared with raw eggs that ate into the paint.

The same evening I found the KKK business card stuck in the front door, fearful our sweet, friendly shepherd was at risk, I moved him to the back yard. Within three days Fernando and I had built a dog house Zeus could grow into. Before work and after school, my son and I taught the dog simple obedience commands in German, confident it would stop fast talking assailants from confusing the shepherd. We played and talked with Zeus every free moment. He became Fernando's four-legged playmate and constant companion. At nine months old, Zeus had become very protective of the family and the back yard. I was reluctant to allow him back into the front yard.

My instincts were accurate when, three weeks later two shots fired from a handgun ripped through my living room window. Zeus could have been a target had he been patrolling the front fence. One week after that, Marie, Fernando, and I returned from grocery shopping to discover our living room window broken out. A water hose had been placed through the opening and turned on, flooding several rooms in our home.

'The Vandals' I've called them in my own mind. Each time something happened, I would report it to Sergeant Barry Armein, my immediate supervisor. Short and stocky, fair haired and freckled, Barry said he would check into the matter. We would then talk about our upcoming fishing trip outside Newport Beach. Three of us shared the joy of the fishing experience. Sergeant Joseph "Joe" Smith, a clean-shaven, easy-going guy joined Barry and me on these infrequent trips.

On one such trip Sergeant Armein, casting his reel, said, "We'll catch the bastards that's doing it, Harlen." I would ask several times on and off the job what the status of the investigation was, and Barry would repeat the same tired reply, "We're working the case."

On a week-day off I looked forward to playing basketball at Jerome Park. Fernando was in school as I secured Zeus with food and water in the back yard and kissed Marie goodbye.

I opened the door and discovered feces smeared on the front door and piles left on the steps. Marie and I had returned only minutes before, after taking our son to school. How was this possible?

It took a good hour to hose and clean up the foul mess. I found myself probing the whys of the situation as I drove to the park.

"Okay." I actually talked to myself, until the stares from a couple at the second stoplight cooled me out. "Okay, I continued silently, consider the fact that I am dealing with White people, who both socially and geographically long ago staked out their own turf, which means "No niggers, negroes, colored, Blacks or Afro-Americans needed or wanted in Orange County, and especially not in any position of authority." The types who treasured this mode of thought hated me. But then, their hate was traditional and I understood it.

The understanding that I created for myself, out of a search for some kind of reason, just wasn't enough to justify having shit smeared on my front door. It merely explained it. They had to get in the shit, too — never wrestle with a pig. You both get dirty and the pig likes it.

Chicanos and Blacks disliked me. "Was it simply because they felt I had been made another authority figure in their lives, but without the color pattern that they had always been taught to tolerate and endure?"

I was developing a headache.

I thought of the "overseer" tradition, a bitter legacy from the plantation days. On the black side, I understood how a Black might be viewed as the overseer for the plantation owner, our tradition being what it had been.

The Chicanos brought a whole new set of energy into the picture. They had another cultural pattern in a different ethnic framework. They had been suspicious of and victims of white police officers for decades. How many times had I heard officers call Chicanos "greasers," "beaners," or other racial slurs? When they saw me, they saw the uniform, which represented a host of emotions, including prejudice, fear, a history of mistreatment, and perhaps false arrest.

I reasoned, "No one likes the idea of having a stranger (a Black, cops in general) placed in charge of his or her misadventures with the law." Nor did I assume that men automatically appreciate having someone tell them that they should be attentive to guidelines that they had not lain down.

It was, indeed, a tough row to hoe on both sides, but it still did not justify what I called the poisoned minds: The Vandals.

"Motherf-----r! I'm gonna get you when you get off!" The unpleasant voice of a neighbor, or one who should be a neighbor since we only live blocks away from each other, shouted at me from the sidelines as I went up for a jump shot. Was he the one responsible for the antennas being crumpled on my car, the side view mirror twisted off?

Later at home when the phone rang, I heard, "Listen closely, you big black ape! We'll be at the intersection of First and Bristol tonight, waiting for your black ass!" Click! Oh well, at least this was one that my wife or son didn't have to hear.

"Hello, Officer Lambert?"

"Yes."

"F--- you!" So much hate in a voice that sounded so young.

"Daddy, a man tried to stop me on the way from school today." I don't know what kind of fear can grab at you harder than the fear of your child being harmed. I knelt down and reached to lift my son on my knee. I asked, "Do you know what he wanted, son?"

"I don't know. He just asked me if I was Officer Lambert's son and I said yes." Forcing myself to be calm, I asked Fernando, "Would you know the man if you saw him again?"

"I don't think so, Daddy. He had a stocking on his face and a cap pulled down on his forehead." Son of a bitch.

With a sigh of resignation, Marie let the drapes fall into their natural folds. "Harlen, they've thrown garbage all over the front lawn again." Six months on the job and the strain of our everyday life was beginning to show itself in a number of ways. Marie was becoming withdrawn and anxious.

"Yes, honey, I know. I looked out a few minutes ago and saw it." On my way outside to begin cleanup, for the umpteenth time, I noted they also turned my water hose system on. If this keeps up, I'll have the greenest lawn in Orange County.

~~*~~

I called in to Sergeant Armein, reporting these latest incidents to be added to the investigation.

It was about this time, during my rookie year, that I can really say that I was on my way to understanding, as well as anyone, what abnormal behavior was all about – both on and off the job.

It will never be possible to recapture the emotional state I found myself in so often, on my way to work, having just answered a hate call. What is the solution? An unlisted number? Somehow it doesn't seem to stay unlisted very long. A telephone service? I could just imagine the messages left. "We're gonna rape your wife, nigger pig!" Or while cleaning my lawn, again, of the crap dumped on it during the night.

Soon, it was obvious that Sergeant Armein was ducking me. We rarely spoke, and never went fishing together anymore. I guess he didn't have answers for me, and it was easier to see me during a briefing, where he did not, and could not, speak with me one on one.

It was appropriate for me to go through the chain of command, which was to report incidents to my supervisor, Sergeant Armein, who was in turn responsible to investigate. I knew I couldn't be objective by investigating on my own. And I knew if I circumvented the Sergeant by going directly to my supervising Lieutenant with a complaint, a whole new set of problems and issues would arise.

I analyzed information and incidents and took necessary precautions and actions to assure the safety of my family. My justification for remaining on the police department was my willpower to be a winner, not a victim. I made a commitment to my family and myself to do the job and to protect them at all costs.

If I was going to make a difference in the world, I had to be involved to make it happen. And I think I was too hard-headed and heart-strong to fail and to allow a few non-law abiding citizens run me away from the job I was hired, and committed, to do.

I couldn't speak for anyone else because I didn't know the extent of the experiences others have had of such behavior in his or her life, other than those shared by Bennie Wilkey and other African-American officers from Los Angeles and Long Beach.

Bennie and I had just finished a cup of soup and a ham sandwich, after a bewitching hour of his stories about the history of Blacks in the LAPD. As we pulled money from our pockets and placed it on the table, I secretly glanced at Bennie and suddenly knew: the 'grit and grain,' as my grandmother used to say, of what a man is built, soon becomes evident.

Would I have the backbone and endurance of men like Bennie?

~~*~~

In March and April 1967, west-side gas stations had been robbed repeatedly. Along with a number of other officers, I responded to the call from Lieutenant Chrockran to volunteer our personal, off-duty time to stake out the stations in the hope of capturing the elusive robbers.[3] We knew that our time would not be compensated with overtime pay or additional time off. Although we were commended for our spirit and willingness to freely give of our own time, the criminal was never seen or caught.

Perhaps our extra efforts were appreciated more by the Department than by my family--or any of the other officers' families.

~~*~~

It had been a long midnight to 4:30 a.m. stake out at First and Bristol. I hadn't had time off for three weeks and as I drove home I looked forward to a two-hour nap before reporting to duty at 7:00 a.m. I heard Marie as soon as I opened the door.

"What's the matter? Why've you been crying?" Oh God, what can it be this time? She sat in our dark living room crying her heart out.

"I was in the beauty shop minding my own business, but I couldn't help overhearing two women gossiping about you. One of them said that you're so mean you would incarcerate your own mother."

As absurd as it sounded, there were still enough moments like this to make life humiliating at times.

"She also said that you're harder on Blacks than Whites."

These two items, plus several other bite-sized pieces of gossip almost made me join my wife in her tearful state but, once again, I thought better of it. I knew a nap was out of the question. I went to the kitchen, made two cups of hot chocolate and returned to the living room, ready to sit down for a soulful talk with the only other person in the world who knew the nightmare we were living.

During this talk I realized that the move to Southern California had severed us from the world of our early years, from the roots we had always taken for granted until those roots were gone. Had we not been bombarded with unceasing hostility from unknown sources, we might still have felt marooned far from the scene of our shared background, the culture and traditions of Black people from the Deep South.

At 5:30 a.m. I grabbed for the telephone, halfway through the first ring. Heavy breathing followed by laughter. Then the line went dead. I'd been up since midnight and going to work at 7:00 a.m. would prove to be a very long day.

And if all that wasn't enough, here I was, ready to give my free time or actually to aid in some way one of the same people who had been trying to make my life miserable. Talk about justice being poetic.

~~*~~

I stopped at Winchell's Donut Shop for a hot chocolate to go, hopeful it would help keep me alert. Roll call was short and by 7:20 a.m. I was back on routine patrol and within ten minutes, I was dispatched for a "male trying to kick in the front door of a house" on Myrtle Street.

On my arrival, an elderly Hispanic male was sitting on the porch, drunk and having lost control of his bladder. Shoulders hunched, he watched me approach with bleary-eyes. I could see no damage to the door.

As he struggled to his feet, I asked him for I.D. He put his hands in his jeans' pocket and pulled out something and asked, "Can you hold this for me so I can get to my wallet?"

He placed a bag of marijuana in my hand. Priceless. He realized what he had done, so turned with hands clasped behind his back to accept the handcuffs waiting for him.

Later that morning, while patrolling the extreme north side of the City in the Heliotrope area, I noticed two school-age boys about 14 years old, noisily giving the finger to pedestrians around them as they attempted to stop oncoming vehicles from the middle of the street. One of the boys waved a jar over his head.

The residents here were older, established, wealthy, and did not have young families, so I knew the boys were not from the area.

I confronted the two middle-class white boys and took possession of the slop jar full of red devils. I counseled the two hitch-hiking, hooky-playing potential dropouts before I arrested them, then escorted them to Juvenile Hall.

With their eyes dilated, goofy grins on their faces, and unsteady movements, it was not hard to know if either one heard me. It was obvious they were tripping on the acid in the jar - the current drug of choice.

At 3:00 p.m. I was dispatched on a 925 call (unknown trouble call) to a domestic situation two blocks from my home. A second car had been called, but I was the first to arrive. As I approached the house, it was quiet. Too quiet.

The front door was ajar, broken furniture immediately visible, and several children cowered in a corner of the living room. I heard low talking somewhere and suddenly screams erupted. I raced toward the sounds. Inside, a man and his wife faced each other in a bedroom. She was black and blue, with a face puffy from a severe beating.

Seconds later, Officer Paul Nugent burst into the room to aid me in separating the couple. He took the man into another room while I interrogated the wife.

"He's not going to beat me anymore!" she sobbed, in between curses directed at him.

"Ma'am, I want to help you, but to do that you need to sign a complaint and I will place your husband under arrest."

She repeated that he wasn't going to beat her anymore and nodded her agreement.

In the living room, informed that he was going to be arrested, the man lunged for his wife. As we restrained him the children, ages five to thirteen, began to cry.

The wife shook her head. "I won't, I won't!"

She looked at me, "I've changed my mind."

The older children screamed that they didn't want their Daddy arrested and ran at me, tearing at my clothes and hitting me with pieces of broken furniture.

Officer Nugent bolted for his police car and placed a "patrolmen in trouble"' call and returned to the house to help me in the struggle with the family. He pulled the thirteen-year old off my back and was rewarded with a kick to the face.

Nugent and I were grateful for the arrival of seven back-up police cars and a supervising sergeant.

The man was arrested and some order was restored. As Nugent and I stood in the same room, nursing our bruises, the sergeant-in-charge walked directly to the man to inform him of his rights. Without warning, the man kicked the sergeant in the groin. The fight began all over again. Officers restrained him and immediately took him to the car.

The sergeant was taken to the hospital. As the assigned officer, I returned to the station to file a report after making a quick stop at the cleaners on 17th and Lincoln where I routinely went for fresh uniforms.

I was grateful I had a uniform in the laundry, because the one I was wearing now had several rips and was dirty from the whipping I took from the kids. Mrs. Hunter, the owner, and I laughed together as I told her why I looked so disheveled.

As I was leaving, Sergeant Webb raced in to drop some cleaning before starting his patrol shift, and brushed shoulders with me. He smiled and greeted Mrs. Hunter, ignoring me. He laid his pile of clothes on the counter, then leaned over and said something to the owner, who giggled and blushed.

The only thing I knew about Sergeant Webb was from gossip in the locker room. He had served in the military and had relocated from Pennsylvania (PA) to California. He wasn't well-liked, and hearsay was that he was an opportunist, earning him the nickname "The Vulture," after a bird from the city of Phoenixville, PA who descends on his prey with enormous wings and carries them to where they belong.

It would be some time before I learned details about Sergeant Webb and that he was one of the five officers hell-bent on assuring my failure.

What a pain in the butt it was to get a new uniform. The Policy was you went to the basement and looked through the hand-me-down locker full of worn, sometimes dirty and torn shirts and pants. If nothing fit, authorization was given to go to Harris & Franks to purchase a new uniform.

At the end of my patrol shift, I typically sat at one of the metal desks in the report room. I referred to my notes for the days' activities and tickets issued before preparing my written reports.

Each day Sergeant Bellows, a short round man with gray hair and bushy eyebrows, peered over his heavy eyeglasses to critique the reports. He had been nicknamed "House Mouse" because he was a cop on full duty, but never left the station for patrol. Bellows was assigned clerical duties and was generally disliked by the cops who did patrol and made collars.

Anything with my name on it was returned to me for a rewrite. "House Mouse" chose the time to return the report. He threw the paperwork towards me, letting it land wherever it might – on the desk, in my lap, on the floor. It didn't matter. He made sure other officers, my peers, were in the area to see his disrespect.

Sergeant Bellows raised his voice in mockery. "It takes an idiot to hand in a report like this. Rewrite it. I want it on my desk within the hour. And don't even think about giving me another shit report."

After a month of Bellow's ridicule, I asked Lieutenant Chrockran why the reports were consistently returned for rewrite. "It's part of the training exercise, Lambert." But I noticed nobody else was getting his reports back.

The Lieutenant continued, "We want you to be better than the other officers."

Four white peers noticed how many rewrites I was doing. They were supportive officers who believed in right and wrong and would, under cover, attempt to make a bad situation better. They decided to write my reports to see if this was training or harassment.

The next day, Bellows returned the "…piece of shit…" domestic dispute report, authored by a peer with my name at the top, for rewrite.

Four different reports, written by four different white officers over a two-day period, were submitted with my name attached. "House Mouse" returned the same four reports for rewrite in the same manner and the same words for me, as always.

After picking up the reports from the floor where Bellows had thrown them, I rewrote the reports and left the station to start my day on the streets.

My report-writing co-conspirators were supportive of having a Negro on the force, but maintained distance from me. After all, their supervisors were the same as mine and I understood their conflict about supporting me and staying on the good side of our superiors.

I was reminded even more graphically that I remained unseen, and unrecognized.

~~*~~

Thoughts of the rewritten domestic dispute report earlier in the day were forgotten as my attention was drawn to the speeding car. I sounded the siren.

The 1965 Rolls Royce pulled to the curb at Fifth and Bristol. My intention was to cite him for speeding. As I walked up to the car, shock registered on the fleshy face of a man dressed entirely in white. His panama style hat hid his eyes. I knocked on his window, indicating to roll it down. He pushed his hat upward and stared at me. His face turned bright red as he mouthed, "No nigger cops." The window of his car immediately glided back up. He turned and stared ahead, refusing to say anything directly to me. He continued to mouth, "No nigger cops" over and over.

I called for a tow truck from East Fourth Street and watched as the Rolls Royce was hooked up and towed away -- with the gentleman still seated at the steering wheel. I followed, chuckling, as the man continued to mutter.

At the garage, a white back-up policeman encouraged the driver to get out of the car and told him that if he didn't sign the citation, he would be arrested. He refused to speak, but glanced in my direction as he signed and paid his tow charge.

My stomach growled with thoughts of a ham sandwich and a bowl of hot clam chowder. As I passed the auto dismantling company on East Fourth, I observed a man in a gray sweatshirt with a hood covering his head duck behind an impounded black Chevrolet. For weeks officers had been making on-site arrests for auto parts thefts and thefts from the vehicles on the lot.

I crept up behind the man and shouted, "Police! Stay where you are!" The suspect dropped the screwdriver he was using to pop the hubcap from the tires. He fell forward onto his stomach, splayed like a starfish. He groaned as I cuffed him, read him his Miranda rights, put him in the rear seat of the patrol car, and carted him off to jail.

Chief Allen wrote a commendation for several patrol officers, including me, for on-site arrests of auto parts thefts and thefts from vehicles resulting in crime clearances.[4]

My stomach contracted and growled from lack of food, but lunch was not on the menu this day.

~~*~~

The department received a call from an elementary school. The school nurse reported attending to Trudy, an eight-year-old complaining of stomach and pelvic pains. Upon questioning, the young girl said that her father had been having regular "nookie," and he hurt her with "his thing" in her.

I was dispatched to interview the mother, Helen, who was alone in a modest house on the west side of the city. I studied her face. It was weathered and lined, but she had delicate features.

She said her husband Gary, a construction worker, was laying brick on a new site in the city of Tustin.

Helen was not surprised with the questions I asked her. In a resigned, worn way she said that her husband had been having intercourse with their eighteen-year-old daughter since the girl was ten. "Sara left and moved away as soon as she graduated school last year. We haven't seen or talked to her since."

When asked why she hadn't reported the ongoing molestation, Helen said, "I considered it a family matter." Her head dropped into her hands. She had no more to say to me.

Eight-year-old Trudy was returned to the home.

The father was arrested later and charged with incest. He had no known criminal history. The judge set bail at fifty thousand dollars. Hearing this, I felt little satisfaction. I never went to court on this case, but later learned that the father pled to a lesser charge and would perform community service as punishment. I spent several minutes gulping deep breaths to keep myself from vomiting. If I did what I really wanted to do,

I would beat the living shit out of that slime bag and probably get eight months to a year myself.

~~*~~

My work-day was finally over and I was on my way home, my stomach still grumbling. At the corner of Myrtle and Raitt streets, I spotted a group of males milling around in a circle. I could imagine the fight going on in the middle. I was reluctant to get out of the safety of my car to stop a fight, but I did -- and discovered that the two combatants were gang members I'd had contact with before. They traveled in groups with pack behavior and mentality.

It was too late to be reluctant. After a short talk with the leader, relative peace was restored. Benito and Carlos shook hands as I went back to the car.

Benito, a member of the FxTroop (pronounced F-Troop) was one of those kids who wouldn't hesitate to pull a gun and shoot someone for simply staring at him, or kick their head in for pocket money. Benito was only twenty-three years old, but had been a member of the primarily Mexican-American FxTroop since he was twelve. By twenty-three, his rap sheet included serious stuff: assault charges that had been bartered down, robbery charges that had been reduced because the juvenile facility was bursting at its seams, and a rape charge that had been dismissed. By age eighteen Benito was convicted of two counts of possession of heroin and sent to state prison for two years.

Back in his neighborhood, he resumed his gang activities. The FxTroop generated large amounts of income through car theft, burglary and muggings. They were known as 'neighborhood' gangs and were careful about committing criminal activities outside of their own neighborhoods. The FxTroop members were one of the most visible aspects of the cultural war raging between the wealthy Anglo community and the poor Hispanic community. The gang had an unspoken commitment among its members to invade defenseless Anglo neighborhoods and claim victory.

Like Benito, Carlos was an FxTroop member, but he wasn't as obvious as Benito when he pushed drugs. Carlos didn't have the prison-swagger or tattoos that Benito proudly displayed.

Carlos, a good looking junior high student and track star athlete, was the youngest of eight siblings and the first in his family to attend high school. His sunny smile and pleasing personality attracted others to him, making it easy for Carlos to mingle and make drug deals – always outside his own neighborhood. Carlos didn't use drugs himself. He knew that was self-defeating, and he wanted the good life. Going to school and making fast money was, he felt, the easy way to get where he wanted to go — out of the neighborhood after graduation. Besides, the FxTroop discouraged drug sales within their own neighborhoods, and Carlos respected the gang pact. He was aware of the "green light," or death warrant given to others before him who had sold drugs in their neighborhood. He thought it was okay, however, to sell drugs in other neighborhoods.

What the hell am I doing? I asked myself as I drove towards home. What impulse operates inside a man's skull to force him literally between two people making war? I began to understand why so many off-duty policemen were killed performing their duty.

This understanding prompted me to take a Civil Disorder Control class at Fullerton Junior College.[5] I didn't know then that this training would be helpful to me in the future as protests into the 70's escalated.

Six months into my rookie year, and the satisfactions in my job were not as abundant as I thought they would be, but I was getting a real education on what goes on inside law enforcement and criminal activities.

CHAPTER THIRTEEN
July - December 1967

At the end of July, a letter from a citizen whom I had cited during a routine traffic stop was read at roll call.[6] The purpose of Mr. Bruce Albert's signed letter, addressed to Police Chief Allen, stated, "I have never seen any police officer, Negro or White, do his job in a finer way. Officer Lambert handled his job intelligently, courteously, humanely, and decently."

Not long after, another letter, this time from the Orange County Council for Better Education was read at roll call.[7] Ted Gillett, Director of the Lincoln Headstart Staff, wrote a thank you note for my "superb job" and participation in speaking with the children about community services.

Four officers shoved their chairs back, got up, and headed to the door. "We don't have to listen to this shit."

The shift Sergeant bellowed, "Roll call isn't over, gentlemen. Get your asses back in your chairs! Time to talk about activity level."

Ticket quotas were loosely calculated by the minimal number of tickets to be issued by a law enforcement officer for stopping people for moving violations, issuing parking tickets and quality of life summons, and even for making arrests. The Santa Ana PD set "productivity goals" but denied having specific quotas. If an officer fell below a goal, he got pressured and chewed out for performing below average or being non-productive. We were reassured daily that the activity log was not a measure of an officer's worth.

I soon discovered the Activity Log – that single piece of paper – had been responsible for more petty tickets, unnecessary arrests, and pure downright police harassment than any other single factor in police work, plus it fostered an antagonistic relationship between police and the communities they served.

The sergeant pointed to me, "Lambert's activity logs are examples of the effort he's putting forth. How about some of you fine officers consider raising your activity level. Now get out of here!"

As we filed out of roll call, I was brushed against and elbowed.

"Since when did the coon-ass become our police poster boy?"

and other snide remarks about my activities on the job followed me into the hallway and reverberated down its walls.

I had been on the department long enough to know what would come next.

~~*~~

Since the officers had been challenged to raise their activity levels, I knew they would go hunting for the most vulnerable folks like jaywalkers, someone spitting on the sidewalk, a kid riding his bicycle on the wrong side of the street, the homeless man foraging in a trashcan, the driver caught in a speed trap – all would be cited and perhaps arrested simply to bring up their numbers for the night.

Captain Tracey, in the hallway near his office, approached me with arms crossed over his chest. Without prelude, he asked, "Have you given some thought to resigning? Maybe this job is too much for you. Maybe it's not for you."

I was momentarily speechless. Where the hell did this come from?

I tried not to change my expression, but I felt my neck stiffen. "Well, sir, I've not given any thought to resigning and I don't think the job is too much for me." I felt my face flushing, but added, "I've made a commitment to myself and my family that not only am I going to be a police officer, but a damn good one."

Hurt and stunned by his questions and suggestions, I just turned and walked away, as Captain Tracey stood in the hallway and stared after me.

This hallway meeting was at the beginning of my shift. My throat grew thick as I went to the garage to get my patrol car. As I drove to my district my eyes became so watery I had to pull to the curb. Anguish filled me. I wanted to understand why the captain said those things to me. I wanted to yell, but couldn't.

Two years passed before we spoke to another again, even if we happened to meet in the hallway. But I would remember that first encounter in the years ahead, a warning light going off before I even knew to look for one.

I tried to consider Captain Tracey's medical problems for his behavior. He had had a heart attack and God knows what else. It was not out of the ordinary to see this 5 foot 10 inch, balding, slender man, walk in the city with his muscular back and shoulders hunched. I supposed because of health reasons.

After the short exchange with Captain Tracey, I retreated into my protective shell – that part of me that closed off open sharing and vulnerability - because I did not know which other supervisors and officers felt as he did, or if I would get assistance in the field if I needed help.

~~*~~

That time came not long after. Southbound on Pacific at First Street, I observed two Hispanic men sitting in a four-door blue Chevrolet at 1:30 a.m. From their parked vehicle, they watched an open liquor store.

As I turned the corner and came up behind their vehicle, I notified Dispatch of my location and the description and license plate number of the car before I exited my patrol car. I detected an odor of marijuana as I approached the driver and asked him to step out.

"Passenger, please remain seated," I said.

The driver, I identified as Juan Herrera, and I walked to the rear of my patrol unit.

"Mr. Herrera, why are you and your partner sitting in the car this time of night?"

He obviously understood English better than he could speak it, "We sit, talk."

I explained to him the liquor store had been robbed several times in the past few months, and that's why I had made contact with the two men.

"Sir, do you have a weapon or anything else in your pockets you don't want me to see?" He patted his right front pants' pocket, "Marijuana."

I placed him in the search position on the trunk of the patrol unit. I removed the bag, cuffed him and told him he was under arrest.

As I opened the left rear door and asked him to get in, he yelled, "No!" and began struggling, trying to move away from the car. My right hand grabbed the cuffs and I turned him so my left arm now had him in a headlock. I moved him towards the open driver's door and reached for the microphone, which I'd left hanging over the doorframe.

While I requested assistance, the passenger jumped out of the Chevrolet and raced towards us, obviously ready to help his companion.

I held the radio mike and listened for a response from Dispatch.

I said, "Sir! If you come any closer or try to hurt me, I'll shoot you. Stop where you are!"

Still no response from Dispatch, but I was relieved to see a black-and-white pull up behind me to assist with the arrest of both subjects. Officer Burgess told me he heard my calls for assistance and responded. Before we left the area, headed to the police station, I expressed my appreciation and called for a tow.

At the end of my shift, I entered the communications room. I said to the dispatcher seated there, "I was trying to reach you…"

The brunette interrupted, "We didn't hear you. We didn't know you needed backup help."

She hadn't let me finish what I was going to say. How could she know I needed assistance if she didn't hear me? And how was it that Officer Burgess heard me?

I stared at her. It took every ounce of effort I possessed to not say another word and to quietly close the door behind me.

One day after playing basketball at Jerome Park, the four men who referred to themselves as the "Nightcrawlers" because they were socially active in the early evenings told me they preferred not to be friendly with me anymore. We had been playing together regularly for months. I was surprised to hear that coming from my friends and basketball buddies. I asked why.

"Man, since you became a cop, we fear for our lives and for our families if we're seen talking or socializing with you. Rumors are that you've arrested a lot of Black people in the neighborhood, and you're harder on Blacks and Mexicans than on the Whites."

At that point I confess I got a little attitude because I knew that wasn't true. "You can be black, blue, green or techni-color. If you break the law, you'll go to jail."

From that time forward, whenever I went to the park to play or watch a basketball game, the Nightcrawlers instantly scooped up their ball and left the area. I understood their fears, but it didn't take away the pain of losing their friendships. I relived the loss of my fishing buddy, Barry Armein's friendship, and others who would only acknowledge me covertly.

That incident caused me to recall a quote from Martin Luther King Jr's speech at a Montgomery Baptist church ten years earlier: "In the end, we will remember not the words of our enemies, but the silence of our friends."

~~*~~

So many threats were made to me on the telephone – never in person. I was told that I would be killed if I played basketball in the park. People I had arrested threatened my wife and son. They told me that they knew the direction my son took to school, the license plate of my personal car, when my wife left for work and the time she returned home.

The threats prompted me to trail behind Marie as she drove through my patrol district to the city of Orange for her job at the Laura Scudders potato chip factory. I knew when she was due to come back, and when I saw her car enter the city limits, I watched her drive to our home, park the car, and unlock the front door. I waited for the 'all okay' signal we had established as she entered.

I then returned to my patrol duties once again.

~~*~~

With the threats of being beaten or possibly killed if I continued going to the park, I began playing basketball with a 357 Derringer tucked inside the jock strap of my gym shorts. I knew my Derringer would not automatically fire, since the hammer had to be cocked first. The weight of the weapon was uncomfortable, but the comfort it brought in terms of what it could do to protect me was worth the pain of wearing it.

Sure enough, two weeks after the Labor Day weekend, my teenage charges - Clarence, Oscar, Willy and Ron - walked with me from the basketball court. I counseled as we walked, "This is a tough park. If you can play here, you can play with anybody, anywhere. Practice well and remember, basketball can be your springboard for so many things to come later."

As we reached the parking lot, I saw seven male Blacks dressed

131

in sweat pants, t-shirts, and knitted caps pulled low on their foreheads leaning on and standing around my new Pontiac. They were tall and looked like weight lifters. Some clenched sticks and bottles in their beefy hands. This isn't looking good - but sticks and bottles mean no guns.

As I approached my car, they fanned out to surround me. One of them snarled, "We told you your ass was going to get kicked."

Another chimed in, "Now's the time, Uncle Tom. We're going to kick your ass here and now."

I slid my 357 Derringer two-barrel pistol from my jock strap. The click of my cocking the hammer sounded in the quiet. I raised the pistol and pointed it in a slow, sweeping motion to cover as many assailants as possible.

The move surprised them. "I have two bullets, which will prove fatal to the first two of you who attack. Who wants to be the first to die?"

It took only a matter of moments to see behinds dispersing in different directions. Oh God, thank you.

~~*~~

Ironically, basketball brought me to Santa Ana and to the distinction of being Santa Ana's first Negro police officer. I had so wanted to be a policeman. I knew it would be difficult, especially for a black man, but I didn't know it would be this hard – or set me on an entirely unexpected course.

My wife of seven years couldn't hold it in any longer. "First, I followed you to Germany for the Army and basketball. Then you brought me all the way out to California. Why? To pursue YOUR dreams and do what YOU want for YOUR life. I understand things didn't turn out as you planned. But you've made being a cop your latest priority. Now your job is your life and your family is second –AGAIN!"

Fists clenched, rage and hurt etched in her face, she spoke in low but emphatic terms, not wanting Fernando to hear. "What next, Harlen? When will your superiors do something to protect you – and us? I never know if you'll get home safe. Or if you'll come home and find Fernando and me dead because of your job." She collapsed on the living room sofa, sobbing.

Before I could respond, eight-year-old Fernando burst into the room inquiring, "Why can't I go to the park, Daddy?" He was wearing his favorite tennis shoes, his basketball tucked under his arm, his hand resting on the door-knob. He was ready for what should have been a routine late afternoon basketball play between father and son at Jerome Park, a block away. Fernando would come home from school, have a snack, and pick up his ball for some playing tips. How to shoot, dribble, guard and complete finger-spins – moves that he could later show off to his classmates.

I looked down into my son's questioning face and thought of the dozens of complex reasons I could give him for not allowing him to go to the park that day, but I knew each of the reasons was too heavy, too scary for his beautiful, uncontaminated mind.

The past few weeks had gotten progressively worse at the park. I thought about those men I had become friends with, played basketball with, but who now were fearful of associating with me. I thought about the threats on my wife and son – the information those faceless voices derisively laughing on the telephone gave me about my family's routines, the direction my son took to school, the routes my wife drove to and from work.

There was no way I could tell my son I was threatened with death, that I now carried a 357 Derringer while on the basketball court, that the usual activities we had enjoyed as a family were slowly, but surely, becoming things of the past.

So, as fathers have done since time began, I laid a stern, parental face on him and said, "Because I said so" and pretended to continue reading the newspaper. Inwardly, I was embarrassed and upset that I couldn't think of something more profound, something he could understand.

Marie, in the kitchen, heard this exchange. "Fernando, take your ball to the back yard and practice shooting at your hoop, while I talk with Daddy."

In a minute I could hear Fernando outside. He wasn't throwing the ball into the hoop I'd put up for him. He was throwing it against the house. With force. I dropped the newspaper on the coffee table. Should I go to Fernando, or to Marie?

I went to Marie, taking her in my arms. She smelled of the tangy oranges she had been cutting. It hurts to see those you love grieving – for you and for the family. There were times she was troubled to the point of being sick.

I knew what I had to say wouldn't make her feel better, but I had to try. "Marie, I do take the threats seriously. You will never know or understand how sorry I am you're in this situation. I'm taking steps to make sure you and Fernando WILL be safe." I tilted her head up and looked in her eyes. "I need to make sure one of you doesn't serve as a substitute for me. You know there's no way I can explain to Fernando that he can't go play in the park with other kids because his daddy is a black pig."

Moving out of my hug, Marie raised her hand. "I don't want to hear any more. I can't continue to live in fear forever, Harlen. I won't!" That was the second time she used my given name, rather than, Sunny, my childhood nickname. She meant business.

She stood up, making her way through the kitchen to the back yard where Fernando continued bouncing his basketball, against the back of the house – hard.

Following Marie, I watched our son from the doorway. With the sun shining out of a clear blue sky on a warm afternoon, tears of frustration coursed down his cheeks with each furious throw of his ball.

I was a green cop, a black rookie, but nothing in the training guided me in explaining to my child the ugly, belittling effect of the hatred that targeted me.

It frustrated and grieved me that I couldn't comfort my wife and my son. To survive, I knew I had to enjoy part of the weekend away from daily pressures of being the Santa Ana Police's Jackie Robinson.

~~*~~

Jackie Robinson was controversial in his time as the first Black recruited in organized baseball, and later into the White Major Leagues. His arriving in baseball on April 15, 1947 was a powerful moment in baseball history, and was a major breakthrough of the color line in sports. Robinson knew that his presence on the playing field would cause resentment. He anticipated that some pitchers would aim balls at his head and that other players would try to injure him on the base-paths. Ballplayers and fans alike would shout epithets of "nigger" at him when he came to bat. He also was aware that a few rabid racists might try to kill him – or at least scare him with death threats.

I escaped to the bathroom to wash up, still feeling like exploding.

Jackie Robinson, despite all his pressures, played extremely well. He was a solid hitter, an outstanding base stealer, and he excelled defensively. And he handled the pressure well even though at times - he felt like exploding.

I wondered, could I continue to remain professional and perform my duties to protect society even as a variety of incidents terrorized and isolated me - and my family too?

The mirror reflected my usual image: a 6'2", 220 pound, muscular man accustomed to working out in the gym. I examined my reflection in detail. I have what is known as "good hair": soft, wavy and cut close to my head. My teeth are white, strong and boast a small space between my two front teeth. I wear a mustache and have been told I look like Richard Roundtree, the actor, known as the "first black action hero" for his portrayal of private detective, John Shaft.

While I usually felt good about what I saw in the mirror, I didn't feel good that day. My appetite began to diminish. I soon began to lose weight and to have difficulty sleeping. I was fighting depression. But, by God, I refuse to let bigots define who I am. I refuse to be baited with racial and physical assaults. No-matter-what!

I removed my black-rimmed eyeglasses to rub my tired eyes, and turned my thoughts to my son Fernando and my first basketball.

~~*~~

During the nighttime hours while in bed I mentally recapped the day's activities. I could no longer talk to Marie, who had become afraid. She didn't want to know about the street life. We no longer socialized with friends nor attended activities we once enjoyed together.

Marie spent numerous hours each week attending the Second Baptist Church in Fullerton. She slipped out before the services ended because of the paranoia she now felt around strangers.

Another time and under different circumstances, I might have chosen to talk privately with our minister. Thank goodness I didn't.

It was 1:30 in the morning and I was on foot patrol at the Greyhound Bus Station. Marines waited in the lobby for transport to the

El Toro Marine Base. A 5'8" male wore a long navy blue coat, the collar pulled up around his neck, and a dark cap pulled low on his forehead. He sat on a bench in the center of the station.

I had observed him as he walked around in the station intermittently talking to Marines. I flashed my badge and casually asked some of the marines about the man in the blue coat. I learned he was soliciting sex.

He identified himself to me as William Wood, which didn't fit the description on his I.D. card which stated that William Wood was 6'5" and 233 pounds. This man was shorter and much slimmer, at about 150 pounds soaking wet, so I knew then he wasn't telling me the truth and didn't want to be recognized.

I asked him to remove his hat and turn down his collar.

There stood the man who had ministered to my family and me over the past year and a half. He hung his head in shame as I arrested him for solicitation. Records revealed the Vice Squad had arrested this man of God previously for the same crime in Birch Park.

He resigned his position as pastor of our church shortly after his arrest and left the city for parts unknown. Because Marie found so much comfort in the church, and believed the minister was all knowing and good in all things, I thought it best not to tell her about the arrest.

Over breakfast, I feigned innocence as we wondered why he would suddenly resign and leave the community.

~~*~~

On a quiet, uneventful night in January as I patrolled, I congratulated myself. The air was misty and cold at 49° when I stopped at Winchell's for a hot chocolate and thought about the last four months as a rookie cop. A lot had happened.

Four teens had started hanging around the basketball court at Jerome Park a week before the Labor Day incident, when I had scared off some threatening thugs.

The following week Oscar approached me, basketball tucked under his arm. "Officer Lambert, we saw what you did to those guys! I told my Dad and he said to thank you for teaching those thugs a lesson."

He pointed to his buddies, standing at the edge of the court. "Can we can play with you?"

Clarence, Oscar, Willy, and Ron crowded around me, firing off questions about the pistol I carried in my shorts and would I teach them basketball? Each expressed a desire to play professional ball one day.

I watched them on the court for a few minutes. I saw young men with talent who needed help. Their skills on the court were special, but they would need more than that to reach their potential.

"In high school all you think about is the ball," I said. "You think it's going to take you to the promised land. It doesn't always happen that way, and it's important you know you can be successful at other things."

"Think seriously about going to college," I continued. "If you make it on a college team, that's where you'll work on discipline, which leads to working as part of a team. Whether you play professional ball or do something else, teamwork is important."

We talked about character being essential to success. "Some might not agree, but I think everybody wants good people around them."

It was then I took on the role of big brother, provided fatherly counsel and guidance, and shared basketball and other lessons I had learned from my time playing.

As I sipped my hot chocolate, I couldn't help but smile as I recalled our "Jump Back!" play and a group invitation that changed our lives.

Oscar dribbled the ball toward the opponent, who guarded him defensively. Our team yelled and clapped, "Step back, baby!" as Oscar quickly stepped back, and shot the ball into the basket. Oscar, Willy, Ron, and Clarence practiced the play over and over, and became known as the "Jump Back" team.

We couldn't know then that our lives would cross paths in unexpected ways on and off the court for the rest of our lives.

One day, one of these young men would be the messenger behind saving the lives of my family and me.

~~*~~

On Wednesday morning, the watch commander brought the previous day's newspaper into roll call. I had not seen the paper and didn't expect what happened next.

On September 10, 1967 *The Independent Press-Telegram of Long Beach* ran the story, "Orange County Racial Tensions Become Apparent."[8] It was a two-part series on the "Orange County Negro community, its problems and the problems it presents to the surrounding White communities."[9] The commander read the following excerpt from the article:

> Harlen D. Lambert is a Santa Ana Negro. He may never gain national prominence as others of this race have done, but he did establish a precedent by becoming Orange County's first Negro police officer.
>
> Until his appointment to the Santa Ana Police Department, community Negroes had complained that no Negro was on the police force because there were two sets of tests, one for Whites and another for Negroes.
>
> When Lambert was hired last December, ghetto residents said, "The city thinks it is doing the big thing by hiring a Negro to satisfy our demands. In reality, they are only tossing us a bone to keep us quiet. Although concurring that Lambert is doing a good job, Negroes still question, "Why no more Negro police officers, or firemen, or city white-collar workers?"
>
> City officials contend such jobs aren't being filled by Negroes because Negroes with adequate background do not apply. "Actually," city personnel director Donald Bott said, "Very few Negroes seek city jobs. We do have a few working in the streets and parks departments. Another thing, the turnover in the so-called white collar area of city government is low."
>
> Many Negroes still feel there is discrimination in the city employment so "what's the use of trying to get a good city job when we know beforehand that a white man will get it."
>
> Former Mayor Harry Harvey, however, said he personally was aware of prejudice by the city against the Negro seeking fireman jobs. "Something to do with white firemen objecting to sleeping in the same room with a Negro, or something like that," Harvey stated.

On reading the article, The Vulture complained, "The ghetto dogs don't know how good they have it, and they need to stop whining." I suddenly understood the nickname given to Webb—like a vulture, he meant to pluck and tear.

Chief Allen received a letter from the vice president of the Bristol Drug Company at West 4th and Bristol.[10] They considered my work "… superior… and (he does) marvelous work in public relations with all people living here as well as with the various businesses located in this area." They ended with the comment that they looked forward to my continued work in the city.

The letter was read in roll call, which resulted in my being reassigned to another district the following night. I was informed that Sergeant Webb would be my shift supervisor.

For the next few months, when I made a stop or took any police action on the streets, he remained in the shadows. He watched me, and left the area without a word after the activity was done.

I thought back to the locker room gossip about the Sergeant— and the warning that he was hell-bent on assuring my failure as a police officer.

~~*~~

The San Diego Police Department hosted the first year of the State of California Police Olympics.[11] It was a three day event that began October 12, 1967. I filed my application to compete and for weeks I trained at Jerome Park where I stretched, jogged, ran, and played basketball to prepare myself for the 100 and 200-yard dash events.

I was privileged to compete and felt confident that, at thirty-one, I could get out there and run my best against the competition.

As it turned out, my competition was largely an indoor and outdoor track team from Los Angeles PD. Most looked to be in their mid-twenties and had probably never been out of condition in their lives. Eleven men joined me at the edge of the track to warm up. We greeted one another and chatted amiably as we lined up for the 100-yard dash.

The whistle sounded to sprint. I was practically left at the starting line coughing and choking on the dust the LAPD team kicked up as they charged ahead of me.

After I checked the roster for the upcoming 200-yard dash, I saw it was the same squad that had destroyed me earlier. Well, that didn't go as planned. I decided I had suffered enough humiliation, so I packed up my tennis shoes and sped home.

~~*~~

Ministers from surrounding African American churches requested that I speak to their youth. The department "loaned" me to the First Methodist Church on Spurgeon at Santa Ana Boulevard. Their letter of October 25, 1967 was read in roll call.[12]

L.E. Romaine, Youth Director stated, "His (Harlen Lambert's) presentation, demeanor and real enthusiasm was received by the youth of this church in a most fabulous way." He also said they planned to request my services again and appreciated my time and talents.

The First Methodist Church had a party planned for Halloween. Parents and teens hung spider webs and orange crepe paper from the banquet hall ceiling. Paper witches, broomsticks, and ghosts were taped to the walls. Carved pumpkins with candles overlooked the huge bowl of green punch containing plastic worms floating haphazardly. Plates of assorted cookies and candies were in easy reach for the smallest party goer.

The sun had gone down, and I was requested to "Keep an eye out" as I patrolled the area. I saw goblins, princesses, supermen, clowns, witches, and other young people dressed in costume marching together toward the church. The youngsters laughed and chatted.

I made another pass twenty minutes later, and braked hard as a gorilla ran out the front door, narrowly missing my patrol car. I got out and saw an angry youth leader catch up with the ape and pounce. A big, hairy hand flopped onto the sidewalk and, as the gorilla turned to run again, he ran right into my arms.

"Whoa! Hold up. What's going on?"

Michael "Mikey" Carter was an enthusiastic 14-year-old who liked to play jokes - and Halloween was his favorite time of year. He had donned his gorilla costume for the church party, with the intention of scaring the younger kids.

The youth counselor explained the gorilla had been standing by the punch bowl, jumped out, and chased the kids as they came to the table. He had carelessly upended the four-gallon bowl of liquid, which had drenched the cookies, dripped on the floor and pooled in a sticky mess.

"Do you have anything to say to the counselor?" I asked.

With a big smile, he said, "I was just monkeying around!"

~~*~~

I would be "on loan" to respond to questions of concern and interest from youth at a variety of churches and schools for the next year – before I was transferred to the newly-formed Community Relations Department.

~~*~~

It started to drizzle and the air chilled me. I ordered another hot chocolate from the Winchell's counter server, blew on it and sipped, as the hot liquid coursed through my veins. I recalled two November incidents and thought about Tom Parrott.

I had met Tom, a tall, handsome, muscular, and well-spoken man through a mutual friend in 1961. He was a reserve police officer in Los

Angeles, and told me he was testing at different departments to become a full-time officer. Tom Parrott hired on to the LAPD and attended law school. Once I was on the police force, I contacted Tom to let him know our department was looking for qualified black police officers, and encouraged him to test for a position.

Tom transferred to the Santa Ana Police Department in September 1967. Now there were two of us. Over the next two years Officer Parrott commuted from Los Angeles, before he moved his family to a section of northern Santa Ana.

In early November a report was made about a prowler in the 1000 block of West Highland Street. The prowler was surprised in the act and fired three shots at the police officers pursuing him, narrowly missing one of the officers. Following the arrest of the suspect, a line-up was held and witnessed by the suspect's attorney.

The prowler, a black, was about six feet one, 200 pounds, close haircut, mustache and wore black-rimmed glasses. Tom Parrott and I were requested to participate in the line-up. The suspect was positively identified and the attorney was markedly impressed by the fairness displayed. Parrott and I received a commendation for "...(our) demeanor during the line-up was such as to afford the suspect a completely fair and objective viewing."[13]

It would be two years before Tom and I worked together again.

Fullerton Police Chief Wayne Bornhoft wrote to Chief Allen and Captain Johnson – asking if I could assist their department in an attempt to purchase narcotics from a known seller.[14]

Two nights later I met with narcotics detectives to formulate a plan to purchase drugs from a young black male who lived in a Hispanic neighborhood on Valencia, near Euclid. I was to approach the house, knock on the door, and when the subject answered, reach into my back pocket as a signal for the detectives to charge the house.

The gate nearly came off its weak and rotting hinges as I opened it to enter the unkempt yard. Broken glass, a discarded tire, and other trash littered the front yard and porch. I knocked on the door. After several loud attempts, the 22-year-old suspect answered. He opened it wide enough that I could identify him by the description the detectives had given me - five feet nine, underweight, with two front teeth missing.

He was scratching his neck and sporting an oversized cross hanging from a chain around his neck. "Yeah?"

I reached around to my back pocket, "Man, I'm here for some stuff."

"Yeah, sure." The suspect opened the door wider, and in seconds the detectives threw open the doors of their unmarked van, jumped the fence and raced through the yard and up the porch. Officers pushed the door all the way open, simultaneously grabbing, cuffing, and arresting the suspect for possession and sales.

I stayed with the suspect as the detectives searched the house, finding large amounts of cocaine and heroin. With pleasure, I handed the doper over to the Fullerton cops. I couldn't wait to get home to wash off the stink.

On a warm, sunny, Thanksgiving Day I was assigned as Field Training Officer to a baby-faced college-graduate rookie. My initial trepidation about being accepted by a trainee was immediately put to rest. Brandon Parsons was enthusiastic and ready to go to work. Our differences in age and race were never an issue. I had vowed long ago, that if put in the FTO position, to be fair and professional at all times.

Working with Parsons was enjoyable as we discussed not only the text book requirements of police officers, but the everyday hands-on role police officers face daily on the streets. Parsons took notes on three-by-five cards with information I gave to him. His field notebook contained only official notes that pertained to his police work.

"Which of these situations would you have more control over," I asked. "A determined assailant lying in wait, who is willing to die in his quest to kill a police officer, or the actions that you take and the decisions you make regarding safety equipment, how you drive, and how you handle a call?"

His face lit up. Parsons was eager to say, "My actions, sir. I have to make sure I wear my seat belt, because seatbelts save lives. I have to watch my speed when responding to a call."

Interrupting his answer, I said, "Cops drive fast because they can, right?"

"Well, yes, Officer Lambert, sir. But driving faster than conditions warrant is a sure way to get in trouble. You said there are times when getting on scene quickly is critical, but those times are rare."

He referenced his field notebook and added, "Cops who speed – just because they can – put themselves and the public at perilous risk for no good reason."

"What's important now?" I asked.

Parson's said, "Deliberate action, not reaction. I can't constantly prioritize what's most important, because if I do I won't have time for the distractions that can get me in trouble, hurt, or killed."

"Remember, Officer Parsons. Complacency is among the most dangerous and insidious threats we face. It lays us open to all others. Complacency is why officers think they can go without helmets and seatbelts. It's why they think they can speed and allow themselves to be distracted. Complacency can kill."

I emphasized safety and would repeat, "You were hired to protect the life and property of the citizens of Santa Ana. This does not mean because you fail to use common sense you have to give your life." Every other note-card of his had the word Safety written on it, and underscored numerous times.

I also trained so my rookie was comfortable asking questions about what we were doing and why. In less than a week, my trainee, holding the keys to the squad car said to me over the roof of the car, "Officer Lambert, I want to thank you for making me feel like your real partner."

With genuine pride, I smiled. "Just get in and drive, partner." I truthfully assured him that driving was part of the training, learning the city streets and neighborhoods while being aware of his surroundings and communicating with dispatch - all at the same time. Parsons wasn't aware of my less than stellar driving abilities—minor incidents, to be sure, but incidents nonetheless—or that I had an underlying purpose in allowing him to drive so frequently.

It was Officer Parsons who started my FTO nickname of "First Aid." Over the next five years while in patrol capacity, I was assigned as FTO to other young rookies, who somehow learned of my nickname.

Police officers are notorious locker room gossips, so I learned some of the rookies specifically requested that I be assigned as their training officer because I emphasized safety. I had gained the reputation of being fair, competent, and always willing to sit down and discuss what had happened during their shift, how they handled themselves, and sometimes how it might be better handled in the future.

As a police officer, the role of Field Training Officer was one of the duties I loved best.

CHAPTER FOURTEEN
January - June 1968

Rain poured down outside, bringing in 1968. I crushed the empty Winchells cup and threw it into the trash can before getting back into my patrol car. Here I was - no longer a rookie. Twelve months and several pounds lighter, personal relationships eroding, constantly under surveillance, low pay in proportion to the work involved, and coping with an intense emotional adjustment.

My thoughts were interrupted as Sergeant Robert Stebbins pulled his squad car alongside mine. We rolled down our windows. Only the rain was heard as it hit and jumped off his out thrust hand.

"Officer Lambert," he said, "Let me be the first to congratulate you on passing your one year probationary period."

We laughed together as we wiped rain, now blowing into our cars, from our faces. He slicked back a lock of blonde hair, and suggested we go inside Winchell's.

I followed the sergeant, about 5'10," slender build, shoulders straight, head slightly bent against the rain, into the doughnut shop. I declined an offer of a cup of hot chocolate – my gut gurgled from the two cups I'd just finished.

The sergeant had been on the department since 1958 and had seen some changes – in his view, both good and bad. He spoke in a down-to-earth, friendly, self-assured manner. I quickly recognized a faithful Christian and sensitive man.

When Sergeant Stebbins asked me a question, he made me feel my answers were valued – that I was of value.

Suddenly, the Winchell's door burst open and a petite, barefoot, gray-haired lady ran toward us. She shivered and tried to smooth down the rain-soaked night shirt she wore. Her eyes were wide. She appeared genuinely frightened.

We quickly rose from the table at the same time.

"Please! Help me! I just moved into an apartment around the corner on McFadden." Her voice escalated, and she began wringing her hands. "There's a ghost! He broke in and he won't leave!"

146

Sergeant Stebbins assured her we'd take care of it as he escorted her to his patrol car. I followed them to her apartment, where we arrested the invisible ghost and carted it out so she could relax in peace. She was smiling and happy when we unceremoniously shoved the ghost into Stebbins car and left.

So ended my first of many meetings with Sergeant Stebbins over the next eight months.

~~*~~

The following night was quiet, but for The Beatles Magical Mystery Tour album, which was #1 on the charts. I stopped at a red traffic light and listened to the lyrics of "All You Need Is Love" coming longingly from somewhere within the apartment complex.

The light turned green. I heard "*All together now…*" as I stepped on the gas pedal.

My thoughts turned to the realities of the Santa Ana crime control strategies I had observed since my first days as a ride-a-long.

It was simple, if not simplistic: Kick ass and take names.

Mike Doran had been on the SAPD for eleven years and he was the first officer to openly share that tidbit with me. The big, ruddy-faced, forty-something former marine reminisced about his time as a cop with a certain nostalgia.

"That was it," he told me. "That was one of the appealing things about it, though. I knew when I went out on the street at night, starting my shift, there would be a lot of activity. Santa Ana's a high-activity town and because we're undermanned, there's always something to keep us going."

He looked at me and sighed. "Time was we had a lot of fights, especially in bars. We'd get in a lot of stick time. I was big, strong, and I loved to fight. Besides, cops always win."

In those days relations with the public were unpleasant and often antagonistic. Police were openly and frequently called "pigs" on the street, and police returned the compliment with epithets of their own or, more likely, with the end of the nightstick.

Since my first days as a ride-along, I had heard officers express either 'considerable' or 'extreme' prejudice against minorities. Blacks (1.2%

of the population) and Hispanics (42% of the population – and 17% who spoke English) in particular did not embody the average policeman's idea of the worthy citizen whose rights and property were to be respected. It was well known that Santa Ana had the highest minority population in the county, a heavy concentration of drug addicts, and substandard housing.

Even though the majority of patrol work involved noncriminal matters, I watched cops frequently stopping, frisking, arresting, and charging minorities. Many supervisory officers shared the same idea of who was a worthy citizen, so they did not regard their rank-and-file responses against Blacks and Hispanics as a problem.

One night riding with Officer Doran, we saw a lone black male walk out of an apartment complex on McFadden Street. The young man didn't appear to be concerned as the patrol car drove by him and came to an abrupt stop. Doran retrieved a pair of black deerskin gloves from the dashboard and carefully put them on. I had thought the gloves were intended to keep his hands clean when he handled a derelict or someone particularly filthy.

In a flash Doran was out of the car and headed toward the slightly built, 5'9" boy. I stepped out and walked to the rear of the car. The young man froze. His arms were held slightly away from his sides, palms open, so we could see he had no weapon.

The size difference was striking. Officer Doran weighed about 250 pounds. Without any discussion or warning, Doran walked up to the pedestrian and knocked him unconscious with a single crashing blow to the jaw. The young man's arms flew in the air as he smacked the sidewalk spread-eagled on his back, out cold. Doran turned around and walked back to the car. Apparently whatever business he had there was finished.

Officer Doran meticulously removed his gloves one finger at a time. He gave me a warning look and motioned me to get in the car. I dropped onto the seat and heard him mumble, "You can't teach those f---ing niggers a thing."

~~*~~

I was jolted out of that painful memory as I neared the empty lot off North Grand. With headlights off, my spotlight hit the backs of two teenagers running. They jumped the concrete wall and disappeared into the night. As I turned and looked away, my vehicle struck the curb.

This accident would be written up as driver inattention to private property and would earn me a written reprimand.

"There's nothing you can do that can't be done. All you need is love, love. All you need is love." The Beatles song I had heard earlier in the evening ran through my mind continually like the leaves that fell silently from the California sycamores on that clear, crisp night.

~~*~~

The following night, Officer Doran and I patrolled East Fourth Street. As night fell, the business people had left the area for their ranch homes and suburbs. Those who remained, and those who arrived, were mostly Mexican.

At night, the street transformed into a time-honored feature of Spanish life. The character was almost that of a stage set. Mariachi bands whose members dressed in native costumes played folk music in the bars. Their button accordions, trumpets and violins brought yells of excitement—a known behavior in the Mexican culture. Guitarists and singers emerged and played in the street, reminding me of a parade. Lines between inside and outside, public and private became blurred.

Doran, scanning the street activity, said, "We use discretion out here, Lambert. If we see a man weaving down the street, we arrest 'im. Most of the drunk driving happens after these people leave the bars to go home to the city's worst shit-hole."

"Where's that?" I asked.

"Few miles away on Minnie Street. Stinking slum." He slowed the car to point out young women lounging in front of the bars, "Look like school girls dressed up for a Saturday night, don't they? Some are hookers, though, and as long as they're not using or dealing drugs, we leave 'em alone. You'll decide eventually who and what to tolerate on the streets."

I saw a more public spirited and patronizing side of Officer Doran when "Tawney" crossed the street in front of us. She was dark-haired, dark-eyed, and petite at five feet tall. She was dressed in tight jeans and a low-cut white blouse cropped to reveal her belly button.

"Now, see, Tawney's twenty-one with three small kids. Leaves 'em with a babysitter when she's working the streets. She's cagey, smart, and good at talking. Her "old man" cares for the kids when he's not in jail for burglary. We leave her alone to get the twenty bucks she earns for every alley visit. Been told most nights she averages more than $200. Not bad for non-taxable income, 'eh?"

We saw a young man approach Tawney, talk for a few seconds, and arm-in-arm they strolled around the corner. We continued to patrol for a few blocks observing, occasionally flashing our lights into dark, garbage littered alleys and back streets.

Doran turned the patrol car around and within minutes Tawney and the young man emerged from the dark. She was laughing and waved goodbye as she crossed the street to take up her post once more.

"We don't arrest these young men," Doran explained. "They work hard and save up money to bring their families from Mexico. In the meantime, they're gonna have sex. No point in arresting people for having sex!"

The night was a lesson in who owned and made rules on the streets. It was clear police officers exercised considerable authority and personal discretion.

~~*~~

The Independent reported "Freeway Pursuit Jails 2."[15] My neighbor, Don Sanders, and I had left Jerome Park after a game of basketball. I was a passenger in Don's car, and he said he needed to fill up before we headed home.

I had met Donald and his family when I first moved to Santa Ana. He was a former marine, now employed as a salesman with Budweiser. A good looking, respectable guy who lived with and cared for his aging parents. Our families spent many hours together in each other's homes.

We stopped at the service station at Fifth and Fairview Streets. We were regulars, and Sammy, the attendant, told me a man had just left without paying for the gas he received. He gave a description of the car while Don pumped gas.

After we left, I spotted the car turn north on Fairview. My friend looked at me with a grin, and said, "You know, I can't let this go!"

Don followed the vehicle for several blocks, before he pulled alongside the auto at a red light. I stepped into the street, showed my badge and ordered the driver to halt—Charles Donnelly—a familiar name. I recognized and had previously arrested his passenger, Paul Donnelly, for being drunk in public.

The driver hit the gas, and narrowly missed striking me before he sped off. I jumped back in the car. Don hit his gas pedal, too, and the chase was on. We pursued the car onto the Garden Grove Freeway at speeds up to 70 miles an hour.

Without warning, the fleeing driver applied the brakes, and caused Don to ram into the escape vehicle and force it off the freeway. Both Donnelly brothers were uninjured. They tried to assault me, but in their drunken states I was able to subdue them. The front end of Don's car had sustained minor damage.

A CHP officer came on the scene, took an accident report, and arrested William Charles Donnelly, 35, on a felony assault charge and his brother, Paul, 32, for drunkenness.

Don and I went to our neighborhood mechanic, who fixed the damage to the pursuit vehicle for a grand fee of $50.00, which I happily paid.

~~*~~

One Sunday afternoon in February I half-listened to the radio as I shaved. Former U.S. Vice President Richard Nixon announced his candidacy for president, and Vince Lombardi had resigned as coach of the Green Bay Packers. Maybe Lombardi would be a better candidate for president, I mused.

During hostile encounters from citizens and officers within the police department, my son was always at the center of my thoughts and I worried about his safety. Fernando, standing in the open bathroom door while I shaved, expressed his own worries.

"Dad, why don't you quit being a policeman? If you quit, Mom and me won't have to worry about being hurt or killed, and maybe you'll let me go to the park."

When did my son stop calling me Daddy? And what the hell does he know about being killed!

In a rush he added, "And maybe I can have my friends come to our house and play."

I quickly set the razor down and dried my face. Kneeling, I put my arms around the little nine year old. Since Labor Day when thugs

151

accosted me on the basketball court — I no longer allowed Fernando to go to the park without me. That made him frustrated, confused, and angry.

"How about you and me going for a root beer?" During the ride to the A&W drive-in we talked about school and his friends.

After we finished our root beers, we drove to a nearby park to play a little 'round ball.' We played until he was tired. "Great game, son!" I took his hand and led him to a picnic table. "Fernando, I'm proud of you and your Mom. And I'm really proud that you want to protect us."

Again I pulled him close, as I had done so many times before. "So you want me to stop being a policeman."

"Yes, Daddy, because I'm afraid." My eyes stung as my son slipped into his little-boy reference to me.

I held him a little away from me and looked into his eyes. "I'm always careful to be safe and come home to the two people I love most in this world – you and your mom."

He leaned into me as I continued, "Someday you'll understand that my job is to protect everybody, and when you hear bad things about me putting people in jail, it's because they did bad things. But I always come home to you, don't I?"

My heart did flip-flops when Fernando wiggled out of my arms, stood in front of me and kissed my cheek. "Just promise to come home, Dad, and I promise I won't be afraid anymore."

That night, *in dreams I'm flying from something. I don't know what. I'm not afraid. I launch myself with a short run, arms spread wide, face down, head moving from side to side. I fly high in the air over fields, suburbs, and the city. Sometimes I stop on top of a building. Other times I dive over a lake. I take a breath and fly on. I have to see what's on the other side. Suddenly I land on my feet, then I wake up.*

~~*~~

In March of 1968, Robert F. Kennedy announced his presidential campaign. Then President Lyndon B. Johnson announced he would not seek re-election. He also authorized a troop surge in Vietnam, bringing the total number of U.S. soldiers to a peak of 549,500.

Martin Luther King Jr. was planning the Poor People's March. Before the march, King traveled to Memphis, Tennessee, to support the city's garbage workers' strike. On April 4, 1968, Dr. King entered a second floor hotel room. As he walked out onto the balcony to greet his driver and other friends, a sniper's bullet struck him in the jaw. Ralph Abernathy and Andrew Young, two of his closest colleagues, were with him as he died. It was five years after his famous "I Have a Dream" speech. The speech expressed his hope for a better future when there would be no barrier between the races and everyone would be equal.

News of his death flooded the nation with shock and anger. Riots, protests, and sit-ins erupted and lasted for months.

On April 8th a "predominantly White audience" of 3,000 mourned the murder of Reverend King in a 90 minute memorial service at the Santa Ana Bowl at Flower and Sixth Streets. *The Los Angeles Times* reported, "Many were crying openly in the closing minutes as Negro and White filed hand-in-hand from the stadium as they were singing We Shall Overcome."

~~*~~

At 4:30 a.m. Saturday morning I got a call to follow-up Officer Hamilton, who had responded to a disturbance at Walnut and Sycamore. I arrived to see six males, ranging in age from sixteen to thirty-four, standing in the intersection cursing loudly. Hamilton was leaning over a male on the ground. Hamilton tapped the man's cheek, and talked to him, in an attempt to rouse the apparently unconscious man.

I glimpsed one of the older men facing Hamilton pull a pistol from his pocket. I immediately tackled, disarmed, and arrested him for disturbing the peace, and possession of a loaded firearm. I didn't know at the time what his intention was, but later he was overheard saying to one of his buddies, "I'm sorry I didn't shoot that cop."

Three back-up units arrived. Together, we arrested the other five for disturbing the peace and booked them into the Orange County Jail.

Sergeant Williams, Watch Commander on this shift, commended my alertness and quick action in a memorandum to Chief Allen and Lieutenant Chrockran.[16] He stated, "This is but another example of the quality of field police work which has become quite common for Officer Lambert."

During this tumultuous time, Chief Allen informed me that I had been elected to attend an awards dinner at the Saddleback Inn, hosted by the Insurance Agents of Orange County on April 22nd.[17] I was to represent the Santa Ana Police Department for my "outstanding police work and participation in the "Stamp Out Crime" prevention program."

Chief Allen and I made our appearance and individually assured the association members that they, the insurance agents and brokers, could do much to assist law enforcement in the prevention of crime. I left with the honor of being publicly recognized both as an outstanding person and as a representative of the Santa Ana Police Department.

The honors were even more personally significant, because Mr. King was being remembered generally as the most important voice of the American civil rights movement, which worked for equal rights for all. I wondered if one day my police officer peers would judge me by the content of my character, rather than by the color of my skin.

One day Sergeant Stebbins waved me into the Spires Restaurant parking lot on East McFadden.

"Hey, buddy, this came to the station for you." He handed me an envelope, gave me a quick wave, and nosed his car back onto the street. My confidence was boosted again when I read a letter from James Prager, on behalf of the Insurance Agents of Orange County, praising me for the awards.[18]

~~*~~

Suddenly I was surrounded by women in shades of purple and red. Ladies of the Red Hat Society talked and laughed. One pulled a feather from her bright red hat and, with a queenly bow, presented it to me through the open car window. The Society of women had been created to connect with like-minded women to make new friends and enrich lives through the power of fun and friendship.

"This is a token of friendship for you on our official Red Hat Society day, Officer."

I thanked her and waited. A line of fifteen women strode in front of the patrol car, and were ushered into the restaurant by the queen, who wore the largest hat plumped with brilliant roses. I wondered how she kept it on her head.

The last person into the restaurant, she turned and waved.

A letter, a feather and a wave in one parking lot. I felt special.

CHAPTER FIFTEEN
July - December 1968

On a hot, humid late afternoon in July, a light blue Ford coupe sped toward me in the 5500 block of Ronda Lane. I whipped a U-turn and followed for three blocks at 60 mph, in a 35 mile posted zone. I put the siren on, and the driver pulled to the curb.

We exited our vehicles at the same time. The female driver, a chunky, poorly-dressed blonde stood at the rear of her car. As I walked toward her she began screaming epithets at me.

I attempted to explain to her why I stopped her. Before I finished, she spewed out, "Mother f----r! You black son of a bitch. You're only stopping me because I'm a white woman and you're a nigger trying to be a cop."

She was so loud, residents began spilling out of their homes to see what was going on.

I waited. She finally stopped screaming to catch her breath.

"Ma'am, you were driving in excess of fifty miles an hour in a posted 35 miles-an-hour speed zone." I asked, "May I see your drivers' license?"

She stomped to the driver's door, reached through the open window, pulled her oversized handbag out and rested it on the hood of the car.

As she dug through the contents and retrieved her license, she cursed me once again. Shoving it towards my face I could see she was Ms. Jan Smit.

Ms. Smit refused to sign the speeding citation I presented to her. She crossed her arms and gave me a look of defiance, calling me more names.

I advised her that if she didn't sign the citation, I would cuff her, put her in my patrol unit, and take her to jail. This got her attention.

She signed the citation.

The residents returned to their homes.

She drove way.

When I could no longer see her vehicle, I left the area.

A few days later, Ruth Gallo, one of the residents who witnessed the traffic violation, called the department and spoke with Sergeant T. Dakin. "We were all amazed at Officer Lambert's cool and calm fashion in which he issued the citation ... in any other fashion than that of a professional police officer."[19]

She told the sergeant that I should be commended for my display of patience with a traffic violator who yelled and screamed at me in a loud, derogatory fashion to the extent that various residents in the area, including her, left their homes to investigate the problem.

Mrs. Gallo may not have called had she witnessed an encounter, not long after that with Mr. Femrow.

~~*~~

I was dispatched to assist a California Highway Patrol (CHP) officer at 17th and Tustin. The officer had stopped a vehicle with three men inside. All three had warrants ranging from outstanding traffic violations to burglary.

The CHP had the driver, a beefy, disheveled white male handcuffed and sitting on the ground. The other two offenders were cuffed and sat in the back seat of his patrol car.

"I need help transporting this smart-mouth punk to jail."

As I bent to assist the arrestee to his feet, he kicked me square between the legs. I fell and landed in the dirt on my knees. By reflex my hands tried to contain the searing pain in my groin.

The CHP kicked the offender's feet out from underneath him, and rolled him over with a command to "Stay put!"

He then came to help me to my feet - and the fight started. The punk hadn't stayed down, but sprang to his feet, and rushed me with a head butt. The three of us rolled around in the dirt, as the CHP and I tried to get the guy under control. Finally subdued, he was put into the rear of my patrol car. We added the felony of assault and battery on a police officer to his arrest citation.

The ride to the Orange County jail was quiet, except for his feet thumping against the back of my seat. My shift wasn't over, and I was irked that I needed another clean uniform – the one in my police locker had just been picked up from the cleaners the day before. Crap. Drop the hoodlum off and change once again in less than 24 hours.

The next day I returned to the dry cleaners with my dirty uniform. Sergeant Webb was leaning comfortably on the counter talking with the owner. Conversation abruptly stopped. I laid my clothes on the counter. Mrs. Hunter wrote out a ticket and said, "They'll be ready tomorrow after two."

As I closed the door behind me, conversation picked up again.

~~*~~

A couple weeks later, on patrol in the 1500 block of West 11th Street, a middle-aged woman in hair rollers, slippers and a housedress, waved me down. A water hose was flipping around haphazardly, shooting water willy-nilly onto her porch, across her lawn, and into the street.

I captured the green monster and turned it off. Mrs. Swearingen thanked me profusely and we talked for a few minutes before I mounted my black-and-white steed and sped away.

In the following afternoon roll call, Sergeant Smith read a citizen commendation from Ellen Swearingen.[20] She related "...That officer Lambert was the nicest, kindest, and most polite officer she had ever talked with, and that she just thought we (SAPD) should know about it."

~~*~~

The next four weeks were an assortment of calls and falsehoods.

I was sent to guard a prisoner in the hospital for one full shift. The guy wore a gown three sizes too short, so I ended up with a view of his scrotum for the better part of eight hours.

I helped Ethel, an eighty-year-old woman stranded on the sidewalk because a branch had wedged inside the spokes of her wheelchair, making it motionless.

Another officer and I found a naked, knife-wielding rape suspect hiding under piles of laundry.

While on the job, I heard lies all the time. The lies accumulated like bugs on the patrol car windshield. Of twelve assignments a shift, half of those assignments featured lies. The car burglar swore he thought that it was his cousin's car. The husband insisted he didn't hit his wife. The john claimed he picked up the girl because she looked lost, and he felt sorry for her. The junkie caught with heroin in his pocket emphatically denied that it belonged to him.

Often I wondered what angle someone was working when they called the police. Did this woman's boyfriend really threaten her with a knife, or was she just mad because she caught him cheating? Did they report their car stolen because they were just involved in a hit-and-run with it? Is this a legitimate armed robbery, or did the alleged victim get rolled by a hooker and now needed a cover story to explain to his wife why he no longer had his wallet or wedding ring?

I had the option to arrest suspects and alleged victims alike, for obstructing an officer. It's not against the law to lie to your host of the dinner party when she asks how the Brussel sprouts tasted, but it's illegal to lie to the police when they're acting in their official capacity and conducting an investigation.

The police locker room was noisy during a shift change. A fellow officer shouted, "Got me another liar today," as if he'd just snared a prized rabbit.

~~*~~

Early in October, Don Smith, a *Los Angeles Times* Staff Writer, contacted me for an interview. We sat together in an empty conference room at the police station. He wanted to do a piece on "…the first Negro ever employed by the Santa Ana Police Department…"[21] Don had the headline drafted as we began to talk: "Negro Policeman: Minority Within a Minority."

Sitting in the living room at home, after the article was published, I thought about what I didn't reveal to Don Smith. *If I publicly acknowledged what my family and I had been exposed to for the past two years, would we be vulnerable to even more danger?*

~~*~~

The November air was comfortable with a slight breeze, as I patrolled at 1:30 a.m. and thought about the past months. 1968 had been a year of turmoil. The Vietnam War, Martin Luther King and Robert F. Kennedy assassinations, racism and sexism all played out on the evening news and in our hearts, minds and emotions. Yale announced plans to go coed. In Mexico Olympic athletes lost medals for their black power salute. It had just been broadcast that Richard Nixon narrowly won the Presidential election over Hubert Humphrey by a mere 500,000 popular votes.

Suddenly, a green Buick going northbound on Main Street at a high rate of speed, ran through the red light at the Edinger Street intersection. I turned on the siren and stopped the car near First and Main. I approached the vehicle and immediately I saw the female passenger, hands around her huge stomach, her face scrunched up in pain.

The driver, in rapid gulps cried, "Officer, my wife's water has broken. We're going to the hospital."

I ran back to my patrol car and contacted police dispatch. I got permission to use the red light and siren to escort the woman to the hospital. In several minutes we arrived safely at St. Joseph's. I assisted the mother from the car and into a waiting wheelchair supplied by emergency personnel.

The nurse rushed the wheelchair through the emergency doors. Her husband ran along-side holding his wife's hand. I returned to the patrol car to finish out my night.

A couple weeks later Chief Allen received a letter from Mr. and Mrs. James Johnson, who related the incident and said that forty minutes after arrival at the hospital, her daughter, Sherry Lynn, was born.[22] She weighed eight and one-half pounds, measured nineteen inches, and was the first girl in their family of three boys. She ended with a kind, "I can't say enough about how thankful we are and how much we appreciated a helping hand from a wonderful person. The Santa Ana Police force can be very proud to call Officer Lambert one of their own."

~~*~~

The following night the air was humid, although a warm breeze continued from mid-day. I was dispatched on a disturbing the peace complaint to the northwest corner of Bristol and 4th. The bar was a local hangout known for its pimps, prostitutes and back room gambling. I'd been there many times for a variety of reasons.

A hooker named Doris huddled behind the open door of the bar. Seeing me, the black prostitute stood up to her full six foot height, slender, and nude. She was bruised, scratched, and bleeding. Her normally pretty face was streaked with mascara, and her shoulder length hair had been pulled out, leaving patches of skin on one side of her head. Even from a distance, she looked older than her 25 years.

I groaned inwardly as I put on my helmet and approached her. I had talked with Doris many times for many reasons.

She sobbed, "Chester, that sonofabitch, did this do me! He's mad at me for not bringin' in enough money tonight. He took my clothes, and beat the crap out of me."

Doris took the paper blanket I had removed from the rear of the patrol car. She wrapped it around her as I helped her into the back seat to wait.

I entered the bar. At 6'4" and 250 pounds, Chester wasn't hard to find. He wore loud clothes and gold chains around his neck and rings on his fingers. His hair shone with excess pomade. Blood stained his red shirt and gold slacks.

"Chester," I said, "Why don't you step outside with me?" He put his cue stick on the pool table, and quietly stepped ahead of me as we left the bar. Blurry-eyed patrons looked after us.

Outside, he said, "I know why you're here, and yeah, I beat the stupid bitch's ass. I send her out, and she's not to come back without more than she's comin' in with."

He looked at Doris in the car, and yelled over to her, "Next time you come home with what you brought in tonight, I'll kick your ass again!"

As in the past, we did the same verbal dance. I asked Doris if she wanted to sign a complaint. This meant Chester would be taken into custody and booked for assault and battery. "If I do that, he'll just be meaner next time."

Doris stayed with Chester out of fear.

I couldn't do anything more. Chester went back into the bar. Doris got out of my unit, and blanket around her, started walking westbound on 4th Street.

Pimps and prostitutes both were aware of the way the game was played. The working girls were required to sell their bodies and bring their earnings back to the pimp. If that didn't happen, they would be punished with a beating.

The law stated that the victim had to make the arrest and sign the complaint for an assault if the crime happened out of the presence of a law enforcement officer. Prostitutes knew that if they had their pimp arrested and sent to jail their punishment would be far worse.

Over the next several months I would have similar encounters with Doris and Chester. She was always bleeding, had swollen and bruised eyes, and new scars. The ending was always the same. The day came when I would see Chester, but not Doris.

Could she be one of the Jane Doe's found in the Santiago Canyon or the Santa Ana River?

~~*~~

In December the Police Benevolent Association presented me with the Meritorious Service Award "for unfailing personal sacrifice in pursuit of his profession."[23]

This is one of the awards I received that I'm not sure what it gave reference to.

CHAPTER SIXTEEN
January - June 1969

In January 1969 it rained hard for over a week, filling Irvine Lake and the Santiago Reservoir. The spillways opened and the Santa Ana River and Santiago Creek flooded.

I was assigned to downtown patrol. Both Main Street and Bristol were closed to traffic at 17th Street as the creek and river continued to rise. My black-and-white stood sentry at the intersection of Main Street and 17th. The headlights faded, the circling red lights alternately beamed and disappeared into the pouring rain, as I made the best of directing traffic to motorists who couldn't, or wouldn't, follow instructions.

Using conventional hand signals hadn't worked. Using some unorthodox gestures hadn't worked. Getting angry would be futile. The rain slapped against me as I walked alongside the motorists as they made a turn. It worked. Three hours later I was dispatched to Bristol and Santiago Creek, and worked alongside other officers filling sand bags.

As Santiago Creek rose, the banks crumbled and the newer homes north and west of Bristol were in danger of falling into the creek. The Marine Corp out of El Toro Marine Base airlifted junk cars from a lot near Memory Lane and Bristol, and dropped them along the creek side in an effort to fortify it. Water, brush, and mud raced at break-neck speed along the creek.

Our shift was due to end four hours earlier, but we stayed. Our arms and backs ached. We were cold and muddy. Three officers and I were dispatched to pick up pizzas donated by Shakeys. After delivering the pizza and water to a central location, our night ended – but the rains and flooding continued for the next two days. Thankfully, I had been assigned for only one long night.

~~*~~

Later that week, before my shift started, I headed to the 600 block of 17th Street to pick up my recently altered and cleaned uniforms. I looked around the parking lot for The Vulture's presence before turning off the ignition. No sign of my shift supervisor. *Shake off the anxiety, Harlen.*

Mrs. Hunter, the blonde, overweight wife of the owner smiled, "Heavy starch, just like you like it, Officer Lambert." Didn't she know that I knew she smiled and chatted with me when Webb wasn't around? I thanked her, and as I left the cleaners and got into my car, I received a radio call to meet with now-Lieutenant Stebbins.

At the station I was ushered into his office. "Congratulations on your time as an officer, Harlen. I can't understand how you've managed so well during the past months. By observing and talking with other officers, I do know some of what you've been going through."

He stuck out his hand for a shake, and finished with, "You're a hell of a fellow and I want to thank you for sticking it out."

I returned to my patrol car, thinking that all those things the lieutenant said sounded good, but only I knew how my insides felt. The 35 pounds I'd lost during the past twenty-four months were physical evidence of my turmoil. Driving to a secluded area, I gave in to the need to be alone. Stebbins words and handshake were appreciated. I had believed no one knew, much less cared or understood, my distress.

Okay, shake it off, Harlen! The ten minutes I had permitted myself to grieve for what ifs, and feeling sorry for myself, was over. I had a job to do.

~~*~~

Just then, the handheld receiver squawked. I was dispatched with a code 10-54 (possible dead body) to the 1200 block of South Standard to the two story, run-down apartments in the mostly Hispanic neighborhood. I had been here before. This time I was directed to the alley behind the Standard Apartments by the elderly tenant of apartment 1C. She reported that the white female lying behind a trash container had not moved or responded to her voice.

When I knelt down, I immediately recognized Katherine, whom I had arrested for possession of crack cocaine two weeks ago. I checked for a pulse, remembering the last time I saw her, she was being processed into a rehab facility. But here she was, lying in a puddle of vomit and urine, unable to move or speak, and she was not breathing.

I picked up my receiver and contacted communications, "I have a female down who's not breathing. I'm applying chest compressions without response. Please send medical assistance."

"10-4."

The medics soon arrived. As they unloaded first aid equipment and administered oxygen, I recalled Katherine's story. She was nineteen and had a five-year-old son. At thirteen, she used her school lunch allowance to buy small amounts of marijuana and alcohol outside the school yard from guys like drug-dealing FxTroop member, Carlos.

But Katherine got progressively more dependent on both drugs of choice, and once she took her first hit from a crack pipe, all good things for Katherine were over. She quit school, stole, and prostituted herself for drug money. She was raped, beaten for the twenty bucks in her pocket, shot at for attempting to rip off a dealer, and lived in crack houses.

After months of searching, Katherine's mother found her, admitted her to a mental institution, and took her grandson home to live with his grandparents. Katherine left the care center and hit the streets she had come to depend on.

And now here she was again, in the alley nearly lifeless, with bruises covering her skeletal frame, her once pretty face now pitted and scarred.

I wondered, too, as I watched the medics lift her onto the gurney for transport to the hospital, what would happen to Katherine. Would she be one of the overdoses I would find in the Shell Station restroom? Would she get the help she needed and finally get clean and sober? Or would she go to prison, and once free, start the cycle all over again?

~~*~~

The following week I was summoned by Lt. Stebbins once again. "Harlen, I've been assigned to head up Community Relations, a newly formed department. I've cleared it with the chief to ask you if you would be interested in working with me in this organization."

"Yes, sir, I'm very interested, but I would like to know more."

Lt. Stebbins said, "First things first. You'll receive a pay increase and you're now considered an "advanced" officer. You'll work in plain clothes and have various hours due to the nature of the work. You'll have tomorrow off and we'll get to work the following day. Sound good?"

Sound good! I couldn't wait to get home to share the news with Marie.

The lieutenant had been an officer for twenty years and had the reputation of being tough, but neutral. Those he came in contact with loved him – me included - and confided in him, yet there was an element of formal friendship that quickly evolved into the personal.

"You might be interested to know that Webb's been reassigned. He's going to the Crimes Against Persons (CAP) unit."

Good. "The Vulture" wouldn't be standing in the shadows watching my every move.

"We'll work together, Harlen, but your primary role is to form a rapport with the Panther members, and to work with the community and schools for a better relationship between them and the police department."

The lieutenant and I shared enthusiastic possibilities for what the new department could accomplish.

"You need to know, too, Harlen, that I've had a couple of run-ins with Michael Lynem, the head of the Santa Ana Chapter of the Black Panther Party," the Lieutenant continued. "Once I walked into the Panther headquarters in uniform to burn him. I asked to see Michael, and in front of everyone, I said, 'Thanks, Mike, for the info' to make others think he was an informant. Another time, he came to my office, and basically said that we cops better change or the Panthers would burn the city down. I told him he'd better have a lot of gas because we're going to blow you off the face of the Earth.'"

The next day I worried about what I knew of the Black Panthers. Before I became a police officer, I knew some members who played basketball with me. Most were in their teens, and at no time did anyone attempt to discuss their beliefs or to recruit me into their organization. I only knew that they were founded in Oakland during the 1960s explicitly to defend the impoverished Black community from what was perceived as police harassment.

When I became an officer, I still wasn't familiar with the Black Panther motto, beliefs, or objectives. I learned they used propaganda and poster art, and wore black jackets with faces of young warriors to attract Blacks from all over the country. The group used strong words which gave a forceful message, such as "Power to the People." The raised fist of glory, arm fully extended, was their most compelling symbol. For them, that iconic fist represented history, glory, and power and became known all over the world.

The Black Panthers had been organizing in Santa Ana and were becoming more vocal about their rights for exclusive use of public facilities and centers. Black unrest in Los Angeles and Orange County was becoming more frequent. Santa Ana began to experience weekend mini-riots, where situations in the streets got out of control, but were handled quickly with the policing approach of the good-ol'-boy tradition of lock 'em up and throw away the key.

I didn't know that morning, as I casually sipped a cup of hot chocolate, that in six months a midnight telephone call would change my understanding of the Black Panthers and their motives.

~~*~~

On January 16th Lt Stebbins and I gave a one-hour presentation of the Introduction to Law Enforcement class at Orange Coast College in Costa Mesa.[24] The school video-taped the program for future Police Science, Psychology and Social Sciences classes. All believed that such exposure would help their communication with the larger student community.

That was the beginning of meetings with students, other law enforcement agencies, the press, the Community Action Council, and other knowledgeable people who could provide factual information that supported their diverse goals and roles in society.

Together, Stebbins and I developed the "Brown Bag" lunch program for day care programs, and elementary school grades one through seven. We went to the schools in our black-and-whites, ate a sandwich and an apple with the kids, played sports with them, allowed them to sit in the car while we described the function of the police lights and sirens, and answered questions. Donald Tibbetts, Principal of the Roosevelt School, wrote that the children thought, "Police were neat."[25]

The "Let's Talk" program was designed for students in grades 8 through 12. That program was directed toward establishing mutual understanding and communication between students in the Santa Ana Unified and Junior College Districts, and the Santa Ana Police Department.

We went to high schools and held assemblies which featured a question and answer period. Students had a hundred problems and a thousand questions. Their basic complaint was that "Nobody listens."

"I'm listening now and will always have time to listen to you," I assured them. I stressed the importance of staying in school and adjusting attitudes toward their futures and the law.

I went on, "Your education is most important for preparing you to become responsible adults and leaders in your community. If you have a problem at school, let's talk about it and see what we can do to resolve it together."

The teens asked questions regarding the law: how, when and under what circumstances they could be arrested, and what a police officer's responsibilities were to them as citizens and as juveniles.

We created an environment where they were able to express themselves and say anything they wished without restriction.

The youths were open to what we had to say. I often wondered how much they were listened to at home. Many children had non-English speaking parents, abusive parents, single parents, were neglected, on welfare, and worse.

The Lt. and I made commitments that we would always listen to what those kids had to say, no matter how much time or effort it took. The "Pal Program" resulted from our commitment. Any boy in trouble - at home or with the law could be heard by a "pal" from the program. We spent many an hour, on and off the job, listening to the youngster as if we were filling the role of a father, brother, guide, or counselor.

I realized my hours at work were taking more and more time from home and my family. When I arrived home here and there, my prolonged absences probably contributed to the occasional outbursts of disrespect from my son, and the frequent, silent tears my wife shed.

Over the next few months the lieutenant and I received letters of appreciation and thanks, not only for our roles in meeting with school children, but our time and effort in appearances at neighborhood meetings, conducting group counseling sessions, and teaming with Vice to give narcotic presentations in southwest Santa Ana.[26]

Speaking with young people was just part of the job – but it was the part I enjoyed most. Before the year was over, we would go to four high schools, and nine elementary and intermediate schools communicating with over 24,000 young people.

My work as a complaint officer was the least enjoyable. We heard grievances about noisy neighbors, abandoned cars, transients in the park, welfare fraud, neighborhood raids for undocumented persons, and speeding cars. What the lieutenant and I could not handle immediately, we wrote out in a report which was handed over to the appropriate department for resolution.

~~*~~

A month before, during court practice at Jerome Park, we heard loud clapping after I had executed a "jump back" shot. Clarence, Oscar, Willy, Ron, and I turned toward the sound and saw a young man with short blonde hair, a square face and huge smile rushing toward us.

He stuck out his hand, "Hi, I'm Paul Peak, coach at Southern California College. I was passing by and saw you playing. Very impressive!" He went on to tell us he had been coach for just a year and, although the college had a basketball team, they needed a winning basketball team.

And just like that, the five of us were offered athletic scholarships to the private Christian college in Costa Mesa.

Oscar piped up, "Man, you have to talk to my daddy about this!"

So the coach, Oscar, and I walked the two blocks to his home, and after the initial shock of a white college coach visiting them about their son, they agreed Oscar could attend college in the fall.

Although thrilled to be offered the scholarship, Ron's goal was to be a fireman, so he declined the offer. Willy, for unknown reasons, decided not to take the opportunity.

As a full time police officer, the coach and I agreed that I could schedule practice and play with the team on my off hours.

Over the next few months, we continued practice at the park. Paul gave us a schedule of the college games, and when my work schedule permitted, Oscar, Clarence, and I attended those games to check out our future competition.

~~*~~

On June 4th, 1969 at 11:30 p.m. I lay in bed sleeping. A shrill ring of the phone startled me awake and I answered. One more of those nasty calls! They were getting less frequent, but I still got them. And I didn't want Marie to be on the receiving end of another threat. The stress and silence between the two of us was now deafening.

The dang thing rang again, but it was the Watch Commander, asking me to come in. "Officer down! Get in as soon as you can!" His voice was tearful when he hung up.

Everything seemed to move at the speed of thick syrup, pouring out ever so slowly, as I pulled on civilian clothes and explained to Marie why I had to leave. I dashed to look in on my sleeping son, and checked once again that all windows and doors were secured. I tried to calm the thoughts prompted by this disturbing late night call.

I drove to the station at breakneck speed. I arrived and entered the roll call room. I saw shock and tears on the faces of the team of officers assembled. The air was thick with a combination of sorrow and anger.

The words, "Officer down!" chilled the blood of even the hardiest and most cynical of cops.

CAP lead investigators Webb and Cornelison briefed us on the intelligence available. They reported that 24-year-old Officer Nelson Sasscer, while on patrol, had been gunned down. He had driven his one-man patrol unit in the vicinity of Third and Raitt streets about midnight when he radioed in that he was stopping to question a group of men walking on the street.

Officer Sasscer was shot through the chest with a Browning 9mm as he approached the men. Police were notified of the shooting by a nearby resident. The young officer was rushed to the hospital, but within half an hour he died.

Investigators suspected that it was a Black Panther execution because of the political conditions at the time, street tensions and "off the pig" rhetoric. A month previously, known Panthers had been arrested for disturbing the peace. They gave speeches in front of the Orange County Courthouse and at Cal State Fullerton with the same chant: "Off the pigs! Kill the police!"

I thought back to when I first heard about the Black Panther Party in late 1966. Bobby Seale and Huey Newton, with the idea of self-defense in mind, organized a group that would protect the Black community against police brutality. There were charitable acts on the part of the Panthers, but their raw side and the negative media attention overshadowed any good they may have done.

The brief encounters the Black Panthers had allowed me while in

Community Relations hadn't provided much insight into their activities or beliefs.

I was immediately reassigned from Community Relations to assist in locating the suspects responsible. All officers were given the green light to aggressively pursue the killer, or killers of Nelson Sasscer. He was the first Santa Ana police officer killed in the line of duty in 38 years.[27]

There were no witnesses to the murder, but there were a few people who had publicly and fiercely professed their desire to kill a cop.

We knew where to begin the search. The following morning squad cars raced to the home of 22-year-old Daniel "Michael" Lynem, the head of the Santa Ana Chapter of the Black Panther Party. A team of officers, weapons drawn, covered Tom Parrott and me as we banged on the door and called for him to come out. Lynem slowly opened the door, and stepped out with his hands in the air.

I immediately turned Lynem around to handcuff him, "Sir, you are under arrest as a suspect for the murder of a police officer." Tom recited the Miranda rights to Lynem as we escorted him to a squad car for transfer to jail.

During the investigation, Lynem's recollection of the night led to a connection with the Tice Brothers, Otis Grimes, and Ernest Bodiford that eventually led to the identity of Arthur Dewitt League as the shooter. League was a high-ranking official in the Santa Ana branch of the Black Panthers.

The investigating superiors told us, "If League is our man and you find the f----r, don't bring him back alive!"

The murder of a police officer set off a law-enforcement frenzy to find and prosecute the killers. The district attorney charged Grimes, League and Lynem on June 6th. A grand jury indicted the trio on June 16th. Officers stormed Black neighborhoods looking for League and Grimes. They interrogated any black man they encountered, and kicked doors in without apology.

Protests, riots, and racial tension exploded. Police encounters with black militants resulted in a steady escalation of conflict, hostility, and sometimes outright violence.

The city's emerging black leadership was enraged that the police were intimidating and harassing people just because they were Black. Jail guards put Lynem in isolation, while hundreds of supporters attended rallies and organized a Panther defense committee based at Anaheim's Unitarian Universalist Church.

Three weeks later, Ricky and Steve Tice were taken into custody and sang like birds. The teenagers had been in the garage where Black Panthers had gathered earlier to listen to Malcolm X speeches on a turntable. They said they were with Arthur League when he shot "Whitey," meaning Officer Sasscer, and that League had been dropped off at an unknown location in Los Angeles.....

For lesser charges, the Tice brothers were willing to testify on the State's behalf against League. That was, if League was found.

CHAPTER SEVENTEEN
July - December 1969

In a surprise move on July 1st, the district attorney dropped all charges against Lynem and Grimes. Grimes and League were still at large, but the FBI tracked and arrested them at the home of actor Donald Sutherland, whose wife allowed them refuge. Sutherland was out of the country at the time.

We learned the Tice brothers changed their stories before the grand jury three times before going with the version that implicated League as the shooter. The brothers were granted immunity and protection.

~~*~~

Officer Tom Parrott and I were reassigned to the Orange County District Attorney's office (OCDA) and given the job of taking Steve Tice and his brother, Ricky, into protective custody. Our assignment was not only to keep the Tice brothers safe, but happy.

That same day our first stop was at an unkempt, uninhabitable Oceanside motel the OCDA sent us to. Parrott and I tried the sink faucet, which wouldn't render water. The light switches didn't work and the door had no lock. Steve Tice complained about the conditions he was forced to endure in our custody. At the same time Rick Tice whined about wanting yet another burger for what seemed an endless pit in his teenage stomach.

While Officer Parrott stayed with the Tice's, I went to the San Diego Police station, contacted the watch commander, and told him our situation. He said he understood and would contact an officer to help me relocate "the boys" to another, more habitable location. The watch commander picked up the phone, and it was obvious the officer on the other end of the line was telling him, "Sure, he would meet Officer Lambert at the motel after he took care of some last minute details."

Coleman Young, a tall, husky black sergeant in plain clothes came to the motel. Running his left hand over his semi-bald head, he said, "You all gather up your gear, get in your car, and follow me."

Ten miles later in the hills of San Diego, the sergeant pulled a key from his jacket pocket and quickly ushered the four of us into larger accommodations. The room was clean, with two queen size beds, and had a telephone, television and a separate kitchenette.

Rick Tice perversely reminded Tom and me that our assignment was not only to keep them safe, but happy. Rick liked his food, amusement parks and talking on the telephone. Steve, who complained a few minutes every hour about anything and everything, liked watching television and eating French fries. As he laughed and joked on the telephone with an unknown person, Rick instructed me to find him a hamburger, loaded, along with fries and a coke.

Officer Parrott said he needed fresh air and took the assignment to find some fast food. Steve, eyes glued to a "Never Pester Chester" episode of Gunsmoke, bawled, "Bring back extra fries, man!"

After allowing older brother Rick to talk on the phone 20 minutes, I told him to hang up so I could contact my department to advise them of the events leading up to the location where we now held the brothers.

Lieutenant Ernie McDowell said, "Okay, Harlen, I'll call you back after I confirm."

Thirty minutes later, he called. "Get out of there immediately! You're in a Panther location setup!"

Officer Parrott was coming through the door as I hung up the phone. The four of us quickly pulled our few belongings together, along with the food, and left in our unmarked car for a military base in Long Beach for safekeeping.

I learned that Sergeant Young, the San Diego officer who relocated us was, in fact, a Panther who had just returned to duty after disciplinary action. After that our rest periods were short, and we were constantly on the move. If we were at a site during the day we never stayed overnight.

The only contact I had with my wife and son was over the telephone. I made empty promises to be home soon.

Mercifully, in mid-July Steve and Rick Tice were returned to jail for protective custody.

The judge instructed Parrott and me, with a room full of Black Panthers looking on, to take the Tice brothers out of jail each day for recreation.

The activities of the day were directed by the brothers; they favored amusement parks, the theater, and the beach. Each evening we returned them to the jail for the night.

Officer Tom Parrott and I returned to Community Relations part-time—and part-time escorts taking the Tice brothers to their favored destinations.

~~*~~

While still a full-time police officer, in September, 1969 I had enrolled in Southern California College, which became Vanguard University of Southern California, (on the basketball scholarship offered by Coach Peak earlier in the year) with a major in Business Administration and a minor in Religion.

Since I worked part-time in Community Relations and escorted the Tice Brothers at differing times my work hours were flexible, allowing me to attend classes two times a week. My primary focus was religious studies. Thus far, I had been drawing strength from my early upbringing, and Christian beliefs in ultimate goodness. It wasn't always easy, but it got me through.

It was a class requirement that each day at 11:00 a.m. all students attend chapel. The student body was 1,500 strong. I attended classes on Tuesdays and Thursdays, so I saw the same two hundred fifty or so students each week in chapel.

Seating consisted of benches and was limited. I sat on a bench alone. Students filled up the rest of the benches. They stood around the chapel, backs resting on the walls, arms crossed. The minister welcomed the students and said, "Shake hands with the person behind you, beside you, in front of you."

I had a lot of backs turned to me, openly ignoring me. My smile was frozen as I dropped my hand of welcome in embarrassment, many times.

Have I been in 'this place' before?

In the classroom I asked questions of the minister-instructor, a fair-skinned, older gentleman of portly stature. He wouldn't look directly at me when answering. But a strange thing repeated itself. His face and neck always turned a shade of pink when speaking at me, never to, me.

Have I seen this before?

I looked forward to the Social Sciences classes. The class narrative drew me like a magnet as soon as I read it:

A time to investigate, analyze,
a time to study the most
difficult; man in relation
to his fellow man.
A time of involved study covering
the many facets of society:
economics, politics, history,
philosophy, anthropology.
A time as well, to think, produce,
and hopefully create new
answers and solutions to
age-old questions and problems.
A time to act, a time to react,
"a time to build up, a time
to tear down."
A time to see wrong and right it,
see suffering and heal it.

Mr. Austin, the instructor, taught to the class description. He was tall, bald, and constantly pushing his glasses back from the tip of his nose. He listened with interest to his students and responded to questions with a generous dose of humor, or seriousness, as appropriate.

~~*~~

Later, I headed to the gym where men were already in practice. Clarence, Oscar, and the Payne brothers stood out among the white players.

I met nineteen-year-old Jimmy Payne the first day on court. He soon confided, that when he first saw me, he wondered, "Who's that old dude trying to play basketball?" I watched Jimmy's older brother, David, a lean 6'5" and tallest on the Vanguards basketball team, easily steal and drop the ball into the hoop.

Jimmy and his sister, Juanita, were the first Blacks enrolled at the college. Their mother had insisted on a Christian education for her children. Jimmy and David applied for, and received, loans and grants to play basketball. Clarence, Oscar, and I were the first Blacks to receive scholarships.

The gym filled with students to watch us practice. We made an impact on the court. Students shouted, stomped their feet, and cheered the teams on enthusiastically.

We soon learned, however, we were called to play only when the white team was losing. After losing three out of its first four games, frustration replaced hope. The Vanguards had lost 51-94 against U.C. San Diego, 62-71 against Cal Western, and 70-80 against Grace College.

It was the last three minutes of the fourth quarter. The home-game score sat at Vanguards 70 and Biola 73. The coach called the five black team members to the floor, hopeful for winning points. Within seconds, a loud whistle pierced the gymnasium, and we were waved to the sidelines, where coaches, referees, teachers, and a group of men in suits huddled, heads together. Voices became loud, but muddled in the noise that surrounded us.

Clarence, Oscar, Jimmy, and I were asked to leave the court. Only David would play the last three minutes. One of the men was overheard, "We can't have all Blacks representing a White college!"

The gym erupted with chants, back-slapping and encouragement when David scored the needed points to win the game. We were proud of him and the team for breaking the school's three-loss streak with a final score of 76.

Clarence, Oscar, Jimmy, and I followed the winning Vanguards to the locker room. Comments and questions besieged Coach Peak. We learned that a number of parents were unhappy with their children, particularly the girls, associating with the Blacks. The chapel minister joined us. The white team members were released.

Jimmy was the first Black male enrolled at the college, and he lived on campus in the barracks-like dormitory. He was outgoing, educated, handsome, and an athletic man who made friends easily, and he often joined groups of young people to study or meet at Shakeys for root beer and pizza, and listen to Creedence Clearwater Revival, "Born on the Bayou." Then back to the dorm to study for class the following day.

Coach Peak said, "Jimmy, I'm getting pressure from the dean of students about your activities with other students, and he thinks it's hindering your performance on the basketball court." Baffled at the innuendo, Jimmy assured him that he and the other students were just friends.

"Yes, I understand that, but some parents are stressing to us that you back off," coach continued.

Disbelieving, I turned to the minister, who began speaking before I could utter a word, "Unfortunately, we've been approached by some parishioners concerned with potential White/Black relationships between the students, and they're threatening to remove their daughters from the school."

He stood behind the coach and said, "Surely, you can understand that the members tithe a lot of money, and we don't want to lose them."

Jimmy looked at the minister, "Now I know the meaning behind the superficial smiles and fake friendships. I can count on one hand sincere Christians who see me as a person, and don't see the color."

It was clear the black team made an impact off the court, too.

We considered Coach Peak a nice guy from the south. I understood he was at risk, and therefore saying and doing what was expected of him. Later that evening I tried to explain the coach's situation to the other four young men, but they each expressed, in his own unique way, that Coach Peak's influence was losing its luster.

~~*~~

Two weeks later, the Vanguards scheduled a trip to play opponents in Azusa. Because of my erratic work schedule on the SAPD, I no longer officially played on the team, but I bought a ten-dollar ticket to support them at every opportunity.

The college had a station wagon to transport the basketball team. Coach Peak would not allow the Blacks to drive, or ride in, the school car – it was for Whites only.

Oscar's father allowed Oscar to drive the family vehicle, if I were to ride with him, so the black team could participate. I took time from the police department and rode in the back seat with Jimmy and David, while Clarence rode shotgun. We followed the station wagon north on the 605 freeway, and stopped at a roadside diner in El Monte for lunch. Once inside, we were again directed to separate from the white team members, who chattered excitedly about the upcoming game.

My normally happy-go-lucky group were quiet and becoming more discouraged with each passing minute. The light was slowly disappearing from their eyes. I went into adviser mode, reminding them of their talents and aspirations – and that they were bigger and better than the prejudice that surrounded them.

At the game our Vanguard team went on to beat Azusa 99-73 – with only one Black on the court at a time.

Crap just didn't stop.

During the next year, David dropped out of school, and "Just decided to move on." He married, got into drugs and became a drug distributor in Los Angeles.

Clarence got into some minor trouble. I talked with him, urging him to do the right things, but he eventually dropped out of school, too. He was an angry young man, unable to leave his hostilities on the court. He became a member of the Black Panthers.

Oscar had dropped out of junior college when he accepted the scholarship to Southern California College. He passed up receiving a degree a few short months before graduating to "Do the right thing." He found a good job in aerospace and married his pregnant girlfriend.

Jimmy graduated with a Bachelor Degree in Physical Education and pursued his dreams of playing and coaching basketball.

I wondered how their lives would have changed if they had been treated differently.

Meanwhile, my private struggles became overwhelming and I left college nearly two years later with my Associate Degree in Religious Studies. I had started work on my Bachelor, but I became so frustrated, I decided to leave.

~~*~~

On my way home one evening in September, after returning "the boys" to jail, my friend Clarence, walking down the sidewalk, waved me down. I slowed my car to a stop, "Hey, bro, what's up?"

He slid into the passenger seat of my car. "Man," he said to me, "I'm going to make this quick and simple. You want to live, give up the bodyguard job now! Don't wait 'til tomorrow or the next day. Do it now!"

With that, Clarence was back on the sidewalk hurrying away.

I sat in the car for a few moments remembering how I met

Clarence. I had become friendly with him when he was just sixteen. He had showed up on the court at Jerome Park with Oscar and Willy a week after I had pulled my derringer on some thugs in the park, and the three boys asked if they could play ball with me.

I watched this 6'7" slender boy shoot and dunk the ball almost effortlessly. I applauded his ability to dribble, shoot and stuff the ball. Clarence joined the other boys and me at a park table, where he told us he had recently moved here from Texas and was attending school.

Unlike the other boys, Clarence was quiet and he didn't share personal information. Over the next several months I counseled, laughed, talked, ate, hugged and played ball with these young men. I often wondered why Clarence left the park alone after practice – and never in the same direction.

One day I asked him to tell me about his family, and he said, "You're my family."

Later, after Clarence dropped out of Southern California College, I learned there were warrants out for his arrest. If the warrant was for an unpaid traffic violation, I would find him, give him the warrant number and tell him where to surrender himself the following day.

If the warrant was for a felony, I would find Clarence, arrest him, and take him to jail. Sometimes I helped him pay his bail. Each time I had a fatherly talk with him.

Eventually, I found out he had taken the Muslim name of Mustafa (the Chosen One) and held a ranking position with the Black Panthers in Orange County.

Clarence risked his standing in the organization, and possibly his own life, when he told me to give up the bodyguard job. The warning was his way of thanking me for months of friendship.

I told Officer Parrott about the forewarning. With Mustafa's words on my mind, I knew it was only a matter of time before an adversary would figure out our paths of operation, and something would happen to either Tom or to me.

I requested to be removed from the case, citing anonymous warnings of imminent danger to my family. So the graveyard watch commander placed me back on patrol and reassigned Tom to Community Relations.

As a result of their zealous tactics in pursuit of Officer Sasscer's killers, lead investigators Webb and Cornelison were later charged with specific civil rights crimes and stood trial in a Los Angeles federal court.

At the end of the trial, they were cleared of charges by the presiding judge. Later, Webb was overheard alleging the judge had said, "I find these detectives not guilty of the charges brought against them. But if they did what they are accused of, I would not blame them."

~~*~~

During the sporadic hours that I spent at home, Marie and I quarreled. We were strained with each other. We repeated the same heated arguments.

"You're hardly ever home, and you have no idea what's going on in this house! You're more concerned about everyone but Fernando and me!"

I had to face the fact that she was right on point one – but not on point two. I hadn't been able to blend the demands of my job, school, and the needs of my family. The constant tension of 360 degree rotation, looking for the bad guys, wore thin. Very thin.

"Marie, I'm going back on patrol so I can be home more," I assured her. I didn't tell her the reason for the change, just that I missed time with my family.

Zeus waited in the back yard. He stood on his rear legs as I opened the door, and put his front paws on my shoulders for a hug. I scratched his belly and gave him a kiss before checking his water and food, and throwing a few balls for him to chase.

This had become a ritual between us. Come home, learn Fernando was either at school or asleep, argue with Marie, and hug and play with Zeus. On the days Fernando was at home and awake, he and I talked about school. I helped him with homework. We took short trips to the park or drove for a McDonald's meat-and-pickle hamburger. Together we trained and played with Zeus – and kept clear of Marie's unconcealed disappointment in me.

~~*~~

That same night, I dreamed. *I'm flying from something. I don't know what. I'm not fearful. I launch myself with a short run; arms spread wide, face down, head moving from side to side. I fly high in the air over fields, urban areas, and tall buildings. Sometimes I stop on top of a building. I come to a body of water where my altitude drops just above the water. I have to see what's down there and then get to the other side.*

As I land on my feet, I wake up.

I thought about this recurring dream. Are these dreams a desire to rise above my everyday life? I always fly away from something. What is it? Limitations or restrictions placed on me? Am I actually experiencing something out of body or doing a little 'soul travel'? I always land on my feet, so I know I'll be okay.

~~*~~

The following night, while dressing for roll call, Lt. Webb's familiar voice announced from the far side of the row of lockers, "The coal car's back on dogwatch!"

He remained in the Crimes Against Persons unit while I went on patrol. Thank you, Lord, for sparing me!

Dogwatch. Graveyard. Vampire ops. Night shift. Ghost patrol. Zombie shift. Whatever it was called, patrolling the streets while most of the city slumbered, could be an endurance test. On a busy night, patrol units received a fair amount of Code 999 calls from the dispatch operators. These were "in progress" calls for domestic disturbances, fights, alarms, an occasional prowler or burglar. Once in a while enough officers could get in the area fast enough to set a perimeter and catch the bad guy.

I was active in my area and did a lot of pedestrian and traffic enforcement citations on busy nights. On occasion, a stop for speeding made me smile.

It was 1:30 a.m. when I stopped a man for speeding, and asked, "Where are you going so fast this time of morning, sir?"

"I'm on my way to a lecture about alcohol abuse, smoking, staying out late and the effects it all has on the human body."

Suspicious, I then asked, "Really? And who would be giving that lecture this time of night?"

"That would be my wife," he replied. I gave him a ticket anyway.

The summer nights were best for DUI arrests. DUIs are no

laughing matter, but one incident did make me chuckle.

I had pulled a man over for speeding and asked him to get out of the car. He stumbled toward me, pushing a flop of unruly hair away from his forehead.

I said, "Sir, your eyes are bloodshot. Have you been drinking?"

Scornful, he said, "Offisher, yer eyes are glazed. You been eatin' doughnuts?"

During stretches of no activity, I rattled doors on closed businesses just to make sure they were secure. I stopped in on all-night businesses to check on the well-being of the working staff. At 2:00 a.m. I parked in front of the bars on East Fourth during last call, placed cones on each side of the patrol unit, and stood in front of it – and waited for the drunks to come out.

Some nights, there was zero activity and I needed a break from silent night riding. The bad guys knew officers were on patrol throughout the city. So I parked in alleys or behind shrubbery on side streets, so they could guess where I might be.

To keep alert while waiting, I began writing down my personal history from childhood to my experiences as a police officer.

~~*~~

A week later, I was off duty on Saturday night, when the phone rang. The watch commander said, "Lambert, get over to Jerome Park, now. A disturbance has broken out and we need you here."

The nearest parking was half a block away near the school my son attended. I locked my car and walked to the recreation building, where SAPD officers and other county departments assembled in a group to form an attack strategy. In the distance I heard yelling, raised voices shouting profanities, and saw shadows darting about. The sounds of broken glass and hard thuds pierced the night air.

The captain in charge told me the weekly social event in the park was over at 10 pm. "We don't know what the hell started this crap!"

"I'll go in and see what I can find out, sir."

In response, he pointed to a patrol unit, and said, "There's a megaphone in there, if you need it."

I got behind the wheel and drove slowly toward the gathering, with the interior light on, so people would recognize me. A group started to surround the patrol car at the same time that I recognized "Superman." He stood in front of his two-door Ford, holding his hand, a grimace on his face. I pulled alongside him and got out of the patrol unit. Drops of blood were splattered down the front of his jeans. His thick afro poked out the sides of his cap, offering a comical image as I approached him.

"Hey, man, what's going on?" I saw the blood, and asked, "What happened to you?"

The well-known 17-year-old, black local gang leader, celebrated as 'Superman Steen' on the streets, griped, "I slammed my finger in my car door. Slashed it. Hurts like hell." His index finger was puffy and reddish blue. His swollen hand now looked like a blown-up surgical glove.

He didn't tell anyone what had happened. His gang members had seen the blood, and assumed the cops had hurt him. In anger, they commenced to throw bricks, rocks, and bottles at others in the park and at the police. They shouted, "Off the pigs" and waved lewd gestures.

"Steen, we go way back. How're you going to explain this to your Mama?" He hung his head as I continued, "We need to make this right before someone gets hurt or serious property damage is done."

After a quick talk, I grabbed the megaphone as we climbed together on top of the patrol unit. Superman, using the megaphone, was loud and forceful, as he called his gang members to quiet down and to gather around the car. Once rallied together, all sound stopped. The stage was set with the swirling blue lights of the police cars in the distance, and the interior light of the car we stood on.

Superman explained what had really happened, and stopped the vandalism and potential riot on the spot, with minimum damage done. He handed the megaphone to me and jumped off the vehicle. He complained, "Need to get home and take care of this hand." The gang members noiselessly followed his car as he drove out of the parking lot.

I returned to the strategy group, still assembled behind and out of the active area, to report the gang was leaving without further trouble.

"You can leave, too, Lambert. Your assistance is no longer needed." Captain Tracey spoke with disdain. Without looking at me, he jotted notes on his pocket pad. All motion stopped, as the huddle surrounding us became still.

I stood dumbfounded for several seconds. For an instant the group appeared to be caught in a freeze frame. A throat cleared, a mumbled offer of remorse as some of the men hung their heads or turned away in awkwardness as they opened a pathway I could escape through.

I had just resolved a dangerous situation and the way I was dismissed hurt! But not a surprise, coming from Tracey. I recalled him standing in the hall, arms crossed, questioning me about being sure I was "right" for the job. Once again my skin color and the bigoted racial overtones took the wind out of my sails. I was given no thanks for my actions – and at that point, I felt a different attitude begin to emerge in me.

To hell with being Mr.Nice Guy.

~~*~~

The following week I made appointments with every black minister in Santa Ana and asked to speak in their churches. Over the next several Sundays I visited and passed on to the members what had happened after the Saturday night event. The vandalism, the near riot, and the consequences. The bottom line message was to keep your children under control – and safe.

~~*~~

Halloween and Thanksgiving were over, and the year-end holidays fast approached. Montgomery Ward extended their shopping hours to capture both early and late holiday shoppers. The retailer advertised sales on items that enticed people of all ages, hopeful that they would see a significant sales jump at year-end.

My radio squawked, "Radio 3150." (Station 31, Unit 50)

I picked up the receiver, "3150, over."

Dispatch continued, "A 488 report at Montgomery Ward, 17th and Bristol."

"Ten-four." I parked the patrol unit in front of the main doors. Two females and one male strolled through the entrance as I got out of the car. Two store security men walked silently behind them.

I had arrested the trio for shoplifting before. Engaged in

conversation, they did not see me waiting for them at the curb.

Lucy, a real estate agent and a divorced mom, got her own kind of high from filching. For some people, like Lucy, it became an addiction, like drugs, alcohol, gambling, food, or sex. She felt compelled to shoplift because something major had happened in her life – again. This time it was her teenage daughter, who had just announced her pregnancy. Instead of dealing with the stress properly, Lucy went - shoplifting.

Tina, large purse slung over her shoulder, was always alert for opportunities to get something for nothing. Tina saw something and wondered if she could get away with stealing it. She might not need the item, but just the get-something-for-nothing gave her an adrenaline rush.

Thirty-one-year-old Terry, a social worker, knew how shoplifters thought because he had been stealing since his teens. Like Tina, his adrenaline rush was to get something for nothing. He had been caught twice, the last time three years ago at a supermarket when he tried to leave with a bottle of champagne under his coat. After release from jail, therapy, medication, and support group, Terry still faced temptation every day, because - like Lucy - it had become an addiction.

"Well, shit!" Tina was the first to see me. She dropped her purse and raised her arms. Lucy and Terry sighed, and followed Tina's lead.

The six of us returned to the store conference room. The agents had the thieves empty purses and pockets of stolen goods to keep as evidence, filed a written complaint, and turned them over to me.

Back in the patrol car, I picked up the radio. The suspects were silent in the back seat.

"Ten-eight." (call completed) "Dispatch, I have two females and one male on the way for booking. Speedometer reads 68390." It was protocol, when females were placed in the patrol unit, to give dispatch the car mileage, and again on arrival at the station-- to prevent retaliatory accusations against the police officer.

~~*~~

At 1:15 a.m. as I patrolled East St. Gertrude Place, I noticed lights on in the Chandler Research building. That's unusual for this time of morning. I turned off the patrol unit headlights and silently cruised close to the front of the building. I got out of the car and tried the door. It was unlocked.

I heard the noisy, rhythmic cadence of a gun being fired. I drew my revolver. Adrenaline high, I quietly moved up the stairs toward the sound and discovered workmen using a riveting gun as they remodeled office walls.

James Hewitt, President of Chandler Research sent a letter to Chief Allen relating the situation, and said of me, "He came in alert, sized up the situation and adapted with no nervous carryover upon discovering everything in order.[28] He acted as a well-trained officer and furthermore, as a gentleman. Our commendation to the patrolman and our congratulations to the Department on the behavior of their men."

~~*~~

A week later, I was dispatched to the Crown Furniture Store on West First Street to follow up a purse-snatching report. As I entered the parking lot, I saw a hefty brunette sitting on another female's back, holding a red ponytail taut between her knees. All I could see were scrawny legs in tennis shoes, kicking from behind.

As I pulled the patrol unit alongside the pair and stopped, I recognized the red hair. It was Jeanette's second snatch of the day. Earlier, she lay in wait for her robbery victim to walk to her car. As the woman searched her purse for car keys, Jeanette rushed from the side of the building and grabbed the straps of her purse, yanking it from the woman's shoulder. As Jeanette ran, the elderly female fell and suffered abrasions to her legs, hands and shoulder.

Jeanette's first grab hadn't yielded the cash, or checks she could forge, to get the crack cocaine she needed. She doesn't think about the consequences of purse snatching, causing injury to her victim, or committing robbery and check forgery. Her only thought is to get her fix for the day.

"Bitch tried the wrong woman," the brunette sputtered, more for Jeanette's benefit than mine. "She grabbed my purse, but I ran her down and jumped on the bony bitch!"

A small group of people, who saw and reported the incident, clapped. The brunette thanked them and pushed herself off a sobbing Jeanette. "Bitch is yours now, officer."

After completing the victim's report, I took a handcuffed Jeanette to jail for booking.

~~*~~

Back on patrol after leaving the jail, the smell of meat and pickles hung in the air. I drove over the railroad tracks that cross 17th Street and stopped at McDonald's for a hamburger and a break.

I thought about my promise to Fernando that, together, we would find and bring home a Christmas tree the next day. Marie had begun decorating the house, and tree ornaments waited in their boxes. I pondered gift ideas for my family that would surprise and delight them.

School was out for three weeks, and patrol was relatively quiet during the holidays. I was home more often, and we hadn't had to clean up our yard or vehicles from the vandals for two months. The nasty calls continued, but they were not as threatening as before.

My New Year resolve was to get my bachelor degree, keep my family safe, and be the best police officer possible.

CHAPTER EIGHTEEN
January - May 1970

I was ready to leave for work, when Marie asked if I would return the tickets I had purchased to take her to see Diana Ross and The Supremes. It was their farewell live concert together at the Frontier Hotel in Las Vegas on Tuesday, January 14, 1970. When I presented the tickets as a Christmas gift she had been excited.

A couple days off work had been approved and arrangements for Fernando's care were confirmed. I looked forward to our time away together.

But now Marie wanted a new television set, with a larger screen, to watch All My Children. ABC had launched the first episode of the soap opera the day before.

Hands on her hips, daring me to object, she said, "I'll go to Montgomery Ward to find one and have it delivered. The old one can go into Fernando's room. He'll like that."

There was nothing to say. I pocketed the tickets before closing the door firmly behind me. I walked next door to Samuel and Jackee's home, the middle-aged couple we considered friends and who had agreed to care for Fernando during our trip to Las Vegas.

When Samuel answered my knock, I held out the tickets, "Sam, there's been a change of plans. You and Jackee take the tickets and have a great time in Vegas. I'll watch over the house while you're gone."

We exchanged some pleasantries before I returned home, climbed into my car and drove to the police station to begin my day.

Surprisingly, I felt free and at ease, but from what? I didn't understand, nor could I put it into words.

~~*~~

Two weeks later during roll call, the briefing sergeant read a commendation letter from Lt. Stebbins for Tom Parrott and me. The Lt. had received an award of merit for "the most outstanding law enforcement program in Orange County for the year 1969." He graciously pointed out the roles we had played in that assignment and our efforts in Police Community Relations.[29]

Later that early Monday morning I was the only thing visibly moving. I drove slowly along West Bishop Street in my patrol car while shadows danced on the pavement in the headlights' glow. The crackle of the radio broke the silence, and I was dispatched with a Code 415 Disturbance two blocks away.

As I turned onto South Parton Street, shrill cuss words reviled someone named Ernesto: most likely the man standing in an undershirt and checkered boxers. He turned, shading his eyes from the glare of the headlights, and jogged toward me. As soon as I got out of the car, he started talking.

His finger stabbed in the air toward the one-story bungalow where my car was parked. The bungalow's door opened, a screeching voice becoming louder, rang out, "Ernesto, you f----r! You lying sonofabitch! You drunken coward!"

Ernesto explained. He and his live-in girlfriend had been fighting about his frequent late night absences from home. The girlfriend had trained their prolific blue and green Amazon Parrot to curse Ernesto. The noise roused a sleeping neighbor, who had called the police.

The girlfriend appeared in the open doorway with the bird, shushing him. "It's okay, officer, Harley's going to be a good boy now. No more fighting, I promise."

Ernesto looked at me imploringly, as I asked, "Can you keep Harley quiet, or will your neighbor have to call me back here again?"

He assured me the bird would not disturb the neighbor and the police wouldn't be called back out.

And I wouldn't have to arrest a talking bird.

~~*~~

Other humorous incidents and incidents not so funny ones provided me quirky insights into people.

On a warm, clear February afternoon I drove across the Santa Ana riverbed on Edinger Avenue toward South Fairview Street. Mobile-style special education classrooms for teenagers dotted the south side of the field.

I stopped my patrol unit alongside the fawn-colored four-door Jaguar illegally parked on the lot at South Fairview and got out to

189

investigate. The white noise of traffic whooshed past in both directions. Somewhere a dog barked. Two young mothers, one pushing a stroller along the sidewalk, and the other watching her toddler skip in the grass, casually made their way toward me.

In the back seat of the Jag, a nude couple relaxed, the man's head between the woman's legs. The windows were down. Eyes averted, I announced myself. The man made a muffled squeak and abruptly fell into a curled position on the floorboard. The woman slowly sat upright on the seat, glaring at me, her dark brown eyes narrowed to slits.

I said, "Sir, miss, please put your clothes on. You're in a public park where a child, or a senior, anyone – can stumble across you. Exposing yourself inappropriately in a public place is against the law."

The woman became irate, but dressed anyway, along with the mustached man. Then, when I asked to see some identification, she cursed me and refused.

"Sir, miss, please step out of the car, and show me some identification." The young mothers passed us, the toddler pointing at me and giggling, "Puhweesman! Puhweesman!"

The man insisted that she show me her I.D. Spewing epithets, she presented the top half of her driver license from the wallet, refusing to remove it completely. I assisted by pulling it away from her.

Because of the verbal abuse, it was all the more difficult to overlook the fact that they were breaking the law. Both were arrested and taken to the police station for processing. The booking officer took their personal information, recorded particulars about the alleged crime, performed a record search of their backgrounds, fingerprinted, photographed, and searched the suspects. Their personal property was confiscated and each was placed in a holding cell.

The female was given permission to call her husband, a colonel in the Marine Corps. Further investigation revealed her lover was also her husband's best friend.

Later that evening, I was advised that the colonel, a tall, distinguished gentleman, was looking for details surrounding his wife's arrest and wanted to speak to the arresting officer. I agreed to speak with him, and returned to the station lobby, where I tried to explain as evasively as I could.

"Yes, but Officer, I would like to know what they were doing!"

After several rounds of this, I gave up. "Well, sir," I said, trying to look at the ceiling, walls, through walls, anywhere but at him, "Would you like to know in clinical terms or everyday street language?" I could see him brace himself.

"Give it to me straight." A little play on words here, I thought to myself.

Pausing, I slowly said, "Well, sir, he was performing oral sex on your wife while parked in public."

I was prepared for an explosion, but there was none. The Colonel instead assumed a puzzled expression.

"After all these years," he said, shaking his head, "I never knew she liked sex in public."

~~*~~

Later that month I was assigned to work a special detail in Birch Park at West 3rd and South Birch streets. Residents living around the small, leafy city park with walkways and picnic areas, had been complaining about the drugs and illicit sexual activities observed near the public restrooms.

At 11:30 p.m. the night air was calm under a quarter moon. I draped paper towels across the closed lid in the first of two stalls, and gingerly sat on the toilet with my pants down around my knees. A dim light flickered over the single sink, sending shadows across the tiled floor.

I wondered how long I had to sit in this rat-hole and speculated on the name and phone number scratched on the latrine door.

Looking down at the khakis I wore when I worked in the yard, I vowed they would see the fire when this assignment was over.

Minutes passed at a snail's pace. *What was a snail's pace, anyway?*

Lost in thought, it took a few seconds for me to become conscious of the white hand from under the partition of the next stall rubbing my calf. A soft, small hand.

I gave long, low moans as consent for more gentle strokes before I pulled up my pants and abandoned the toilet seat. I stepped out and faced his closed door. As it opened, I took two steps back to grant the lecher an unhampered view of me.

The 5'4" blond man wore a short-sleeved t-shirt and loose blue jeans with his fly open, swollen penis exposed. He looked up at me hopefully with a huge grin.

The grin quickly faded as I flashed my badge, identified myself as a police officer, and removed handcuffs from my back pocket.

"Sir, you're under arrest for lewd and lascivious acts in a public place." I read the offender a Miranda warning. I asked the standard questions about his name, age, and address. He said his name was Markine.

No way was I going to search Markine, with his now flaccid penis.

I notified communications on my handheld. "Dispatch, I'm at Birch Park with a 647a (Penal Code for lewd or dissolute conduct in a public place) in custody, and request follow-up."

Sergeant Armein arrived, and after a situation exchange, the downcast hopeful was going for a ride to jail and booking. As Markine wriggled into the back seat of the unit, the sergeant said, "The guys downtown can do the search on this one! I'm not getting near that!"

The gay community was foreign to me. I didn't understand them or their way of life. But once Armein uttered those words, I sensed in Markine the same familiarity of being on the down side of hatred and prejudice that I had been fighting.

In a subconscious gesture of disgust with myself, I watched the tail lights of the transportation car disappear onto West 3rd Street. Sighing, I entered the first of two stalls in the public restroom, and gingerly sat on the toilet with my pants down around my knees to wait for the next seduction.

~~*~~

A week later, Brandi waved me down as I patrolled the West 3rd Street side of Birch Park. Brandi was a neighborhood prostitute and could be found walking the streets, when not in the park. The long-legged, skinny hooker in a too tight, too short, neon-tan sheath looked like a walking condom. She was clearly agitated.

Holding her three-inch spike heels, she sprinted to the car barefoot, shrieking, "I got ripped off. Bastard raped me!"

Her almond eyes were sullen. One side of her head was shaved, displaying her most recent tattoo - a botched purple and yellow butterfly.

She now had three botched butterflies.

She howled, "Sonofabitch! Didn't give me my money! That means he raped me!"

I mentally counted to ten, to give her time to get hold of herself. "Take a deep breath and slow down, Brandi. What happened?"

"This john had sex with me and didn't pay me! That's rape, right?"

"It could be, Brandi. Where did it happen?"

She gave me a teasing look as she gestured to her crotch. "Right here in my p----."

Ask a dumb question.

~~*~~

Sunday the first, was the beginning of March Madness month.

At 11 p.m., at the start of second shift, I responded to an unknown trouble call, possible 417 (man with a gun) at the Alamo Bar on North Harbor. The suspect was described as a male white, brown hair, 6'2", 220 pounds, wearing blue jeans and a blue plaid shirt.

On the way to the Alamo, I requested a follow-up unit. I parked my patrol car across the street from the entrance. Officer Tony Condello responded and positioned his unit behind mine.

Tony had been on the force for three years. He was born, schooled and raised in New York. After high school graduation Tony moved to California in search of a career in professional wrestling, but he was injured early, so he decided to get into law enforcement.

At 5'7", Tony wore his brown hair swept high in front in an effort to add height. His flat, crooked nose drew immediate attention and he spoke with a nasal Bronx accent. Tony's lean size belied the strength he possessed.

"Well, let's find out what we have waiting for us, Tony." Not knowing what to expect, and as trained to do, we each rested our shooting hand over the holster of our weapons and entered the run-down bar.

The smell of alcohol and cigarette smoke made my nose sting. My eyes got accustomed to the darkness as we made our way to the rear of the bar, where we saw the barkeep serving a beer to a guy with a cowgirl pin-up tattoo. Drops of the beer spilled onto the counter. A few customers sat on bar stools, focused on the drink in front of them. We heard the buzz of chatter from patrons sitting at grimy tables littered with endless glasses.

We approached the bartender, who said he called the police because, pointing to the suspect at the other end of the bar, "I think I saw a gun in the waistband of his pants, fellas, and I don't want any trouble here."

Looking at the man pointed out to us, hunched over the beer mug held close between his hands, Officer Condello and I looked at one another, shaking our heads. Our first impression was that the bartender had underestimated the man's size by a good margin. This was the biggest male I had ever seen. He stood 6'4" and at first guess, he weighed 325-350 pounds. His plaid shirt was tight across sizable biceps. He looked like he could easily lift a ton.

The bartender continued, "He comes in here about once a month. Sits in the same place and drinks alone. Sometimes he gets nasty - and he hates cops."

"Thanks a lot," Tony said. "You're just one hell of a swell guy."

"No problem," replied the barkeep. "I got my job, and you got yours."

We pulled our guns as we approached the huge man from both sides. Customers, seeing the .38s come out, fled through both entries, or slipped to the floor and vanished under the table nearest them.

Officer Condello and I simultaneously put a handgun into each of the hulking man's ears. Tony, barely detectable at the suspect's elbow, announced, "Sir, we are Santa Ana police officers. Please remain where you are and put both hands on the bar where we can see them."

As long as this man had his back to us, we were just two bad cops. But if he chose to put his hands up in the air and turned to us, we would probably have had a major problem with him.

With that thought in mind, I asked, "Sir, please place your right hand behind your back."

"Sure. Okay." One enormous arm clumsily moved to his backside.

While I remained on guard with my gun still in his left ear, my partner holstered his gun, cuffed the giant's hand and eased the other arm around the back of the body and finished the cuff. I holstered my weapon and turned the giant on the swiveling bar stool, bringing him to his feet. The big man was docile, eyes blurred, his breath sour. He mumbled, "What you want with me?"

"Sir, we got a call you might have a gun. We just want to make sure you and others are safe and there are no weapons. My partner is going to search your person, and if you're clear, we'll be on our way."

Officer Condello did a body search, and found a five-inch hunting knife sharpened on both sides of the blade, one hundred eighty dollars, and a driver's license, which identified him as forty-three-year-old, 231 pound Santa Ana resident, Gordon Belstock. Obviously, the man had put on significant weight since he had renewed his license.

With each of us taking an arm, I said, "Let's go outside and talk and let the other customers come in, okay?"

I looked at my partner, thinking that this was going too smoothly. My gut was telling me something was going to happen. Sure enough, this amiable giant, upon seeing the black-and- whites, had an instant personality change. The big man roared like a wounded bull elephant ready to fight for his life.

"I ain't going to jail, you sonsa bitches. You ain't takin' me no place, and not to jail!"

He lunged forward, his elbows swinging out with a power and speed that knocked both my 165 pound partner, and me, away from him. I jumped to get my arm around his neck to take him down in a chokehold, my feet dangling two inches off the tarmac. The man began spinning as I swung around, holding on like a pit-bull.

Tony hammered his nightstick against the mammoth's calf and shin bones, with no outward effect. With effort caused by fear, I got my arm properly positioned around Belstock's neck, and applied pressure to cut off the blood supply to the man's brain, while Tony threw a football tackle on his legs. We both went down like fallen redwood against the police car.

He roared four-letter words nonstop.

Somehow the door was opened, but we couldn't pull, push, or maneuver the suspect into the police car. From sheer exhaustion, we were unable to utter those famous words, "You're under arrest" or to advise him of his rights. After fifteen minutes of this, which seemed like an hour, we radioed for more help. Another three officers arrived, and between the five of us we dumped the handcuffed Mr. Belstock into the back seat of the car.

I thanked the backup units, and could hear Officer Condello begin a replay of the night's events in the bar. I perceived chortles of amusement as I pulled away from the curb.

My passenger cleared his throat. A blob of slime hit the back of my head, followed by another clearing and a second blob.

"Prick! Wait until you take me out of this car. I'm gonna kick your ass, you yellow f----r. You couldn't do it on your own before, and you won't have more help!" Throat cleared. A gooey, ropey blob dribbled down my neck.

My fingers gripped the wheel. It took all the self-discipline and inner strength I could muster to wait until I went through the entry gate of the Orange County Sheriff's Department. While he spewed out profanities, I radio'd in my situation and requested backup to remove Godzilla from my black-and-white.

I secured my helmet and waited outside the car. When reinforcement officers arrived, I opened the rear door and was immediately met with a head butt to the gut. The massive Mr. Belstock was rowdy, menacing, and fast.

Rolling over, I went for my hard sap, a ten-inch leather baton, and lunged right back with blows to his shoulders and back. Dropping to a crouch, I hit him behind the knees, which didn't drop him. So I hit him in the kneecaps, which gave my back-up the opportunity to subdue and remove him to a holding cell. And his mouth didn't stop, even after the iron door slammed behind him.

Later, I found out Gordon Belstock was a retired warehouse worker and part time delivery driver for a beer distributor at the Port of Long Beach. He was booked for public intoxication, carrying a weapon, and assault and battery on multiple officers.

I wondered how a man his size could fit in the seat of the delivery truck.

~~*~~

For two weeks into March Madness, officers were advised that armed robberies had been occurring in the wee hours of the morning. At midnight on the twelfth I observed an older model white Corvair acting suspiciously in the area of the all-night service station at First and Raitt. Because of the hour and the number of occupants in the vehicle driving slowly back and forth, lights flicking on and off, I had reasonable suspicion that a crime could be committed.

I contacted the owner of the service station and told him I would maintain a stakeout, unaware the occupants of the vehicle observed me talking with the attendant.

They left the area. An hour later, dispatch assigned patrol Officer Bailey to an unknown trouble call at a service station on North Bristol. I contacted the sergeant on duty and alerted him to the description of the suspect's vehicle. Within moments I heard the description broadcast on the unit radio. "…Five male Negro suspects in the Corvair were taken into custody…"

A memorandum of commendation for the arresting officer was issued and included me for my "alertness."[30]

~~*~~

Over the past few months the Lyon Street Apartments, on the east side of Santa Ana, had had a rash of burglaries. The offender scaled the walls to the second floor and entered through open apartment windows while the residents slept. He quietly took valuables and left through the front door and out of the complex.

The task team assigned to the detail captured and arrested a nineteen-year-old wearing dirty black construction boots, blue jeans and white tee shirt. I was dispatched to transport the offender to the police department for interrogation.

When I pulled up, the kid was sitting on the curb, hands cuffed behind his back. He had a smirk on his face. As I got out of the patrol car, I had a feeling, a case of familiarity, from my rookie days. The officers on scene gave me a quick rundown, and we turned to assist the perp to his feet, when he suddenly lifted a leg that hit me square between the legs, forcing me back and onto my knees. The kick was strong enough and painful enough to cause me to momentarily black out. Two officers quickly restrained him and put him in the rear of my patrol vehicle, while another officer tended to me. It took a few minutes for me to regain my composure and wait for the pain to subside before I could get behind the wheel and take the kid to the station to be booked.

Back on patrol, confident the night couldn't get any worse, I was dispatched to carry out my first-ever notification: make contact with the Femrow family and advise them the police department had received an emergency telephone call. Mr. Femrow's elderly father had been involved in a fatal car accident. I took a deep breath and mentally prepared myself to address the son with sensitivity and to offer an escort, if needed.

As I knocked I took notice of the peephole in the door. The house was a small, comfortable-looking bungalow. I noted the manicured lawn and newly planted flowers along the front of the home as I waited for an answer to my knocks.

I heard a loud, nasal, male voice, "What are you doing up here? We don't allow niggers. Now get out!"

I flashed my badge quickly to the peephole. "Sir, I was sent to tell you that the police department has an emergency message for Mr. Femrow regarding his father."

Again, the nasal voice said, "I told you we don't allow niggers. Now get out!"

Unsure what to do, I flashed my badge once again to the peephole before turning away to leave the premises. I repeated, "I was sent to tell you that the police department has an emergency message for Mr. Femrow regarding his father."

The frowning, middle-aged white male, khaki's belted below his protruding stomach, opened the door when I was half way down the walk. He had told me to get out.

"What is it, nigger? What about my father?"

Trying to control myself, I opened my vehicle door, ready to slip into my seat, one hand on the steering wheel. Stiffly I said, "You may call, or go to the police department, and they will be happy to personally give you the message. Have a good day, Sir." *Not my finest hour.*

~~*~~

In addition to patrol, I was assigned the dual roles of field training officer and crime scene investigations (CSI). I completed the forty-hour

CSI course the department offered.[31]

The quote on the certificate had special meaning to me: "Let the yardsticks of knowledge, character and experience gauge a man's fitness for the job."

During the sixties, the patrol division had their own crime scene investigators who carried CSI kits in their patrol cars.

I was dispatched to answer an unknown trouble call to a one-story stucco in the 200 block of West Pine, where I was met outside the home by neighbors who had called the department. They had heard screams coming from the home occupied by a single 75-year-old Hispanic female. She did not answer the front or back doors when neighbors attempted to contact her.

Concerned, they started looking in windows – the kitchen window framed her body, wedged between her small dining table and two-burner gas stove. The neighbors said it was Mrs. Martinez who was lying on her back, her arms in a defensive position across her chest and face.

Given the information from the neighbors, I called for back-up before entering the home, where we found Mrs. Martinez just as the neighbors described. I was somehow thankful that the neighbors hadn't seen the blood pools that came from her neck, shoulders, and abdomen, or the blood spatters on the table, chairs, counter-tops, icebox and stove. It was a horrific scene.

My back-up, Officer Doran, returned to his car to summon medical aid while I went about the task of securing and protecting the crime scene.

The fire department arrived quickly and determined Mrs. Martinez was dead. Officer Doran returned to his unit to make radio contact with homicide and the coroner. He then cordoned off the area to keep family, friends, and curiosity seekers away from the scene.

As the first officer on the scene, it was my duty to note the time and as many elements of the crime scene as possible without touching anything. While I waited for the homicide detectives, I sketched the crime scene and made notes that included odors, the amount of light present, whether doors and windows were open or shut. I made sure nothing was disturbed.

I stepped outside and thought about the frail, gray-haired Mrs.

Martinez and how she would not have been able to defend herself against an intruder. I also thought about my mother, so many miles away in Arkansas. One day she would be older and frail. I sent a silent prayer that unlike Mrs. Martinez, my mother would never be in a situation where she was helpless and unable to defend herself.

I shook away the thoughts and walked toward the small group of neighbors who now were witnesses. I began the process of separating and taking names of the witnesses. The Crimes Against Persons (CAP) detectives arrived to take charge of the case.

I heard Lieutenant Webb before I saw him. "Lambert, what happened here?" I excused myself from a witness and turned to Webb. I gave him a verbal rundown of what I found on my arrival and my activities until he arrived.

Without looking directly at me, he said, "You can take off outta here, Lambert." Webb and his team would investigate how the crime was committed and try to find evidence that pointed to a suspect.

In a matter of days I learned from one of the investigating officers that a twenty-two year old Mexican male, who had been manicuring the victim's postage-stamp lawn for more than two years, was arrested for the brutal murder of Mrs. Martinez. He was convicted of first-degree murder that put him in prison for life without parole. He never gave a reason for committing the crime.

~~*~~

Minutes before midnight, a thin layer of clouds masked the moon, and it started to drizzle. An elderly man waved me down on South Raitt and West Raymar Street. "There's a bunch of drunk kids making noise over there, and we can't sleep!"

He motioned to a house where half a dozen teenage White and Hispanic males were on the front porch drinking beer, and shouting, four-letter words into the night air. Before I pulled up in front of the house, I called Dispatch and requested assistance.

As I got out of the patrol car, I heard, "Hey, f---you, pig! This is private property, and unless you have a warrant get your f---ing ass out of here!"

A heavy, middle-aged Hispanic man stomped down the steps. I approached the house ignoring the profanity, and said, "Sir, I received a disturbing the peace complaint of loud noise. Please quiet down your guests."

Suddenly the group moved toward me and started yelling, "We know where you live, pig. You were told to get off the property, and if you don't, we'll get even!"

My attempt to communicate with them was impossible. Their screams were loud as they circled around me—just as follow-up officers arrived. Seeing the white officers, the obscenities became hushed. Together, we ushered the men back onto the porch, where they stood, now noiseless.

"Gentlemen, I don't want to have to arrest you. But if you don't quiet down, and if I have to come back, you'll go to jail for disturbing the peace."

As I pulled away I glanced at the group and saw half a dozen middle-finger waves.

~~*~~

It was 2:30 a.m. and raining, as Sergeant Robile and I sat in our black-and-whites, our units' driver-sides facing in opposite directions, about two feet between us. We were behind an apartment building in the 1100 block of McFadden and jolted from our quiet conversation when we saw in the light of lampposts a black man being chased by a barefoot black male wearing only white jockey shorts.

Seeing the car, the chaser quickly jogged to us, rapidly telling us, "My wife and I were in bed. I woke up hearing her scream." Bending over to take a deep breath, he continued, "And when I rolled over, there was a guy on top of the bed, just stretched out there touching my wife!"

Looking toward the street where he had been chasing the now out-of-sight intruder, he said, "I chased him through the bedroom, out the door and through the complex. Then I saw you guys." As Robile called for backup, I exited the police car, took his elbow, asked his name and requested he show me their apartment.

As we entered the apartment, Mrs. Thomas was sitting on their couch with robe tight about her and arms crossed protectively. She said she was awakened when she felt the pressure of a man on top of her, nightgown pulled above her waist, and just started screaming to her husband for help. She pointed at the knife on the coffee table, "This was laying by the bedroom window, and it's not ours."

As I walked to the window, it was evident the screen had been cut with a sharp object, and the Thomas's confirmed their windows were not locked. An area search for the suspect proved fruitless.

~~*~~

Not long after this incident I had a surprise visitor at the police department. Bruce, a personal friend whom I knew and played basketball with on the same team was a high-ranking officer in the Black Panther Organization. He put himself in a very dangerous position coming to the police department to find me.

Pulling me out of earshot of other officers, he whispered, "Move your family now. The Panthers are going to kill you and your family and destroy your home." Moving through the office door he had a final warning, "Move before it's too late, my brother. You don't have much time." As he left the building, I went to my supervisor to tell him an emergency had come up, and I needed to go home.

I knew that Bruce's words "right away" meant right away, not "as soon as you can" or in a few days. I left the station immediately, but on the drive home I was unable to focus around what I had just been told. It seemed almost impossible to move an entire household "right away." I tried to come up with a list of tasks which would accomplish this impossible move.

That was on Thursday.

First, I called Kent "KC" Carmine, a realtor friend. I told him that I had received information from a reliable person that my family and I would be killed if we didn't move from our home immediately. The informant had told me to move now, because our home would be destroyed.

"KC" told me to stand by, that he would call me back shortly. Ten minutes later he called to tell me he had found a place for my family to move to in the City of Tustin. He knew the builder of the tract of new homes and made arrangements for me to begin moving in that same evening. He further told me that if we wished to purchase the home, we could remain in the house while it was in escrow.

I still look back in amazement that "KC" was able to do it, and to keep it confidential. Marie, Fernando, and I took enough items to be able to stay in Tustin that night. In between packing and constant checks out the living room windows, I told Marie about Bruce's visit to the department. Fernando played quietly in his room.

My wife became hysterical, afraid for our lives and our son's life. Tears flowed like I had never seen before. Her hand shot up, as though warding me off. "Harlen, no more talking. Just get us on the plane. I can't wait to leave this place. I need normalcy. I'm just tired."

~~*~~

I believed then, and I believe now, that for her this was the final straw. I knew it was just a matter of time before she would file for divorce.

On Friday and Saturday we moved most of our possessions out of the house and over to the Tustin home. By Sunday I was making reservations for Marie and Fernando to fly out of the Los Angeles Airport in the middle of the night. I made sure that they would have everything they needed packed and ready for a midnight flight to Chicago where they would stay with Marie's sister until I felt it was safe to bring them home.

The drive to LAX was difficult. Marie and Fernando both traveled light, one suitcase apiece, and dressed casually in jeans. Marie sat in the front seat looking straight ahead, saying nothing. Fernando sat in the back seat directly behind me, crying, his arms wrapped around my neck. I can still see them getting on that plane.

That had to be the lowest time in my life, having to sneak my family out of our home in order to save their lives. Over the next two nights after work I moved the remainder of our furniture and personal things out of the Santa Ana home and into our new house in Tustin Meadows.

I wasn't aware I was the first Black to move to this newly built community until I contacted the telephone company to transfer my telephone to the new address. I was told they did not have enough cable to accommodate me at that time. I knew this wasn't true because before leaving for work that morning, I heard my neighbor's telephone ringing.

I called again, "I'm a police officer and I must have a telephone."

The service representative instructed me, "If you want a telephone, you need to supply a letter from your chief of police spelling out the need."

I notified Chief Allen. I got the letter. I got a telephone.

~~*~~

Three weeks later, a family from San Diego purchased our Santa Ana home. Shortly after the new owners moved in, the home was vandalized. Someone broke in, breaking all of their furniture, cutting the carpet in every room, knocking holes in the walls, and pouring flour over the broken furniture throughout the house.

I had heard about the break-in from officers at the department. Was this done by amateurs—the teens who said they knew where I lived and would get even with me? Undoubtedly the Panthers idea of killing and destroying would have been carried out more skillfully.

Wearing civvies, I went by to talk with the new owners to see how they were, and to see what damage had been done. Showing me around the home, the middle-aged black woman expressed her dismay, "The realtor didn't tell us the house was once owned by a black police officer." Not wanting to make things worse, I never told the new owners I was the one who once lived in the house. Soon after, the family moved out, planning to return to San Diego.

~~*~~

It wasn't long—but seemed an eternity—until my wife and son returned to our new home in Tustin Meadows. It didn't take Marie long to make the house a home, with those touches that only she, mother and homemaker, could do—a colorful tablecloth, a well-prepared meal, a clean tub, reading to our son in the evening. She seemed to like the home well enough, but her air of sadness increased day-by-day.

Her fears had consumed her. Talk between us had come almost to a stop, except to argue about the smallest, most unimportant things imaginable. It was doubly hard because we made sure we never entered into a heated talk within Fernando's earshot. But he felt the tension in the home between Mom and Dad, evident in his escapes to another room. If we weren't arguing, it was silent—silent for days on end except for the interaction we each had with our son. The silence became deafening for all of us.

Intimacy between Marie and me had long ago ceased. I had felt, before, that we were going the way of so many others, with separation or divorce. It was now just a matter of time.

As April came to an end, officers were notified that the sergeant supervisory exam would be conducted soon. I immediately enrolled and completed a 24-hour pre-sergeants supervisory instruction at CSU-LA.[32]

CALIFORNIA STATE COLLEGE
LOS ANGELES

THIS CERTIFIES THAT

HARLEN D. LAMBERT

HAS SUCCESSFULLY COMPLETED 24 CLASS HOURS OF INSTRUCTION IN
PRE-SERGEANTS SUPERVISORY INSTITUTE
AND IS THEREFORE AWARDED THIS

CERTIFICATE OF COMPLETION

April 25, 1970
DATE

PRESIDENT   John A. Morton   DEAN

Three days later, as I confidently approached the examination room, Captain Tracey stood at the open door, wiping his bald head with a paper towel. It was warmer than usual in the building.

I was the first of fifteen officers to arrive for the testing. My internal alarm went off as I recalled our hallway exchange three years earlier. Now, like then, arms crossed and shoulders hunched, the captain leaned against the wall and calmly said, "I'm not sure why you're here. Don't count on your score and supervisor evaluations, Lambert."

With that, he indicated I could enter as he greeted the officers arriving behind me.

I said nothing to the captain, and refused to be provoked, as I had been by his earlier derision. But I felt somehow diminished, even though the young, blond officer next to me peeked at my test paper before furiously erasing and writing on his own. We were told we would have results in June.

The following day a letter to the chief from Mr. and Mrs. O'Toole thanking me for speaking to the Teenage Christian Doctrine Class on my free time was read in roll call, and met with silence.[33]

~~*~~

I stumble over piles of dead bodies, black, white, yellow and red. Bodies with broken necks, crushed faces, blood running from wounds all over them. I seem to be in a cave, or some underground place where the only light comes from a mysterious, flickering ball that slowly bounces from place to place on the ceiling, casting down a dim, yellowish light. Where am I?

My wife screams. I call out. But who will hear me? Who CAN hear me?

I stagger around, to somewhere. Suddenly I come to a strange sight. It's almost like a surrealistic painting of a street corner, complete with a lamppost. Just beyond the lamppost, a flickering neon sign over a storefront and leaning against the building housing the storefront are – people! I rush over to them, overjoyed and almost falling as I try to avoid the slippery spots between the bodies where blood has congealed. I stop abruptly as two of the men look up and smile at me – their faces contorted with hate.

The faces are those of the nigger-coon-darky joke tellers. The two cops who are always ready to ask, when they think I'm not around, "Have you heard the one about the darky who didn't like watermelon, was afraid of graveyards and sleeps with his sister?"

I stare, horrified, at their mean, ugly faces, my eyes x-raying past their skin into the bony masks of their faces. I'm unable to move, my disgust and hate for them causing a sweat to break out all over my body.

"Wake up, Harlen! Wake up! You're dreaming."

Yes, damn it, a dream inspired, I'm sure Freud would agree, by the latest nigger joke that was told when ol' Powers and Webb thought I was out of earshot, or maybe were sure I wasn't. Some stupid, idiotic, racist joke about how to get a nigger to laugh on a Sunday.

I pecked a little kiss on Marie's cheek and eased out of bed, troubled and unable to sleep, as badly as I needed it. I went to the kitchen, thinking about the dream. It wasn't the first time I'd had a similar dream, or a variation on the theme.

I'm in this cave-like place, stumbling around and it seems that I am the only living human being on the set and, as usual, I stumble onto these two racist officers lounging around. Of all people in the world, in a world filled with bloody bodies and all kinds of other distressing things, why should I run into these two?

Another variation of the dream was that I would come out of an area of this island we're all shipwrecked on and who else survived, other than me? Right! Cronies Powers and Webb.

I reached into the fridge for a Coca-Cola, but I shook myself away from the thought. Caffeine would mean no sleep at all and, not digging the idea of warm milk (like in the movies) I decided on a glass of water from the kitchen faucet, and loaded it with ice. I removed leftovers of my son's favorite meal from the refrigerator, the foil-covered spaghetti and meatballs my wife had prepared the day before. Using leftovers from the spaghetti, I made a small meatball sandwich before sitting down at the kitchen table. As I began to eat, my mind drifted back to the dream and an incident that happened a few nights ago.

An incident that brought awards for my bravery, a headline that both congratulated and insulted me, and a re-examination of my desire to stay in the Santa Ana Police Department.

***

Officer "Lamb" Lambert:

May 26, 1970 near the end of my graveyard shift. I was patrolling the South Evergreen area, a quiet residential community made up of small, wood-framed ranch-style homes built during the 1950's and occupied predominantly by Hispanic families. Some small yards had grass, some just hard dirt. Some back-yard gardens had fruit and nut trees, or even chickens. Unlike so many other areas I patrolled from 11 p.m. to 7 a.m., I rarely saw the residents themselves, unless someone would be coming home from their own third-shift job, or perhaps making a quick run for milk to the local market, which opened at 6 a.m. I could surmise, given the number of toys, tricycles, and a child's jacket hanging and forgotten on the picket fence that the area had a good number of children.

To help time pass, sometimes I made a game of counting the yards that didn't have kid's toys, when suddenly, to my left, I saw flames leaping from windows of a home in the 2200 block of South Evergreen. Dawn was breaking as I did a U-turn and sped to the home. The street was eerily quiet. I radioed "10-97 at a 904 Res. I've arrived at a residential fire." I gave the address. "Send fire department!" I leaped from the car.

Fear and anxiety coursed through me. A flashback of crawling into a fireplace as a toddler. I subconsciously clenched my left hand into a ball, the fused fingers unable to close completely. A remembered sensation of burning. Of pain. An invisible force propelled me forward. Toward the fire, apprehension forgotten in the moment.

The front of the home was engulfed in flames. The heat and flames were intense. I couldn't go in that way. I raced up the driveway, towards the rear of the house. Someone shouted "There are babies, babies!" More residents poured from their homes. As I ran, I yelled, "Stay back!"

***

Officer "Jake" Jakobson:

One morning, near the end of my graveyard shift, I was driving my black-and-white south on Main Street. The sun had just come up and it was a cool, crisp, bright day. This is when, after working a whole shift in the dark, you sort of fight back that drowsy feeling you get when the daylight almost blinds your eyes.

Suddenly I noticed something off to the east of the city which was an all residential area. I saw a huge billow of dark smoke. A sick feeling came over me. It was someone's home. At that very instant, out of the silence, I heard Lamb radio "10-97 at a 904 Res". I responded "I'm close by. I'll follow-up Officer Lambert."

Lamb Lambert and I had worked the streets together for a few years, but like many officers, we just worked together as that "thin blue line," but didn't really know each other well.

***

Officer "Lamb" Lambert:

As I neared a rear window, I pulled my police baton, and broke out the glass, all of it, to avoid getting cut. Just as I started to climb through, "Jake" Jakobson, ran up. "Stay put, I can hear kids inside," I told him. Just then, a child's cry of "Mommy! Mommy!" became even louder.

I crawled through the window head first, falling to the floor. Trying to stay under the smoke I crawled towards the sounds of fearful cries. Suddenly I felt the child. I grabbed her, and placed the body under my left arm. The girl went limp. I crab-crawled with her to the window, where "Jake" waited, arms extended to take her from me and to safety.

***

Officer "Jake" Jakobson:

As I rounded the corner and pulled up behind Lamb's unit, I saw that the whole front of the one story house was completely engulfed in flames. I glimpsed Lamb running up the drive-way. He disappeared around the rear of the house. As I jumped from the car I felt the blast of heat even from out in the street.

I ran up the drive-way after Lamb. When I got to the smoke-filled backyard I saw that Lamb had broken out a rear bedroom window and was climbing through. I ran up and Lamb said, "Stay here. There are kids in there. I'll hand them out to you!" I assumed neighbors had told Lamb there were children in the house.

Lamb then proceeded into the dark, smoke-filled room and disappeared. He almost immediately reappeared with a crying child in his arms and headed towards me.

He stretched out his arms and handed the child to me. I started to retreat toward the safety of the back of the yard. But then, Lamb yelled, "There's another kid in there. I gotta get 'em." He then turned around and disappeared, once again, into the darkness.

***

Officer "Lamb" Lambert:

Still inside the smoke-filled house, flames ever closer, I again listened for sound. I realized the attic was aflame. Bits of ceiling were falling down into the room. My eyes smarted. I tried not to breathe through my nose, instead taking small half breaths through my mouth. My throat felt so dry. Dropping to my knees, I crawled with outstretched hands towards a door at the end of the room, where I could hear the gagging and whimpering of another child. Choking on the smoke, avoiding hot embers and trying to avoid pieces of the ceiling from falling directly on me, I thought God, help me keep breathing.

It had been months since I had called on Him. Or even thought about Him. But at that moment, I knew it was Divine Intervention when another youngster crawled almost right into my arms. I again tucked the little one under my left arm, where she wound both arms and legs tight around its length. I slowly made my way back to the window, handing her to waiting arms on the other side.

Turning in an attempt to find other victims, I stumbled against the wall, losing my equilibrium, nearly passing out from heat and lack of oxygen, as hot ashes and splintered boards began raining down on me. I collapsed towards the window, barely feeling Jakobson grabbing my arms and pulling me through the same window. From the roof hot tar dripped on us.

***

Officer "Jake" Jakobson:

I will never forget that morning. Up until this point, this all looked like something I had seen in a movie that had a happy ending. Officer goes into burning building, officer emerges with child, officer saves child's life. All is well. Every one escapes without injury. But, now there was a glitch in this all-too-perfect scenario. Lamb was going back in.

The fire had progressed and spread towards the rear of the house. The attic was burning and the ceiling was falling into the room Lamb was standing in. I quickly handed off the child to a neighbor. "Take the child to safety." Then I turned back to the window and focused my attention on Lamb, standing under the falling ceiling in the smoked-filled dark room.

Lamb dropped to his knees, where the smoke was not quite so thick, and started crawling towards a door at the far end of the room.

I was now fearful of Lamb's safety. Had he become "caught up in the moment" and lost his sense of survival? What was he thinking? I yelled, "Lamb, come back! It's too late to save anyone now. You'll just die trying." But, Lamb said, "No, I can get them, I heard them. Just wait here, I'll be right back." And again he disappeared into the darkness.

I felt my back stinging. The fire was so hot it was melting the asphalt shingles and the tar was dripping from the roof of the house onto my back and melting my nylon police jacket as I leaned in the window.

It was time – I had to go in and get Lamb. There is no way he can survive this, I thought. Hell, I could barely keep from being overcome with smoke while leaning in the window, straining to catch a glimpse of Lamb or hear him crawling around in there. But, if I did go in, I'd probably die too. The very thing I tried to warn Lamb against. But, could I stand by and watch a fellow officer die without trying to save him? Could I live with myself? After all, police give their lives for one another. I'm going in!

Just then, out of that death-filled smoke trap, Lamb emerged carrying a limp young child in his arms. He stood up right in front of me and collapsed towards the window onto me, as he tried to hand the child he was carrying to me. By now, the fire department had arrived, and I pulled the child from Lamb's arms and handed her off to a fireman, so she could be resuscitated. Then I pulled with all my might a limp, hot to the touch, fellow officer, Lamb, out the window. We both pretty much collapsed on the ground under that window, under that damn tar dripping from the roof.

***

Officer "Lamb" Lambert:

I was dazed, but felt firemen laying me on the ground, Jake next to me, as we were given oxygen. I could vaguely see outlines of people and heard muted sounds. In the background I heard someone call out, "Where's the baby? There's a baby still in there!"

Still dazed from smoke inhalation, I yanked the oxygen mask off my face, jumped up, unsteady, but ready to head back towards the house. At the same time, I could hear firemen entering the building. We heard more cries. Jake was holding my arm, "Lamb! Let the firemen handle the situation!"

I was put back on oxygen to clear my burning lungs. In and out of consciousness, I felt I was missing pieces of a movie I should be watching. Besides a report of an officer down, the worst scenario, the one that makes percussion drums sound off in your gut, is a working house fire with children still inside screaming. I could vaguely hear a neighbor call out to the firemen where the window to the baby's room was, and heard the distant shattering of glass. I heard someone say we were heroes. I heard someone ask, "Where is their mother?" I could see the flashing blue and red lights of the emergency vehicles, and pick out the horrified faces of random men and women as the lights flickered in circles from the street.

Soon I realized Jake was no longer next to me, but attempting mouth to mouth resuscitation on a tiny, soot-covered, nearly lifeless body. The baby looked like he was melting, and my brain couldn't connect with what I was seeing, and the awfulness I was feeling at that moment. The next thing I remembered was seeing the three children lying side-by-side receiving CPR and oxygen, as I was recovering and removed from the oxygen mask.

Standing near the emergency vehicles as the children were being prepared for loading into ambulances and taken to a local hospital, I overheard Chief Allen state that a female victim, presumably the mother, had perished in the fire. We learned the fire was started by a cigarette. Apparently the mother had fallen asleep on the couch in the front room while smoking.

I knew the road ahead for these babies would be long and painful. I absently massaged my left hand, as I briefly thought of yet another fire. A fire that destroyed our family home, because of a lovers quarrel between my older sister and her boyfriend. He carried out his threat of revenge.

I was exhausted, and sad, as I thought about how a cigarette and an argument could destroy a home, a family, and everything they owned.

***

Officer "Jake" Jakobson:

Some fireman must have helped us back to a safe part of the yard and started giving us oxygen. It was sort of fuzzy as to what happened next. I just remember a lot of people milling around, looking at the fire, and the firemen's hoses pouring water on the flames.

Then one of the neighbors yelled, "Where's the baby? There's a baby still in there!" Lamb, still groggy from smoke inhalation, pushed the oxygen mask from his face, jumped up and started to head back towards the house. A fireman stopped him. I said, "Lamb, let the fireman handle it now." Lamb was still intent on doing everything he could, to do what police do – put their lives on the line to save others.

A fireman, dressed in all his flame retardant gear, hacked his way in the back door and went in the direction the neighbor pointed out as the baby's room. He broke out a window and handed the baby out. I happened to be near the window and took the lifeless baby from him and ran back to the driveway. I looked down at the baby, which was still hot from the fire. He had soot all over him and was not breathing. I began giving him mouth to mouth resuscitation. I remembered I had to be careful with the "chest compressions," so I just used two fingers to push his chest, while gently breathing into his nose and mouth. Suddenly he started crying, and a fireman handed me an eye dropper and told me to suck the mucus and ashes from his nose and mouth with it. Another fireman leaned over me and held an oxygen mask over the baby's nose and mouth.

***

Officer "Lamb" Lambert:

Left standing after the ambulance left the scene, I waited a few moments watching the firemen do their jobs, knowing they would be on scene for some time.

I looked around for Jake, making eye contact. I knew in that moment, had Officer Jakobson not pulled me from the burning home, I too might have died.

The shift was over. We were each returning to our police cars knowing we would meet up again at the station to return the black-and-whites, change into civilian clothes and go home to another day. It was then I could express to Jake how indebted I was to him for saving my life.

Officer Benoit, a good looking, well built, dark-haired man, and Officer Jakobson, blond, tall and thin with a constant smile, and I discuss our "early morning heroics." None of us know, exactly, what a hero is supposed to feel like. We're just thankful for the lives we were able to save.

***

Officer "Jake" Jakobson:

I looked over to the other part of the yard, in Lamb's direction and caught his eye and we just smiled at each other without saying a word. This scenario really did have a happy ending, just like in the movies. It was almost like someone now should have shouted "cut, that's a wrap."

To this day, Lamb tells people that I saved his life. I didn't really save his life, but I did have a front row seat watching a true life police hero in action.

~~*~~

The weeks following the fire were a roller-coaster of activity, and emotional highs and lows. Community appreciation. Newspaper interviews. Top cop recognition. Awards and medals. The "Bircher Group," or the BGs as I referred to them, was openly hostile. *Nothing new.*

Informant threats.

Divorce papers!

It was late evening, May 26, 1970. I had had few hours of restless sleep when I entered the roll call room. Attendance would be taken, and the oncoming shift officers would be informed of any outstanding incidents that may have occurred, or be informed of suspects to look for, and any other pertinent information officers needed before heading out on the streets.

It was unusual to see Chief Allen in roll call. He greeted me at the door and pressed a typed copy of the 904-S Incident Report that had been recorded and filed by 6:25 a.m. It detailed the date, time, location, type of incident, victim names, officers involved, and a brief account of what had happened earlier in the day.[34]

Lieutenant Garrison wrote an officer commendation on my behalf and read it after the standard briefing concluded. He had outlined the actions of the officers on scene at the fire and wrote, in part, "The conduct and actions of Officer Lambert are in the highest tradition of the Professional Policeman. His demonstrated courage and disregard for his own safety while rescuing two children trapped by fire are far above and beyond the normal duty." Chief Allen penned at the bottom of the commendation, "These are acts of high courage and heroism & I am honored & proud to have the opportunity to congratulate & commend Officer Lambert and the others who assisted."[35]

I was then called to the front of the briefing room, where Chief Edward J. Allen presented me with a second Meritorious Service Award "For saving the lives of Angela & Wendy Clune at the scene of a fire on May 26, 1970."[36]

I choked up, and squeaked out a "Thank you." I was appreciative, but still overwhelmed with images of the fire and sounds of the cries of the children.

Seventeen months earlier the Police Benevolent Association had presented me with my first Meritorious Service Award "for unfailing personal sacrifice in pursuit of his profession."

I couldn't remember why I received that award, but I would never forget the events of Tuesday, May 26,

1970.

The following day, I met with Ray Merchant, *Orange County Evening News* journalist, for a sit-down interview at the police station. We shook hands in the conference room, before settling in for the next two hours. The interview covered my role in the fire, the resulting commendations, and the turns my life had taken since hiring on to the Santa Ana Police Department in December 1966.

I talked about how many of the black youth and adults looked upon me as a sellout, a pig, an Uncle Tom, and a lot of other names you could never print. Members of that same community threatened the lives of my wife and son. I told him there was malicious vandalism to my home and car. We talked about my wife and the fear and hardships she had to overcome being a cop's wife.

The death of Officer Nelson Sasscer, killed by Panthers in June 1969, had started a chain of events that forced me to send my wife and son to Chicago, and later to another city. This death also exposed me, and a fellow officer, to a different kind of danger when we were assigned to take two Panthers into protective custody. We talked about why I joined the department to begin with, and my time as a community relations officer. We talked about a book I wanted to write one day.

Merchant said the story would run in the Sunday, June 7 edition, two weeks away.

On May 28, 1970, I was nominated to the International Association of Chiefs of Police for the "Parade-IACP Police Services Award." Chief Allen summarized my work ethics since hired as the city's first Negro officer, "…Officer Lambert has worked hard and diligently to provide to members of our city from all walks of life a fine example of a conscientious policeman…" He sketched the fire rescue, and wrote, "… In courageously performing his rescue tasks, Officer Lambert displayed those qualities of initiative, courage and perseverance which accrue only to the very few and which serve as an ideal to which less gifted men may aspire."[37]

Two days later, on May 30, 1970, Chief Allen received a letter signed from several neighbors recommending special commendation and public recognition for my saving the Clune children:

Without regard for his own safety, and without any fire protective type of clothing, he fought his way into the burning building and carried out two of the little Clune children trapped therein, under conditions which appeared to make rescue impossible. We feel that such unselfish and heroic action merits special commendation and public recognition.[38]

CHAPTER NINETEEN
June - December 1970

On Tuesday, June 2, 1970, while dressing to go on duty, my gut clenched as I focused on ignoring Officer Powers as he hurled ongoing insults. "Nigger thinks an award makes him a real cop. Get your stick ready for the street, boy. You're gonna need it when we stop for coffee." Sergeant Webb doubled over with mirth.

Sergeant? What happened that he was no longer a lieutenant? I wondered.

I focused on getting my uniform on before roll call. Laughter from some. Locker doors opened and closed. The snap of guns being holstered. Whispers. The off-duty officers rushed out of the room, zipping and buttoning up their street clothes as they left for home. They were eager to get out, not waiting to see what I might do.

Some things just don't change. From day one on the job, the BGs ridiculed me, called me names, and presented obstacles. I remained silent. The sergeant I reported to was a BG. My supervising lieutenant was a BG. They ran the job by their self-made rules. I was aware of the prevailing blue code of silence - a cop simply did not turn in or testify against a fellow officer.

I recalled a meeting with Lieutenant Chrockran the day my field training had ended two years earlier. I had requested that Powers receive some counselling to address his behavior before someone was hurt. He had told me then, that I had balls to walk into his office with a crap request and would be unable to prove the claim of harassment.

I remembered, for the umpteenth time, Martin Luther King's words: "Our lives begin to end the day we become silent about things that matter." But I knew I had to remain silent. So hard as it was, I did.

I left to join the on-coming shift of officers in roll call; I knew it wouldn't end in the locker room. As my stats were read, officers smirked and made demeaning comments on the number of citations I wrote, on the arrests I made, on the field interrogations and follow-ups, even for letters of appreciation the department received on my behalf, and even for the success of my special assignments.

~~*~~

A few minutes later in the black-and-white, I adjusted mirrors and checked that all equipment, limited as it was, was operable. I turned the ignition and waited for the engine to warm up. Sergeant McGibbon appeared and called out to me. I rolled down the driver-side window. He poked his head inside, almost nose-to-nose with me. He warned, "It was a good save, with those kids, but knock it off, Lambert. You make us look bad. And we don't like that."

Before stepping back and turning away, he dug in his pocket and presented me with a key. "Take this and duplicate it for entry to the back door. It's yours."

I had a fleeting moment of hope. A step closer to acceptance? But that should have been a red flag.

Had I not been giddy with the prospect of becoming one of the guys, I would have reasoned that the black-and-whites were always parked in the rear of the police station. And on the key-ring of each car was a key to the rear entrance. It would be nearly two years before Sergeant McGibbon's gift of the key would bite me in the ass.

~~*~~

On June 6, 1970, I received a letter from the sister of the deceased fire victim, Bernice Reynolds, who was gracious in her comments about my fire rescue.[39] She had two pages of signatures from neighbors who claimed, "Most of us take the services of our police and our firemen too much for granted and fail to say thank you for the many services and protection we enjoy." That letter and the signatures from the men and women of the community meant more to me than the medals. And there were many more letters to come.

On Sunday, June 7, 1970, *The Orange County Evening News*, Garden Grove, reporting the fire, began the front page coverage with a glaring half-inch headline, "Tough to Be Hero When You're a 'Nigger Cop!'"[40]

On June 8, 1970, a memorandum written by Officer Frank Rocha was read at roll call about threats made towards me. As he waited for the room to quiet down, I recalled a time when Frank and I had waited, straddling our motorcycles side-by-side. We chatted several times about me becoming a police officer before he would rev up his motorcycle to pursue a speeding offender.

Rocha had been contacted by Mr. Jones, a reliable informant, who stated he had heard on the street "that a lot of very young male and female Blacks hated Officer Lambert and that they would not hesitate to shoot him if given the chance." He further stated that a lot of the young Negro youths south of First to Edinger Streets and from Bristol west had been buying unregistered weapons, from shotguns and rifles to hand guns. Mr. Jones told Rocha he liked Officer Lambert and had known him for many years, but he feared for Lambert's safety and felt it would be better if he worked the White section of town because the people he had talked to and heard rumors about stating they were out to get him.[41]

The memorandum was for information only. "You're not dead, Lambert," Webb had advised me. No investigation was conducted regarding the threats, nor did any ranking officer discuss it with me. But this was no different from prior threats or incidents. The content was reminiscent of my visit from Bruce, an officer in the Black Panther organization, warning me to move from my home. Déjà Vu.

It wouldn't be long before I would learn that, indeed, investigations would be conducted if it served Webb and his cronies.

Fifteen officers had taken the sergeant supervisory exam in April. There were three openings, and the test scores were in. When the promotion list came out, fourteen names were on it. Officer scores were listed from one to fourteen, high to low. The top three scores were promoted - one of them the fair-haired officer who surreptitiously checked my test sheets.

I confidently read the list that had been posted but I didn't see my name on it. I read it again, but more slowly – had I skipped over it? I was in disbelief after reading it a third time - my name simply wasn't there.

I recalled Captain Tracey's hallway comment two months before, "I'm not sure why you're here. Don't count on your score and supervisor evaluations, Lambert."

There was no one I could talk with about the test or the fact my name wasn't posted. I felt screwed once again, but a grievance would be ignored, so I chose to preserve the status quo—for my own survival if nothing else.

On June 16, 1970, as a result of my rescuing the children from a house fire the previous month, *The Register*, Orange County newspaper reported, "The Santa Ana Rotary president, Chester E. Horton, along with Santa Ana Police Chief Edward J. Allen, presented Harlen D. Lambert with the '1970 Officer of the Year' award and he received the 'June 1970 Officer of the Month' plaque.[42] He also received a $50.00 check which he said he would donate to the Santa Ana Youth Fund."[43]

Later that Tuesday evening, I entered the locker room to prepare for another night on the streets. A folded piece of paper was scotch-taped to the door of my locker. I pulled it off and opened the single sheet to see a rough drawing of a rope with a knotted noose.

The semi-lit locker room was quiet, since I was the only one there at the moment. I sat hard on the bench, struggling to keep my emotions from erupting into rage. Images of the KKK card stuck in the door of our home, vandalism and midnight telephone threats, abusive language and harassment from fellow officers, threats from members of the community I served, and my fearful wife flashed through my mind.

I sensed that it was the beginning of the end, that my life as a cop would soon change forever.

~~*~~

On June 25, 1970, Lt. Chrockran prepared a citizen's complaint memo.[44] Sergeant Morrissey had received a telephone call from a male citizen claiming he had observed me for several weeks. He claimed I had been visiting a home in the southeast part of the city for thirty minutes to an hour at a time, and appeared to be "making out" with a female at the residence.

The male accuser refused to answer any questions posed to him.

Sergeant Morrissey spoke with me and I told him a childhood friend lived at the location, and I occasionally stopped by to say hello. Never for more than five minutes and always in the front yard. Morrissey verified my story – he did not post the complaint as unfounded.

I wasn't surprised since Lt. Chrockran was the same man who repeatedly delayed my progress as a rookie, saying "I want to be sure you know how to handle yourself, especially with White people on the street." Add to that excusing the harassment on my reports being returned for rewrite, "It's part of the training exercise, Lambert." Priceless, coming from a man known for his skill in passing tests—and as a performance doofus.

This was to be the first of more "investigations" to be proven false, unfounded, or misleading – and the written results hidden in the text.

~~*~~

On June 29, 1970, my wife Marie asked me for a divorce. I felt like I'd been kicked in the gut. Not that I hadn't expected it, but it sounded so final. I couldn't admit to myself then that I, too, was unhappy in this marriage. Or that I felt and still feel guilt when it comes to her and to my son because of all that happened to them. All because of me.

I suggested we get counseling before taking that final step, but Marie said, "We can try, but I can't take any more because of your job! The constant threats, the moves. I want Fernando to have as normal a life as possible. And I want it for myself, too."

~~*~~

After the July 4th holiday, I was dispatched to my son's former grade school to take a report of children throwing rocks over the playground fence, which hit cars on the street. Shortly after taking a detailed report from a middle-aged man standing next to his new Toyota with the passenger window cracked from one of the rocks, a slightly built boy, baseball and mitt tucked under his arm, approached me. "I know

Fernando."

Resting paperwork on the hood of my unit, I extended my hand to the youngster, "I think I might know you, too."

He smiled up at me, "I'm Jessie. Me and Fernando went to the third, fourth, and fifth grades together. Do you 'member me now?" Yes, I remembered Fernando's friend. It had only been three months, since, under threat, we moved out of our home. We had not informed anyone we would no longer live in the area, nor would our son continue to attend that school.

I assured Jessie I remembered him, before he rushed on breathlessly, "I 'member our teacher telling our class that Fernando's dad was a policeman. And you know what else I 'member?" Shifting his ball and mitt to his other arm, "When me and Fernando were outside playing, if Fernando heard a siren coming, he would stop playing and run and stand at the fence over there until the emergency car would pass. Sometimes he cried."

I felt a slow, but crushing, weight in my chest as I listened, and before Jessie could go on, I waved to one of the benches two youngsters had vacated, "How about we sit and you can tell me more?"

He tossed his prize possessions on the bench next to me, and stood directly in front of me, "Well, I asked Fernando why he always runs to the fence when he hears sirens, and he said he was always lookin' to see if the am'blance was for his daddy, 'cuz Fernando said he was afraid that his daddy would be hurt or killed."

Looking me square in the eyes, tears welling up in his, small hands on slender hips, Jessie said, "Fernando was my friend. We sat across from each other in our classroom. He didn't say very much and didn't want to play a lot, but he played ball with me. Then one day I came to school and Fernando's seat was empty and I didn't see him again."

Before leaving the school grounds, I threw a couple balls to Jessie, congratulating him on his skill as an up-and-coming catcher and assured Jessie that Fernando was fine and enjoying a new school in another town.

~~*~~

The mid-July day, not too hot, about seventy-five degrees with a perfect breeze lingered into the early evening as I patrolled, I thought about my dog, Zeus. We had had to put Zeus in the back yard for his safety, and although we spent time training, exercising and playing with him, I worried about his being alone so much of the time. I laughed at the image of Zeus entertaining himself by trying to catch flies and grasshoppers.

I was thinking about my dog as I turned the corner at South Diamond onto Monta Vista Avenue. A little boy sat on the curb crying. He had red hair and freckles and wore a green tee-shirt and blue jeans. He was obviously not in danger, but I was curious why this little boy was sitting all alone, bare feet crossed, and sobbing his heart out.

"Hey, little guy, what's wrong?" I asked before I had considered that this might be opening a can of worms.

He pointed to the sewer drain at the corner and wailed, "My Hot Wheels fell in the drain. It's my fav'rit car!"

"Oh, that's not good." I walked with the little redhead to the drain and looked down. "Don't worry, we'll find a way to get your car out."

Then I wondered how I was going to get down in that drain — and not get my uniform dirty. But as I looked again at the boy's trusting face, I suddenly felt the gravity of the Hot-Wheels-in-the-drain situation. I thought briefly how much Fernando loved his Matchbox muscle cars, especially the Firebird and Mustang.

I knelt down and first put my hand, then my whole arm, all the way into the drain. I maneuvered myself so that I was just barely able to touch the car, caught in a small pile of leaves and paper cups. I pressed my face against the curb, stretching enough that I was able to grab the tiny car, before backing out and up from the drain.

"I got it!" I shouted in triumph.

The little boy shrieked, "You're a policeman. I knew you could help me!" His face lit up as he reached for his model Camaro, hugging my leg as I stood.

A woman's voice called from behind a nearby fence, "Robbie. Time to come in!"

Another squeeze on my leg, and the boy, clutching his bright blue metal treasure to his chest, ran toward the voice.

As I dusted myself off, tucked in my shirt, and watched him run, I realized at that moment what my job was all about. It was all about a little red haired, freckled boy and other little ones like him.

~~*~~

The sun was bright and burning on another sultry, scorching August day. I was full of sweat and perspiration and I had the day off, but it was too hot to play basketball or exercise with Zeus, and Fernando was attending his new school.

Two months had passed since my wife had asked me for a divorce, and although we continued to live together in our new home, attempting to right things between us, little had improved. I tried to think of small ways to make her life a little easier. Amana had advertised a sale on their counter-top electronic oven (microwave). I jumped in my Pontiac with thoughts of surprising Marie and cooling off in the Montgomery Ward building.

I turned the corner from South Diamond onto West McFadden Avenue. The whoop-whoop-whoop of a siren sounded behind me. I looked into my rearview mirror and saw a winking blue siren atop a black-and-white Ford Galaxy. There were no police emblems to identify the department. The uniformed driver signaled for me to pull over.

I coasted to a stop into the Seven-Eleven parking lot and waited. The officer didn't much look like a cop as he approached my vehicle. "Sir, I stopped you for speeding. The fine for exceeding the speed limit by 10 mph is a mere $40.00. I can help you out by handling it for you right now."

This had to be a wannabe cop or a badly scripted joke.

While he was talking, I was observing the officer. He was tall and angular. His name tag read "Maldonado." An unidentifiable blue tattoo ran from his hairline down under the wrinkled collar of his uniform. Had he gotten the outfit from a costume store? He couldn't hide the massive sweat pits that decorated his shirt.

"Officer, I know you want to see my I.D. and write me a ticket." I said, "but I have to get out of my car to give you that and my money."

He motioned me out of my car—his mistake, other than not looking much like a cop. I stepped out and removed my wallet from my rear pants pocket, all the while looking straight into the man's light brown eyes.

My shield was shiny and visible as I casually flipped the wallet open, and held it close to his face. "I believe we have a problem here, Mr. Maldonado." I had him in a headlock before he could respond, and duck-walked him into the store.

I showed my badge to the counter clerk and requested he call the station and let them know there was an off-duty police officer holding a man impersonating a police officer.

While we waited for back-up, Maldonado started talking, admitting he had done this before. "But I had good intentions, man! Usually I pulled people over for speeding. That's good, right?"

I was pleased to see Officer Earl "Woolly" Wooldridge pull into the parking lot. I hadn't seen him for several months and we beamed at each other over handshakes. Slightly shorter than me, I couldn't take my eyes away from his Adams apple, which made his gray and dark brown mustache move slightly when he smiled or spoke. Like Officer Katiz, Earl Wooldridge was one of my early training officers who left a positive, indelible mark on me. Long after we had parted company, I often found myself employing his approaches and mannerisms in the field.

Almost as quickly as Officer Wooldridge got out of his vehicle, the cop wannabe was taken into custody and placed in the rear seat of the patrol unit.

Before the Ford Galaxy was towed, "Woolly" and I checked its interior for evidence. Wedged between the console and driver's seat was a plastic BB gun, a very realistic replica.

I watched the black-and-white leave the parking lot with Maldonado cuffed in the back seat, before returning to my car to make my way to Montgomery Ward.

While I was purchasing the Amana counter-top oven for my wife, Maldonado was being charged with falsely impersonating a police officer and jailed. His bond was set at $2,500.

~~*~~

I met Don Regan, through my neighbor Donald Sanders back in 1968 when I received a letter from "Attorney Don" saying, "It's not every year that I have the honor of having been elbowed, shoved and kneed, by the Policeman of the Year."[45] The Nagel, Regan & Auman attorneys played in the Santa Ana basketball industrial league. We (SAPD) had enjoyed beating the pants off those attorneys on the Santa Ana College court, and now I enjoyed his letter that made my day despite the heat on the beat.

~~*~~

The intense, energy-sapping heat continued through August into September with little respite throughout the evening and nighttime hours. I watched a senior couple walking slowly across the street, looking distressed. The cocker spaniel they walked had its tongue hanging out, panting, in an effort to keep cool. Lord, don't let one of them drop over and stick to the melting tar of the pavement.

My police radio crackled, "10-87 at Hank's Liquor." I picked up the handheld and responded, "10-87" ("I'm there").

Like all officers, I was trained to follow-up fellow officers patrolling adjoining districts. This was an added measure to assure officers were safe when making stops and/or arrests. It was common practice that my peers used minor offenses as a pretext to stop African Americans and Hispanics because they believed that these groups were more likely than others to commit crime.

Shit. I turned into the liquor store parking lot and observed my Mississippi training officer cuffing a young black man. A woman stood nearby, crying and wringing her hands.

Officer Powers said to me, "These two were out here yelling at each other. I asked the little lady if there was a problem."

The woman interrupted, "I told you we were just arguing. It wasn't anything serious!"

"Nah, looked like a drunk in public to me. You're under arrest, boy." Powers pushed the cuffed man into the back seat of his patrol car and slammed the door.

Sobbing, the woman rushed to the car, and pounded on the window. "Let him go! He didn't do anything!"

"Little lady, you back off or you're gonna join him in the back seat."

I watched the woman retreat, her eyes imploring me to intervene. As Powers entered his car, he held the door and turned to me with one last utterance, before driving away. "You know the drill, Lambert."

Yes, I knew the drill.

Each time I witnessed one of these incidents, knowing it was wrong and not based on police practices, I was not able at the time to put a name to, I was warned not to take it to the attention of my supervisor. One, it would be declared hearsay, and two, I also needed my back covered while on my own shift.

I drove away from the incident—as I had others like it—knowing the officer was wrong, and at the same time feeling like a turd because I believed I had to protect myself. I knew one day they would be caught for their wrongdoing. I also prayed that when that day came, I wouldn't be present.

~~*~~

In September of 1970 I attended the Sheriff's Department Chemical Agent Training, which was a requirement to work CSI.[46]

The following week, I pulled the patrol car to the curb on South Main Street, in front of the Sears, Roebuck Company where a middle-aged woman frantically waved her arms, wanting me to stop. She rushed to the door before I could get out.

"Help! He stole my purse!"

"Okay, calm down, and describe him to me."

"It was so fast. He came from behind me and ripped my purse right from my hand! He was my height, had on a blue cap pulled down on his ears, and blue jeans with a ripped gray tee-shirt." She pointed south, "He went that way, just a couple minutes ago!"

I notified communications of the situation, description of the suspect, and that I would attempt to locate the suspect. Three blocks away, I observed a man that fit the purse snatcher's description. With his back to me, he leaned against a palm tree, rifling through a red purse.

I got out of the black-and-white and said, "Police. Don't move. Drop the purse." I walked up to him, "Raise your hands and turn around."

The man dropped the purse and turned to face me, visibly shaking--caught in the act.

"That looks like a purse that was stolen from a shopper at Sears." I picked it up. "And the snatcher she described looks just like you. You don't mind taking a ride, do you?"

He shook his head as I cuffed him, put him in the rear seat of the patrol unit, and drove him back to the scene.

I saw the woman pacing back and forth, where she had first waved me down. I helped the alleged offender out of the car to face the victim for an ID.

The suspect dutifully eyed the victim, and blurted, "Yeah, that's the woman I robbed."

The purse and its contents were returned to her. He was arrested for robbery and escorted to jail.

~~*~~

At the beginning of my shift on October 3rd, after roll call, officers were supposed to examine their squad car for damage, check the fluid levels and tire pressure, search the backseat for contraband, inspect the first-aid kit, and ensure there were enough road flares, reports, and crime tape. The pre-operational check didn't take much time, but was important to assure operational efficiency, reduce repair costs and prevent collisions.

It didn't always happen, especially when the dispatcher had an assignment for an officer right out of the barn, as was the case when the radio crackled as I approached my assigned vehicle. I was dispatched on a Code 288 L & L (lewd and lascivious conduct) at the corner of First and Main Streets. By the time I reached the area, the deviant had disappeared. "Dispatch, 3150 (unit number). Suspect not visible. Enroute to my district."

At the end of my shift, I was fatigued. I slowly drove the patrol unit into the parking lot, with other units following me. I made a left turn at the west end - and struck a cement pillar. I got out of the squad car to inspect the damage. The water bumper, or push bumper, that was installed on the front of the vehicle to protect its front from collisions, was mangled.

"Damage to the front end of your unit would have been minor, had you checked the water bumper," chastised Sergeant Morrissey. I elected to forfeit 14 calendar vacation days in lieu of 14 days suspension without pay and be reduced to "D" bracket.

Two weeks later at 2:40 in the morning the October moon was hidden behind a cloudy sky. The air was crisp and cool at 57 degrees. The windows of my car were down as I patrolled the business complex in the 2000 block of First Street. I heard the muffled sounds of the last patrons as they left a nearby bar, slamming car doors, the occasional giggle as an ignition turned over, and the squeal of tires. In the distance, a dog barked repeatedly, before his bark ended in a lonely howl.

As I approached the exit onto First Street, a short young black male, limping on his right side, made his way across a parking lot near the closed businesses. I reached for the handheld radio and said, "31-15. Pedestrian stop at First and Raitt."

The boy pulled his too-large jacket closer around his small frame as I pulled up next to him and stopped.

He stood quietly, head down, as I said, "Good morning, young man. The complex has been burglarized recently, so I'm checking everyone in the area. Tell me your name and what you're doing out here by yourself at this time of the morning." The boy opened his jacket and spread his legs for a quick pat-down, before answering.

"Yes, sir. My name is Tom Shelton. I just left a friend's house and I'm taking a shortcut home."

"And where is home?"

"I just came to California from Mississippi and I'm staying with my cousin over on Myrtle Street."

As we talked, Officer Larry Cornelison arrived to back up my stop. I quickly told him why I made the stop. After he heard the Black, Tom Shelton, was from Mississippi, he looked from me to Tom.

Crap. This isn't going to go well. I remembered that Cornelison, along with Webb, had been charged with civil rights crimes after their vigorous tactics in pursuit of Officer Sasscer's killers in June the previous year (1969).

The officer stared at Tom for several seconds before he spoke in a guttural sound that came from the back of his throat, "Have you ever seen a nigger or coon shot?"

Tears welled up in the young man's eyes. He began to shake with uncontrollable spasms. He leaned against the police car and locked his arms around the window post that separated the front and rear passenger windows. "He's going to shoot me! He's going to shoot me!"

Trying to remain calm, I turned to Officer Cornelison, "I can handle it from here."

With a smirk, Cornelison got into his patrol car and left. I put my hand on Tom's shoulder and, after several minutes of assuring him he was safe with me, he stopped shaking and crying. But he didn't release the window post.

"Tell me what you're afraid of."

He shut his eyes, "Before I came to California me and my fifteen-year-old brother, Taylor, were walking on a dark road going home from the movies. Cops came speeding up behind us, shining their light."

Tom gulped and continued in an undertone, "We were afraid of being run over, so we ran in different directions. I heard a shot and looked over my shoulder. I saw Taylor fall. I ran into the woods and hid all night. I was afraid they'd find me and shoot me, too."

He fought back tears, saying, "I didn't know if Taylor was alive or not. I waited 'til dawn and made my way back to find him. He was dead with a gunshot wound in his back. I made my way home and told Mama what happened, and I asked her to please don't tell the police I was with Taylor when he got shot."

Tom let go of the window post and dropped to the curb, elbows on bent knees. "Mama cried and screamed, before she told me that my sister, Cicily, had been raped by two white policemen some years earlier and became pregnant from the rape. The baby died at birth. Mama never made a report on that rape, and said she wouldn't report this latest police action, because the family wouldn't be safe if she complained."

He sat silent, until I asked, "How was it you came to Santa Ana, Tom?"

"I worked long hours to save enough money for bus fare to come stay with my cousin. I've been here for about four weeks. When that cop said what he did about a coon getting shot—I couldn't help myself. I'm afraid."

My guts ached for this boy. I helped him stand, and as we shook hands my inner spirit spoke to me. I prayed that God would give Tom the strength to endure. I watched him duck his head and pull his jacket close, once again, as he cut across the lot to continue his walk home.

For three weeks I patrolled past his cousin's home on Myrtle, finally stopping by hoping to speak with Tom. His cousin told me he didn't know where Tom was—he had moved on to a destination unknown.

~~*~~

Not long after the encounter with Tom Shelton, a "complaints of police conduct" memorandum was read in roll call. Chief Allen wrote "… far too many complaints about police conduct, judgement, unprofessional responses, and unacceptable performances…" had been received, and called for corrections.[47]

I reflected on the memorandum and recalled two incidents I had observed while a reserve ride-along, and how I had learned "the drill" from a handful of officers. During that time I was to simply observe and be backup support, and not deal directly with the public unless asked to by the training officer.

Officer Dennis directed me to stand silent, as the African American male stood with feet spread, hands on the engine hood of the police car. Officer Dennis said, "Lambert, I recognize this guy as a known troublemaker. You get on the force, you'll get to know 'im, too."

When asked by the driver why he was stopped, Officer Dennis responded glibly, "What's in your car you don't want me to see?" Turning to smile at me, he went on, "You don't mind me searching your ride, do you?"

"Yeah, man, go ahead. I have nothing to hide. I'm just on my way home from work."

Not finding weapons or drugs in the vehicle and with the trunk of the Ford hiding him from the driver, Officer Dennis reached into his own front shirt pocket and pulled out a baggie of marijuana.

Closing the trunk door, he made contact with the driver. "Nothing to hide, huh? Found this in the trunk, darkie."

Over protests of innocence, Officer Dennis went through the procedure of arresting the young man.

The following night "the drill" continued. Sergeant McGibbon had a teenage Hispanic spread-eagled on the ground as he searched his clothing. He had stopped him as the teen left the corner market.

"You're going to learn how to conduct a field interrogation, Lambert." I stood next to the patrol unit. I hated this supposed training. I couldn't say anything at the time and I dared not report it.

Leaning over the young man, McGibbon pulled a baggie from his own back pocket with one hand while rolling the kid on his back.

"Look what I found in your back pocket, boy. You're under arrest for possession of drugs, kid."

Sergeant McGibbon winked at me as he cuffed the struggling teen and told me to open the rear door.

Yes, I had learned "the drill" very early. And I had sometimes felt like a turd – the most recent time was just two months before, when Powers arrested a man for doing nothing but arguing with his wife.

I reread the memorandum and the call to "…shape up, act like mature officers of the law and perform our serious duties in exemplary manner…" I was thankful, knowing it was only a handful of officers who trained new recruits in "the drill."

In mid-November Marie said she wanted to spend the year-end holidays with her sister in Chicago. Arrangements were made with the school for Fernando, now eleven, to make up three weeks of missed homework. While they were there, I talked with my son on the telephone every other day, and listened to stories about activities he shared with his cousins.

Samuel and Jackee, my old neighbors in Santa Ana, invited me to spend Thanksgiving dinner with them. It was a warm reunion with old friends. Samuel was a boxing and baseball fan. He regaled Jackee and me with a colorful account of Joe Frazier knocking out Bob Foster in two rounds for the heavyweight boxing title.

~~*~~

The Golden West College students greeted me enthusiastically on Friday, December 4th, 1970. I had been invited to join the instructor of the Law Enforcement Program and to present to the Police Community Interaction class.

The students were vocal about social change issues such as the anti-war movement, civil rights, anti-gender discrimination, and confrontational protests. We then discussed how some of the Warren Court decisions impacted police powers such as limited interrogation, evidence seizures not presented in court, and the difference between reasonable suspicion and probable cause to stop a person. Some of the Warren decisions made it nearly impossible for police to fight crime.

~~*~~

The following day, after my shift had ended, I was on my way home wearing civvies and driving my own car. I casually observed two men in a field adjacent to an auto dismantling company. I probably wouldn't have noticed them at all but for their filthy clothes and furtive actions. Then I saw tools in the taller of the men's hands as he attempted to push them inside his shirt, while the shorter man turned to re-enter the auto parts lot.

Oh, jeez, they're thieves! I pulled my car to the curb and stopped an oncoming motorist. I asked the driver to call the police department and request an officer be sent to this location.

I turned to approach the suspects, who were focused on removing parts from the interior of a damaged blue 1963 Ford. They didn't hear me come up to the vehicle. I showed my badge, asked them to come out of the car, and detained them with the show of my duty weapon. Small parts hidden under the taller man's shirt fell at his feet as he had raised his arms.

Both men sat on the ground quietly while we waited. I had made arrests at this site before – but in uniform. It was only moments before Officer Barnes arrived. I stood by as he cuffed and searched the two men, pulling out of their pockets marijuana.

Officer Barnes later wrote up a commendation relating the incident and commented, "It appears Officer Lambert's awareness is extremely commendable while off duty and he should be commended for his actions."[48]

~~*~~

Sunday, December 6th was my day off. I arrived early to find a parking space, eager to hear guest speakers California Governor Ronald Reagan and Mayor of San Francisco Joseph Alioto. They would address more than 600 attendees at the non-partisan intercollegiate conference on "The Political Outlook for California in 1970" at Santa Ana College.

As I searched for an open space, I thought back to February, when the governor visited the CSU-Fullerton campus to address the need to charge tuition. Scores of protesters booed, chanted and screamed obscenities. Reagan finally yelled "Shut up!" and walked out. A few days later, a tactical squad of 20 Fullerton police arrested two students for disrupting the speech, sparking a wave of violent demonstrations in late February and early March.

The Vietnam War protests of 1970 were the largest scale demonstration in CSUF history, reflecting the chaos of a nation in the midst of war.

I pulled into a vacant parking space and made my way inside. The Santa Ana College auditorium was packed. I scanned the area, pleased that only a handful of protestors marched outside the building and were being ignored. The speakers were warmly received by the audience. At the conclusion of their speeches, the Governor responded to questions with a mix of seriousness and humor. That day I was proud of the respect the community-at-large showed to Mayor Alioto and to Governor Reagan.

Later that month Fernando shouted into the telephone, "Dad, Mom and me are going to Louisiana for Christmas, to see Grandma and Grandpa!" They had left for Chicago before Thanksgiving and would not return home until after the New Year. We continued to talk on the telephone every other day, but I missed them at home. Our dog Zeus moped at the back door, listening for Fernando to dash out the door, ball in his hand and shouting a loud, "Here, boy! Go fetch."

On Christmas Eve, as I was getting ready to leave for work, my old neighbor Samuel, a boxing sport lover, called to tell me that Sonny Liston died at 38. "You know, Lamb, he was known for his toughness and punching power. He was fearsome! He was the 1962-64 world heavyweight boxing champion, then lost to underdog Muhammad Ali. That man had heart failure at just 38!"

As I drove through my patrol district later that evening, I thought about Ali. He had been vocal about the Vietnam War and conscription. I remembered back in 1967, after he had been drafted, he refused induction on grounds of his religious convictions.

Ali had announced, "I'm not gonna help nobody get something my Negroes don't have. If I'm gonna die, I'll die now right here fighting you, if I'm gonna die. You, my enemy. My enemies are White people, not Viet Congs or Chinese or Japanese. You, my opposer when I want

234

freedom. You, my opposer when I want justice. You, my opposer when I want equality. You won't even stand up for me in America for my religious beliefs, and you want me to go somewhere and fight, but you won't even stand up for me here at home."

~~*~~

My thoughts were interrupted as I approached West 1st and Main Streets. A lemon-colored Corvette thumped unevenly across the intersection with four flat tires. I stopped the driver and asked him if he knew his tires were flat.

In a slurred voice, he said, "Yeah, thought my car was running kinda bumpy."

"Where you coming from?" I asked.

He told me he was going home from Pepperdine School of Law (previously Orange University College of Law, acquired by Pepperdine the previous year). "I'm a teacher. We had our Christmas party, then I went with some friends out drinking."

He went on to tell me his pals brought him back to his car, where everything was locked up in the school parking lot. "I guess I must've gone out the wrong way."

"Yes," I said. "That would be over the spiked rails where a sign says, "Do not back up, may cause severe tire damage.""

I continued, "Sir, please step out of your car and show me your driver's license."

In slow motion, he staggered out, holding onto the door and fumbling to get his billfold out of his pocket. He stood unsteadily, and finally managed to open it—and dumped the contents onto the street.

"Thas all right, officer. I'll pick it up." As he bent down, he fell flat on his butt for about a minute before he vomited into his lap. Then he fell backward and passed out cold.

I called dispatch, related the situation, and requested a tow truck and an officer to escort the teacher to jail.

~~*~~

The holiday parties had begun.

Holidays were usually quiet around the police station. That's not to be confused with the streets, or the jail when celebrants were brought in. As a general rule, the administrators and most of the clerical and miscellaneous employees were gone. I had requested overtime, since my family would not be home until 1971 had rung in the New Year.

During the wee hours of my shift I encountered derelicts and winos at 4th and Bristol, and pimps, hustlers, and prostitutes in the downtown area. I kept a highly visible presence to prevent robbers, con artists, and other petty criminals from preying on the crowds that frequented the area at night.

Traffic violations and excuses to get out of a ticket were abundant. Few officers enjoyed issuing traffic citations. We understood they could be expensive, but we had seen the results of poor driving too often. It wasn't fun or pretty to see, and neither was having to tell people their loved one had died because of the actions of careless or aggressive driving, and of innocent drivers caught up in the circumstances caused by others. So officers had to balance the case for ignorance with the case for safety of the public at large.

Officers exercised discretion to issue a verbal warning instead of a written summons, often based on excuses.

I sat next to the stop sign on Willits Street at the South Raitt Street intersection. The young man lightly tapped the brakes of his Chevrolet as he passed me, and continued through the stop sign. I hit the siren and pulled him over.

The driver sheepishly admitted, "I apologize, officer. I'm in the wrong." He had no excuse and offered an apology. I issued him a verbal warning, because being genuinely sorry was almost fool-proof.

Within minutes another car failed to stop. When I pulled him over and asked him why he didn't stop, he said "I did see the stop sign, but I didn't see you, and I'm all kinds of stupid." Another verbal warning was handed out.

When I gave a verbal warning, I always said, "This one is on me. Please drive carefully and considerately. The next one is on you."

Stupid excuses or flattery, arguing, denials, and accusations that I "Should be doing real police work instead of handing out tickets" resulted in a summons.

"If it were another time, we could be friends and hang out."

"I have a cold, and when I cough, my foot mashes the pedal."

"Obviously I'm in a hurry. Can we speed things up?"

"I wasn't speeding, I was qualifying."

Attitude was one of the biggest causal factors in determining whether to issue a summons or a warning.

"How much would it take to make this disappear?"

"Met your quota? Happy now?"

"Is this really the best use of my tax dollars?"

When I gave a citation, I always said, "Please drive carefully and considerately, and have a good rest of your night."

CHAPTER TWENTY
January - June 1971

The holidays had come and gone. On Sunday, January 3rd, 1971, I waited anxiously at the Los Angeles Airport baggage area. Marie and Fernando's American flight from Chicago had landed on time. Scanning tired passengers waiting to retrieve their baggage, I heard my son call out, "Dad!" as he raced into my arms. As I hugged my wife, I felt her reserve and lack of hugging back.

We returned to our routine of school and work. Marie and I went through the motions of trying to save our marriage for the next few months. Awkward or little communication, our changing and conflicting schedules that left little time to spend together were problems we found difficult to isolate or resolve. I don't think either of us tried hard to change where and how much energy we could or would put into our marriage.

~~*~~

Bruce Hand, Golden West College instructor for the Law Enforcement Program in Huntington Beach sent a letter to Chief Allen after I had presented a program on understanding problems today's officers faced for our Police Community Interaction class in early December.[49]

That letter was read in roll call. Webb openly looked at me and sneered at the comment, "I especially appreciate Officer Lambert taking his valuable time…"

Although The Vulture was no longer my field sergeant, watching my every move, his attitude had not changed, nor had it improved.

~~*~~

The sun had begun its descent when, a week later, I was dispatched to Windsor Park. At the corner of S. Nakoma Drive and West LaVerne Avenue, a bearded youth with a shaved head sat cross-legged on the grass. He wore beads, khaki shorts and sandals. A psychedelic shirt was folded across his lap, with several clear bags dropped in the creases.

I called for backup and approached him. "Do these bags belong to you?"

He nodded, "I have left the mother house and Father Yod to find my own religion."

I pulled him to his feet, cuffed him and put him in the back seat of the patrol unit.

My back-up, Officer Ensley, and I picked up the heroin-filled baggies.

The suspect complained, "You can't arrest me! These are part of my religious duty."

"And what duty would that be?" Ensley asked.

"To care for and distribute to the sick, lost, lame, and dead members of the kingdom of heaven."

Officer Ensley took the suspect to jail, where he was booked for possession of drugs.

~~*~~

The following month, I observed a Santa Ana College student crossing the street to shop at Roberts Department Store, in the Honor Plaza at 17th and Bristol. She browsed for an hour without making a purchase.

Dispatch called me with a location and code 488 (petty theft). On arrival, the middle-aged store security officer held the girl's arm firmly. Chestnut hair concealed her face as she clutched books to her chest with her free arm. A green canvas bag lay open at her feet. Colorful scarves, a pair of white tennis shoes, and a broken bottle of perfume had spilled haphazardly from the bag. The scent of Chantilly permeated the air around us. I knew the scent, because it was Marie's favorite.

"Girl swiped these things, and I want her jailed to teach her a lesson," growled the officer.

I went through the process of arresting and placing the teenager in my black-and-white. Before I shut the door, I asked, "Why did you feel you had to shoplift from the store?"

"It was a homework assignment," she sobbed. "I was researching a term paper on kleptomania."

~~*~~

A few weeks later, I issued a traffic accident citation for a minor rear-ender on North Euclid. The husband of the violator, his wife, came into the station to file a commendation for my actions at the scene.[50] Mr. Schmidt, a former police officer, stated, "…people are taking "pot shots" at policemen and no one takes the time to thank them."

The memorandum was read in roll call. Lt. Webb couldn't contain his sarcasm, "Pretentious prick."

Always had to have the last word.

~~*~~

One early May evening when I was patrolling Raitt Street near the Monte Vista elementary school, that I heard shouts, "Officer Lambert! It's me, Jessie!"

I saw the boy, a bat slung over his small shoulder, as he motioned to me from the sidewalk. I recognized Fernando's friend from my son's previous school and pulled slowly alongside, stopped, and got out of the police car.

In unison, we had held our hands up into high-fives. "Hey, young man. What's up?"

"I'm on my way home from baseball practice and I saw you." His face was suddenly serious. "Mom and Dad said I might have to go to another school on a bus. Will Fernando have to ride a bus, too?"

So much for an eleven-year-old to be concerned about. "There's a lot of talk about new schools and where students will go, Jessie. It's a while away, and you shouldn't worry. The adults will work it out, okay? And like you, Fernando will stay where he is for now."

After some small talk, we parted with promises of getting the two boys together for a play day before the summer was over.

~~*~~

Rebuilding inner city schools had been an ongoing discussion between the Santa Ana Community Improvement Committee, the School Board, and the community.

On June 28 the *Times* reported that, according to Ruben Alvarez of the Community Improvement Committee, minority residents were unhappy with the city's plans not to rebuild. Their solution was to bus minority students to predominantly Anglo schools in outlying areas.

Alvarez said, "The people in the community feel that if they want to reach ethnic balance, why not build schools here—two or three big ones, in fact—and have children bussed to our community?"

According to Mrs. Halfrid Moore, "This is another White racist perpetuation of their ideals of equity. I feel Blacks and Browns do not want to be homogenized into suburbia." The *Times* noted Moore was responsible for raising public opinion among minority residents, despite being an "Anglo." The vote to send minority students to outlying schools had been made on June 1, and the School Board had not consulted with those who would be affected. Moore was calling for a citizen's committee. "Mrs. Moore says the plan, proposed to achieve ethnic balance, is not equitable because it involves movement in only one direction—out of the inner city."

Fernando was enrolled in Nelson Elementary School on Browning Avenue, a short three-block walk from our Tustin home. It would be weeks before Marie and I learned that all California cities must comply with state guidelines that required individual schools not to vary more than 15% in ethnic balance from the school district average. Did this mean Fernando was an at risk minority student? I made a mental note to look into the ethnic makeup of his school.

The Asian citizens did not participate in the meetings, which didn't surprise me. During my midnight patrols in the Morning Sunwood community near West Warner Avenue and South Greenfield, I never had contact with the residents. The larger Asian communities of Vietnamese immigrants were in the area of Harbor Boulevard and Hazard, which I never patrolled.

~~*~~

The day before the *Times* article was published, I was off duty, ready to exit the 405 northbound onto Avalon Boulevard. A California Highway Patrolman (CHP) on his motorcycle had stopped a vehicle in the center divider. Three weight-lift-looking males leaned against the center divider, and faced the officer, who was on his radio.

Intuitively I knew it was an enforcement stop, and that the officer was in trouble.

As I approached, within seconds one of the suspects jumped, grabbed the officer, and threw him against the center divider, feet off the ground. The other men looked on, their backs to me.

I stopped my vehicle and flashed my badge to the CHP, the only one who knew I was there. I nodded to him, put my badge into my pocket, and removed my duty weapon. I approached the men, "Hey, bro, what're you doing? You don't want to do that. Put him down!"

Again, "Hey, bro, let him go!"

All three whirled around, their eyes wide as they focused on my gun. The subject looked sheepish, as he set the officer on his feet. The CHP rushed to his motorcycle and called for help, while I continued talking to the offender. Within minutes five police officers arrived to wrap up the arrests. The subjects never knew I was a police officer.

The following day Captain G.F Goodwin from the California Highway Patrol wrote a letter to Chief Allen, "Officer Van Voorhis firmly believes that had it not been for Officer Lambert's premonition of trouble and his physical assistance, that Officer Van Voorhis might have been seriously injured if he had had to physically arrest the subject by himself." [51]

As the letter was read in roll call, the lieutenant looked agitated, but said nothing. He reminded me of a frenzied sea gull battling for a piece of bread.

CHAPTER TWENTY - ONE
July - December 1971

The late July evening was humid as I patrolled. I saw an older model pickup truck moving at a turtle's pace erratically from one lane to the other on West Seventeenth. Before stopping the truck, I notified dispatch with the license number and our location. I pulled my vehicle to the curb, bumping up over the curb myself and knew right away that I had some tire damage I would have to report.

The driver, a thick-necked Hispanic male, hung onto the steering wheel as he slowly put one leg out to rest on the running board, and his short-legged body seemed to follow in a rush. I approached him as he placed his hands on the hood of his truck, assuming the position without being told to do so. I could see his droopy eyes were bloodshot and the smell of alcohol was overwhelming.

"Sir, what are you doing?"

He looked up at me with a goofy smile, "Yep, I been drinkin' and you're gonna arrest me, so I'm gettin' ready."

He obviously knew the drill, so I accommodated him with a field sobriety test, which he failed miserably. I then cuffed him and arrested him for driving under the influence. Before leaving the area, I called for a tow truck to impound the pickup for safekeeping.

At 10:45 p.m. I observed a vehicle with headlights off, driving northbound at a high rate of speed in the 400 block of South Raitt. I immediately followed for three blocks, clocking its speed at 62 miles per hour in a posted 30 miles per hour zone.

I stopped the car at First and Raitt. I approached and made contact with the driver, a young blonde with shoulder length hair, fully made up face, and expensive evening attire pulled tight and low over large breasts.

"Miss, may I see your driver's license?"

Her bright pink manicured nails matched her lipstick. The license identified her as Emmy Lou Adair, who asked, "Are you going to give me a ticket?"

"Yes, Miss Adair. Not only were you driving 32 miles over the speed limit, but you were driving with your headlights off."

"Maybe we can work something out."

She then slipped her gown strap down, released one breast out of her bra and holding it, said, "See! You don't have to give me a ticket."

"Miss, let's keep this official, please." I walked to the rear of the police car and finished writing the citation.

When I returned to her vehicle, the top of her gown was down around her waist and both of her considerable assets were exposed. "This isn't hard for you to figure out now, is it, Officer?"

"No, ma'am, it's not very hard for me to figure out."

I pointed to the signature line. "Please sign the citation here."

The coy, quiet-spoken young lady suddenly became loud and aggressive, "You're just what my friends say about you." Miss Adair pulled her gown up, pushed her breasts back into their proper places, jerked the ticket book from my hand, signed it, and had the last word, "You're an Uncle Tom—a white man's nigger."

I tore the violator's copy of the citation off and handed it to her, "Thank you, and you have a safe evening, Miss."

Jesus, I thought as I got into my patrol car, thank you for helping me get through this without making a fool of myself.

~~*~~

On September 15th police presence had been requested at the Santa Ana High School on West Walnut Street. I parked the patrol unit and made my way to the auditorium, where 250 Santa Ana residents waited for the School Board President, Charles Paskerian, to discuss the city's plan for bussing which was scheduled to start in 1972.

Groans could be heard when Paskerian announced all California cities must comply with state guidelines that required individual schools not vary more than 15% in ethnic balance from the school district average. An estimated 1,700 students would be bussed to meet the requirement.

One attendee, Mrs. Mary Pryor, said, "Telling a child he must go to a certain school because he's Black is depriving him of his civil rights. We've formed a group to follow this and other points of law to their ultimate conclusion!"

Shouts of agreement from Hispanics and Blacks reverberated throughout the auditorium, as the School Board President brought the room to order. Once again, the Asian citizens did not attend.

Paskerian and the School Board members encouraged parents to volunteer their children to be part of the bussing program, while the Santa Ana Junior Chamber of Commerce and the Santa Ana-Tustin-Orange Board of Realtors urged the Board to rescind or delay its decision.

The meeting ended without incident, and I continued on my patrol route full of routine speeding stops.

~~*~~

Marie and I had struggled for fifteen months to hold our marriage together. Ever mindful of officer safety, I had become hyper-vigilant, emotionally detached, and even cynical about protecting and shielding myself and my family from the hostilities encountered daily. Coming home, I couldn't turn off the vigilance, let go of the cynicism and connect positively with my wife.

We had rolled up our sleeves to fight for our marriage, but with our stressful experiences of shift work, sleep deprivation, days and holidays apart – we questioned being together at all.

It was easier to bail, so I just moved out.

In October of 1971 I made my fourth move in three years. But this time without my family. I moved into a two-bedroom apartment in the city of Tustin, not far from the last home we had shared. Separate living arrangements, furnishings and another car were required. It didn't take me long to realize that a cop's salary wasn't enough.

~~*~~

Within a month I had purchased a food and vending machine business to supplement my officer's salary. The machines were set up in a variety of business locations in Santa Ana and proved to be lucrative.

Before my shift, I routinely went to the vending machines to clean them, fill them, withdraw the money, and place it in bags, which I then put in the glove compartment of my car.

After my shift ended I went home, wrapped the money and

delivered it to the night deposit.

I couldn't know then one day when I did not go directly home after my shift ended, the bags of money in my vehicle's glove compartment would prove to be a nearly fatal mistake.

~~*~~

One morning in November, the bank notified me that Marie had been writing checks on an overdrawn account. It was my day to spend with Fernando and as I waited for him to finish his bath and dress, I asked Marie to join me in the kitchen. I told her about the call from the bank.

"You sonofabitch," she snapped. "You have more money than you're telling me and you just don't want me to have it. I'll spend whatever I want and you'll pay for it!" She turned on her heel and started up the stairs to the bathroom to check on Fernando.

I started up the stairs, too, to gather up remaining clothing left in the master bedroom closet. Marie came out of the bathroom and stood at the top of the stairs, and yelled, "You're not coming up here!" She raised her leg and kicked at me. In defense, I pushed her away from me. Marie darted into the bedroom and called the Tustin police. I waited for the officers to arrive, write their report, and leave.

Before long, Fernando rushed outside to where I waited. Marie shouted, "You want your crap? Here it is!" She threw an armful of shirts onto the ground. I heard the bedroom door slam.

Fernando screwed his eyes shut and stood rigid as I picked up the clothes. My eyes welled up. I felt inconsequential in front of my son. We entered my car in silence. Sounds of weekend lawn mowers, laughing children, and a piano tinkling made me even sadder. There was happiness out there, but not with us.

~~*~~

That evening, after a day of McDonald's hamburgers, playing ball with Zeus, and television episodes of "Here's Lucy" and "Beverly Hillbillies," I returned Fernando to Marie's care. She opened the door as we drove into the driveway, and shouted, "Don't mind walking him up here!"

I hugged my son and watched him move around his mother before she slammed the door shut for the second time that day.

246

~~*~~

Two days later, Lieutenant Garrison called me into his office and relayed a message from Lieutenant Chrockran that he had had a telephone conversation with my ex-wife. Lieutenant Garrison wrote a "Possible misconduct by Officer Harlen D. Lambert" memorandum for my file.[52] He noted that I had been counseled and that I would comply with Marie's wishes not to bother her any more.

Lieutenant Doug Garrison and I were on a first name basis when in private. Doug was the coach of the SAPD basketball team on which I practiced weekly, and sometimes played when in competition with other teams. Doug and his wife, Bonnie, were frequent visitors in our home before Marie and I moved to Tustin Meadows. After our move, with the rising tension between my wife and me, I had simply stopped inviting people to our home.

Doug motioned me to close the door and have a seat. "I'm sorry to hear about you and Marie. I know things are rough, Harlen, but hang in there, buddy." In an attempt to be positive, he said, "Keep those jump shots coming, man! See you back on the court."

I appreciated his support, unaware that within six months the relationship between Doug and I would become a thing of the past.

~~*~~

On November 17th at 2:50 a.m. I was patrolling northbound in the 500 block of South Main. I used my spotlight to illuminate doors and windows of the businesses in the area.

Concentrating on the view out of my left window, I inadvertently steered to the right—up a driveway into a light standard. The pole sustained no damage, but the front bumper and grill work took a moderate hit. This offense was cited as negligent operation of a police vehicle – and I was suspended from duty for five working days, without pay.[53] This wasn't done with white officers.

As I made my way home, I thought about the officers who had been in drunken driving accidents and covered it up, and about officers I witnessed planting drugs or intimidating minorities. Nothing was done to them. The officers who repeatedly hurled racial slurs at me inside the police locker room were never reprimanded. And, oh yeah, how about the officer who choked a teenager already in handcuffs. Not a thing. Or the police officer who cheated on his wife, or tomcatted, while on the job. Nothing. Zero. Zilch!

I remembered what LAPD Officer Bennie Wilkey had said to me, "Carry yourself and do your job in such a way that you communicate to the worst of the Whites you are an officer above reproach." I repeated this to myself, now eventually becoming calm.

~~*~~

The circumstances of a week from work weren't ideal, but I took advantage of the free time. My dog Zeus had moved with me to the ground-floor apartment. School was out for the Thanksgiving holidays, and I arranged for Fernando to stay with me for the week.

During the day Fernando, Zeus, and I spent time at neighborhood parks playing ball and training the dog. In the evenings, Fernando and I flipped a coin—dinner at home or his favorite treat—McDonalds. I ate a lot of hamburgers and French fries. One night we drove to the Orange Drive-in movie theater on State College Boulevard, attached the voice box to the rolled down car window, ate buttered popcorn, drank coke, and laughed during the showing of Willy Wonka & the Chocolate Factory.

Fernando wanted to go back the following night to see Dirty Harry with Clint Eastwood, but I didn't want him exposed to that kind of action. So, we spent our last day together at Disneyland. After paying $3.50 for my ticket, and half of that for Fernando's, we enjoyed several theme park rides ranging from ten to ninety cents, before heading to the New Orleans Square for food and my son's favorite ride—Pirates of the Caribbean.

Later that night, when I took Fernando home, Marie announced that she was taking our son to Chicago the following day to celebrate the Christmas and New Year holidays with her family. Tears in his eyes, Fernando said, "Daddy, come with us!"

I tried not to sound tone weary, but cheerful, as I hugged him hard, "I can't, son, but we'll talk on the phone every day, just like last year. And I bet your cousins are waiting to see you—just like I will be waiting when you and Mom get back!"

~~*~~

Three days later, after an uneventful night shift, I parked the black-and-white in its assigned space, gathered my gear, and turned the corner of the building to make my way to the front of the police station.

"Hey, Lambert, wait up!" Sergeant McGibbon trotted toward me. "You passed the back door, man. Come on back with me. Where's the key I gave you?"

"I'm embarrassed to confess I must have lost or misplaced it, Sergeant." I followed him through the rear door, and we walked to the locker room together.

"Well, the units all have the building key on the ring, so just make a copy and don't worry about it."

It would be three months before I would remember the sergeant had given me permission to duplicate a key to the rear door of the police building.

A week before Christmas I was assigned a civilian ride-along. As we walked to the patrol unit to begin our night on the streets, twenty-one-year-old Jeffrey said he was a Santa Ana College student studying criminal justice and was interested in a future career in law enforcement. Jeffrey had sun-bleached hair and was athletic. "In my free time I ride the surf and scuba dive. I also teach scuba lessons at Huntington Beach on weekends. That's how I pay for college. I live at home with my folks, not far from the campus."

I unlocked the car and Jeffrey tossed his blue backpack in the trunk, before he settled into the passenger seat. As we pulled out of the garage, I reviewed the standard ride-along arrangement that I had adopted from Officer Katiz. I remembered his friendliness, safety precautions, and observations when I had sat in the passenger seat on my long ago ride-along.

At that moment the radio crackled, and we were dispatched to the Alpha Beta grocery on Tustin Avenue where a suspected shoplifter was being held. Within minutes, we learned the accused, identified as Mr. Grabbard, was a single father who had fallen on hard times and was stealing formula for his three-month-old baby who lay in a shabby stroller next to him. Grabbard's face was lean and haggard; his clothing was too large, and the soles of his shoes flapped when he moved.

Terry, the store's grizzly loss prevention officer did not want to press charges. I asked him to keep the man and baby in the office for a few minutes longer, and motioned my ride-along to follow me. "This is a situation where the officer makes a judgement call, Jeffrey. Citing Mr. Grabbard for court won't do any good. He's already short on money and can't afford formula, so making him appear in court—he still won't have any food for that baby."

I thought, what if this were my son and me in this situation? There was just one thing to do. Jeffrey and I locked eyes, and he said, "Can I get my backpack out of the car? I think I have something in there that will help."

We entered the store a second time, and as I went to the baby aisle to buy formula, Jeffrey waited for my return. A pair of new tennis shoes dangled from his hands. The loss prevention officer left us alone with Mr. Grabbard. Along with the formula and shoes, we gave the desperate father names of people and organizations that could help him.

As we opened the door to leave, Terry arrived with a brown paper bag full of milk, cereal, fruit, and a receipt for a grocery credit of one hundred dollars. He laid the sack on the bottom rack of the stroller. Tears welled as he said, "Merry Christmas, Mr. Grabbard. Take good care of that baby." Terry looked at Jeffrey and me and added, "I'm going off-duty now, so I'll see these two home."

We were quiet, deep in our own thoughts, as we made our way to the black-and-white. Suddenly Jeffrey pronounced, "Yes. I'm definitely going to become a police officer."

I knew then that my career as a police officer was careening in the opposite direction—downhill.

HARLEN "Lamb" LAMBERT

PART FOUR
GONE TO THE DOGS

What we call the beginning is often the end.
And to make an end is to make a beginning.
The end is where we start from.

T. S. ELIOT

CHAPTER TWENTY - TWO
December 1971

The following Monday, five days before Christmas, I woke early. I had several hours of time free before I had to report for duty. After a quick shower, a turkey and provolone sandwich chased with a tall glass of ice-cold water, and a telephone call with my son, Zeus and I set out for a run. We jogged along Red Hill Avenue. At the moment we turned onto the Sycamore Avenue entrance into Tustin Centennial Park, I heard Chuck Minsky's raspy voice shout, "Harlen! Over here!"

Chuck, his signature beard clipped like the jack of spades, smiled widely and waved. Zeus and I waited as he crossed the street, tugging along a muscular, hefty, bulldog with a wrinkled face and distinctive pushed-in nose.

After small talk and introducing the two dogs, which were soon play growling and biting each other's faces and legs, Chuck said, "That's a great dog you have there. You know, we've been having parts thefts at the RV (recreational vehicle) lot, and we can't catch the guys ripping us off. Other local businessmen and I have met and are thinking about some kind of night-time security."

Chuck pulled on his dog's leash, yanking him from Zeus's behind, and exclaimed, "T-Bone! Stop that!" He turned back to me, "Maybe dogs are the answer. Would you be willing to leave Zeus in the yard overnight as a deterrent? Of course, we'd pay you for the service."

The question took me by surprise. Chuck was the lead sales manager at an RV lot located on North Harbor. The police department at large, and I had been aware that a number of businesses ranging from fenced-in heavy equipment yards, service stations, and manufacturing plants, to car dealerships had been subjected to overnight burglaries. The trespassers had not been caught.

"I need time to think this through, Chuck. What I do know is that any dog put in as overnight security must be trained for the job. Zeus is my son's dog and trained to protect him, not unknown property, so I can't help you out there. Give me a couple days, and we'll talk more about this."

Happy coincidences? I thought about two telephone conversations from just the previous afternoon.

The first call was from Mr. Percy, a seventy-two-year-old trainer who lived in Hemet. He had a four-bedroom home for sale and acreage with kennels and twelve guard dogs contracted with several Riverside car dealerships. With my dog in the back seat, I had driven a friend to a Riverside car dealer two weeks before, to pick up his new Oldsmobile.

While there, I observed a flat-bed truck with two rows of five kennels. A rail thin man with bushy eyebrows of white steel wool, opened a kennel door. He ordered the Doberman Pinscher to "stay" as he affixed a leash to his pinch collar before the dog jumped to the ground and was led behind the sales offices into a car lot. I heard the gates close and lock with a loud metallic sound.

I had taken Zeus out of my car to pee. I approached the man as he returned to his truck. He introduced himself as Percy and we struck up a conversation about his dogs, his business, and dogs in general. "I'm getting up in years and ready to retire," he said. "I'll be putting my home and business on the market in the next week or so. I'll give you a call in case you know someone who might be interested."

Maybe dogs are the answer because I was definitely interested

The second call came from my sister Dorethea (Doe) and her husband, Lewis. They lived in Oakland but Lewis found it difficult to find continued employment there. They had called asking if they could stay with me in Santa Ana while Doe looked into a nursing degree program and Lewis looked for work. They planned to arrive in Santa Ana before the New Year.

~~*~~

Over the next few days, I thought about Mr. Percy, his dogs, night-time security, and the opportunity for additional income. The following week was a whirlwind of activity, and by Tuesday, December 28, 1971, I had met with local businessmen ready to sign on the dotted line for night-time dog security. I also acquired Percy's home, his dog business, and made an offer of employment to my brother-in-law.

Doe and Lewis moved into the home in Hemet, and provided dogs to the ten Riverside car dealerships already under contract. I had purchased a Toyota truck and had it modified to transport twelve dogs—Doberman pinchers, German Shepherds, and two Saint Bernards—from the kennel to the job sites and back. Lewis maintained the upkeep of the dogs and the kennels, and Doe assisted in the bookkeeping. I drove to Hemet once a week on my day off to help with whatever needs arose. That took care of Riverside.

In my free time during the next few weeks, I leased an acre of vacant land at South Main Street and Sunflower Avenue, purchased a second Toyota truck, relocated a used, one bedroom trailer on the lot, and purchased fourteen German Shepherds and kennels from a dog trainer in Tijuana, Mexico.

And this was the beginning of the first canine security company in Orange County.

~~*~~

I hired Ernie, a Vietnam Army veteran, to stay six days a week to clean the kennels, feed and water the dogs, and to assist John Davis who I had also hired for preparing the dogs for delivery to their nighttime jobs of securing a variety of Santa Ana businesses.

Ernie was sturdy, his compact body clothed in a dust-streaked plaid shirt and faded Levis. He had answered my ad in Santa Ana's *Pacific Clipping*s newspaper for an on-site kennel keeper. Ernie had handled dogs in the Army, and in a calm voice told me, "I'd rather be with dogs than men."

While serving in Vietnam, Ernie had become friends with a few of the marines. Within a couple weeks, canine handlers from the El Toro Marine Base started training their sentry and attack dogs at the Orange County Kennel site on weekends. They also volunteered in maintaining the training for our guard dogs and were often extra hands when needed.

~~*~~

On rare occasions Ernie spoke about his time in Vietnam. "It was wrong, bein' there. The wrong war! No honor in what we did!" It was after these outbursts I felt Ernie was being held together with the emotional equivalent of Scotch tape, but he remained intact.

I had met John Davis, owner of a janitorial service, while I was on patrol one evening several weeks before. Standing at the sidewalk entrance of the Bristol Drug Company on West 4th Street at 1:30 am, he had motioned me to a stop, pointing to an old hippie vagrant with gray hair and a green and brown army surplus bag strapped to his back. The old man tagged behind John, begging for money.

The panhandler saw me emerge from the squad car, its blue lights twirling quietly. He took off. We heard his shoes slap-slap the sidewalk as he disappeared around the corner on Bristol.

John and I chatted for a few minutes, and he told me the different businesses he and his wife Lenore cleaned throughout the nighttime hours. Somehow dogs entered into our conversation. He had a German Shepherd the same age as Zeus, and we laughed as we shared our dog's antics.

"You know, Harlen, that's a part-time job I'd like to explore one day. Don't know doing what with dogs, but something."

It would be two months before I remembered chunky, square-faced John's wistful comment. What a stroke of luck! We had contracts with twelve of the same businesses, and his work hours aligned with the night-time drop of the dogs. Lenore drove her husband John to the kennel facility, where he picked up the loaded truck and delivered the dogs. He then returned the truck to the lot, where Lenore waited in their station wagon.

Ernie picked up the dogs in the mornings and returned them to their kennels. I frequently drove to the facility after my graveyard shift to help Ernie pick up the dogs, put out water and food, and review paperwork or pay bills.

~~*~~

I often solicited business. Chuck Minsky, who owned the vehicle parts store, signed the contract, and boosted himself from behind his desk. He handed the paperwork to me, and announced to the room of salesmen, "I want the biggest, baddest dog you have. We don't want any more prowlers stealing expensive parts out of this lot!"

I had three dogs to choose from, all residing in Hemet. Toby, the Doberman pinscher, was quick and ferocious-looking, while the two Saint Bernards, Bella and Beasty, appeared docile, but understood guarding against intruders.

Later that day, after my phone call, Lewis delivered Bella to the Santa Ana kennels. Before closing time that evening, John placed water inside the North Harbor RV lot as Bella jumped from the truck kennel. The dog stretched, sniffed the air, and walked toward the gate, where she would spend the next eight hours. I released her with the command, "Bella, wander and watch!"

I locked and chained the gates behind me, and turned to where a group of salesmen stood in a single line. Laughter erupted, as they looked at the laid-back dog, now taking pleasure in rubbing her neck on the steel fencing. Chuck Minsky declared gruffly, "Harlen, I wanted a bad-ass dog, not a bone and bark fur ball!"

"Chuck, walk to the fence quietly." I motioned for the men to be silent as Chuck swaggered to the fence, playing to the salesmen as they waited behind him.

The dog was intent as she watched Chuck approach, one of her forelegs doubled up. We heard a vibrating growl deep in Bella's chest. Canine teeth uncovered, ears pressed close backwards on her head, 260 pounds of bone and fur slammed against the fence, ropes of slobber hitting the steel links that vibrated along the length. Instantly, Chuck and the salesmen recoiled.

No longer showing off, Chuck asked, "What if I call her name and tell her no?"

"She's trained to respond to her handlers only—and that's why your lot is now protected with one of the biggest, baddest dogs we have."

~~*~~

Working on a part-time basis we soon had fifty-five dogs throughout Orange and Riverside Counties for four years. I was blessed with family, friends, and workers that could be trusted with the business while I continued to work as a police officer.

I had had no hint that a chance meeting on a quiet Friday afternoon would begin a chain of events that one day would change my life's work forever.

CHAPTER TWENTY - THREE
January - June 1972

The second week of January 1972, Chief Allen granted me permission to attend advanced officer training at Golden West College in Huntington Beach. The training consisted of updated arrest and control tactics, drug overview, and field training officer and firearms updates.

I knew the bonus training would be helpful to me in the field, and I was hopeful fellow officers would appreciate my efforts. On January 14th I completed the course, and during a late afternoon briefing at the station, I received the Certificates of Completion for Advanced Officer Training from the State of California and Golden West College.[54] Officer Powers and now-Sergeant Webb shoved back their chairs and stood. Webb muttered in irritation, "What Lambert needs is a bust in the head."

Shortly after that the briefing was over. I made my way with other officers to our assigned patrol units. Powers and Webb dogged me like their own shadows. Webb leaned on the trunk of a unit parked next to mine. As I opened the door, he said to Powers, "You know, turds roll downhill in threes."

They enjoyed a laugh over the wisecrack, while I wondered why Webb no longer held the rank of lieutenant. Had someone complained about the weekend swap meet finds he brought to the station for display and sale from his assigned desk? Or did one of his apartment building renters file a complaint about his method of collecting the rent? Oh yeah, or did his wife find out about his frequent "trips" to converse with Mrs. Hunter, sans laundry for dry cleaning?

It wouldn't be long before I realized the turds were rolling my way.

~~*~~

On January 22nd a complaint was lodged against Officer Dan McCoy and me. Mrs. Teresa Wild had complained about a loud television in the next door home of Mr. Laginess, who became belligerent and argumentative when we contacted him.[55]

When I arrived as backup to Officer McCoy, he had suggested Mr. Laginess move his television set from the living room to his bedroom, where the neighbor would not be able to hear it. "No, damn it! I just put in a permanent ventilating fan in the window and I can't close it. The bitch can deal with it."

"Sir, we're not going to stand here and argue with you. If you will calm down and listen to Officer McCoy, there's a simple solution. Otherwise, you're subject to being taken in for causing a disturbance."

"Then I'll get a damn attorney, after I talk to your boss!" The homeowner picked up his telephone and dialed the police department. Mr. Laginess contacted Captain Tracey and shouted that he was upset with the suggestions made to him by the two officers. McCoy and I waited. Mr. Laginess listened, and shortly exclaimed, "Yes, I'm upset. This should be a civil matter, and the police shouldn't even be here." He listened another few minutes, looked at us, and said, "The officers have been polite and gentlemanly. But this isn't over. You can bet on it."

Mr. Laginess withdrew his complaint. The complaint was recorded as unfounded. Captain Tracey later reviewed the Daily Officer's Log, and determined my log time did not coincide with that of Officer McCoy, so I was warned to be more careful in the future about logging entries.

As I reviewed my copy of the memorandum, I remembered that in 1967 Tracey had stood in the hallway, arms crossed, and questioned, "Have you given some thought to resigning? Maybe this job is too much for you. Maybe it's not for you." And later, when I took the supervisory exam, Captain Tracey taunted, "I'm not sure why you're here, Lambert. Don't count on your score and supervisor's evaluations."

Turd one.

I wondered what would come next—and I didn't have long to wait.

On February 19th, Sergeant Hindman, Officer Simmers and I were dispatched on a code 415 call (disturbance – investigate the trouble).[56] When we arrived at the home on South Bristol, Mr. Beasock reported his eleven-year-old daughter, while riding her bike from the park, had been struck by a vehicle. The girl fell off the bike and now her back hurt.

We asked the daughter, Linda, for details about the accident before arranging for an ambulance to take her to Tustin Emergency Hospital. When the ambulance arrived, Mrs. Beasock entered the vehicle to accompany her daughter. Mr. Beasock asked to ride with his daughter too, but the ambulance attendant said they could not transport him. They allowed only one person other than the patient.

Mr. Beasock, already upset, turned to Sergeant Hindman, and commanded that the police follow the ambulance and take him to the hospital. The sergeant said, "Sir, we can escort only in an emergency situation. You will need to drive yourself to the hospital."

All of a sudden, Beasock became aggressive and vulgar. "Then what the f--- are you good for, you bastards." He rushed at the three of us. The sergeant put Beasock in a choke-hold, while I handcuffed the man. Officer Simmers placed the combative father under arrest for disturbing the peace, and transported him to jail.

The following day, the Acting Watch Commander, Sergeant M. J. Smith, received a call from the Tustin Emergency Hospital, advising that Mr. Robert Beasock was in the emergency room seeking medical attention.

On the Sergeant's arrival at the hospital, Mr. Beasock made a formal complaint against three officers who he said physically assaulted him the previous day, for no reason. He claimed the officers were sarcastic and abusive, that he was suddenly attacked by "The black officer wearing black gloves," and that the other two officers "Jumped in and beat on me" before Beasock was transported to Orange County Jail and booked.

He stated he later went to the hospital with complaints of being unable to speak due to being choked and beat on, and that his left arm was hurt and useless. Later, Mr. Beasock's wife and nephew were asked to come to the station to make a written statement. At her husband's direction, Mrs. Beasock wrote in long-hand the offenses that "the colored officer" committed against her husband.

Asked about his hospitalization, Mr. Beasock stated the medics could find no injury but did give him medication for pain.

A week later, Mr. Beasock withdrew his complaint against the officers. Further discussion with the accuser and review of the written statements revealed numerous discrepancies. Later, the complainant admitted that he had used some vulgar language and "...had challenged the officers to remove their badges and see who the best man was."

Turd two.

On February 26th Sergeant Smith recorded the complaint as unfounded.[57]

~~*~~

The first Thursday morning in March, I was on patrol on North Harbor Boulevard. At 2:00 a.m. and the bars were closing. As I passed the Alamo Bar, I noticed a man leaving the bar so intoxicated that he could barely walk. I pulled the patrol unit to the curb to observe him. He stumbled around the parking lot for a few minutes. He tried his keys on a number of different vehicles before he managed to find his truck and fall into it. The man sat there for a few minutes as a number of other patrons left the bar and drove off.

Finally, the man started the engine, switched the wipers on and off, flicked the blinkers on and off a couple times, honked the horn, and then switched on the lights. He moved the vehicle forward a few inches, reversed a little, and then remained still for a few more minutes. More patrons left the bar and drove away. When his was the only car left in the parking lot, he pulled out and drove slowly onto Harbor.

I had waited patiently, but now started up the black-and-white, put on the flashing lights and pulled the man over to administer field sobriety tests. He performed each test without pause, indicating no evidence that he had consumed any alcohol at all.

Astonished, I said, "I'll have to ask you to accompany me to the police station, where you will test on the breathalyzer equipment to confirm my findings."

The man countered with a grin, "I seriously doubt it. Tonight I'm the designated decoy."

At that moment the car radio announced a code 415c (Disturbance – children involved) on West Townsend at the home of Hedda Schneider.

"Dispatch 10-4." The eighty-year-old spinster was one of our "regular" callers. When Hedda forgot to take her medicine, she hallucinated and saw young children in her house. She would call us to report the kids were making noise and moving her belongings around. I had been to her house several times for these calls, but this time was different.

As we sat at her dining room table talking, she soon became annoyed with me, because she could "see" the rowdy children but I couldn't. She looked at me with concern, and chided, "You can't see him? He's been staring at you for five minutes now and smirking." Hedda pointed to a spot about three feet behind me. For the first time on one of my "visits" to her home, I felt a surreal mix of fact and fantasy that raised

262

the hair on my arms.

~~*~~

Two weeks later, on March 16th, Sergeant McGibbon walked into the locker room ten minutes after me. I heard the chinking of keys as he entered, and with a nod in my direction, he opened his locker. We had just finished our shift, and I continued to change into my civilian clothes. I closed my locker and palmed the keys to my apartment before leaving the room. As I left, I didn't see the sergeant put keys on the bench.

Later that night, before my graveyard shift started, I was called into Lieutenant Palmer's office, who told me keys had been found in the locker room and given to Captain Tracey. The watch commander found me in violation of Department Rules and Regulations – possessing a key that had been removed from unit 3180, with the intent to duplicate the key, without permission, to open the rear door of the police building.[58] He also presented me with a key to an apartment complex swimming pool, with "do not duplicate" stamped on it. I told the lieutenant the complex I lived in did not have a pool and that the key did not belong to me.

I recalled how I had come by the first key to the rear door of the police station in June, 1970. I was giddy with a feeling of acceptance when Sergeant McGibbon presented me with a key to the rear door of the police department and told me to keep it. I had misplaced or lost the key, and thought no more about the "gift."

Just three months earlier, Sergeant McGibbon had stopped me at the end of a shift and had given me permission to duplicate a unit key to the rear door of the police building.

I thought about telling the lieutenant that I had had permission from a superior officer to duplicate the key. But I knew that complaining or explaining that I'd been set up was not in my best interest——it was an unspoken rule that police officers didn't rat out a fellow officer.

The violation cost me 16 hours of accumulated overtime in lieu of 16 hours without pay.

Turd three.

Sergeant McGibbon shrugged, picked up his gear, and headed out of the locker room ahead of me.

If this latest incident was a sign of things to come, I was in deep trouble.

~~*~~

On a Saturday early in April, I was training dogs with two El Toro marines. I had just kenneled Fritz, a ninety-four pound German Shepherd, when I heard the familiar voice of Maury Beam, a staff writer for *The Orange County Register*, shout a greeting from his dark blue Chevelle, parked alongside the row of kennels. "Very impressive, Harlen! I'd heard about you training Saint Bernards, and I'm hopeful you'll give me a few minutes to talk about them."

While he grabbed his note pad and camera, I removed Beasty from his kennel. Jaime, one of the marine handlers and I took the Saint Bernard through routine training steps, while Maury snapped photos of the session. Once completed, I gave Beasty a "friend" command, and spoke with the writer while Maury petted and cooed to the massive canine.

Four days later, on April 19th, Maury Beam published an article titled "Image of Docile, Peaceful St. Bernards" in the Pacific Clippings section of the *Daily Register*, along with a photo titled "Who says St. Bernards can't be mean? Here 250-pounder is restrained from attack."[59]

I was pleased with the article because it brought attention to my growing business, and the value of protection without weapons.

~~*~~

While on patrol later in the month, I had finished writing up a minor vehicle incident and was settled behind the wheel of my patrol unit, parked under the shade of a tree to finish writing my field report. I heard the small group of young people before I saw them. They advanced to the driver side of the car like little soldiers—with a mission in mind. The tallest of the cluster, a blonde girl, with shoulder length hair, said in earnest, "Officer Lamb, I told these guys you would have an answer to my question!"

I recognized teenager, Carly, and her companions, and after a round of "high-fives" I said, "I don't always have the answers, but let's give it a try. What's the question?"

Just then, Maury Beam honked his car horn and stopped. "Hey, this is great! I didn't expect to see you. But, Harlen, have you a few minutes? And kids, wanna have a real interview and be in the newspaper?"

264

The youths clapped their hands, and chattered excitedly as Maury joined the group with not only a pad and pen, but a camera. Maury snapped photos as the kids asked questions and I did my best to answer them, as we stood next to the black-and-white.

Soon, the minors headed home, and Maury began asking me the tough questions. "Harlen, I'd like to follow up with how it's going for you—what it's like enforcing the law in a community of some 12,000 Blacks in a sea of 158,000 Whites and Browns."

We spoke on a range of topics, from slang usage to my social life to the million questions kids have, to the manuscript I had started writing for a book.

On April 28, 1972, *The Orange County Register* published the article "SA Policeman Pens Racial View of

OC," with a photo of me speaking with the students and the photo tagline "Person-To-Person" is Theme of First Negro Officer in Santa Ana.[60] The article provoked some officers, as the reporter had highlighted our discussion about the book I had begun writing.

As I read the article, I knew the book title "Nigger Pig" would inflame some. The word "nigger" was slang, while "pig," applied to police officers, was a dirty word—unless it meant what policemen said the letters stood for: pride, integrity, and guts. I had no problem saying it as I knew it and lived it every day.

~~*~~

Back in November 1971, soon after I had purchased those food and drink vending machines, I had also purchased a new 1972 Cadillac. During my work shift I parked my car in the yard designated for police officers' personal vehicles—I ignored the occasional smart-aleck comments about my cream Cadillac. It had been my routine that before my shift, I go to the vending machines, withdraw the money, place it in bags, and then put them in my glove compartment, to go home, wrap, and then deliver the coins to the night deposit.

The first week in May, I drove through the City of Orange on the way to visit a friend after a full day—my head clear and relaxed for a change. That is to say, most of the problems I was facing were pushed to one side for a while. It was a balmy evening, one of those incredibly soft, southern good-gracious-the-Chamber-of-Commerce-was-right evenings. The kind of evening a man from the frozen sidewalks of Chicago's west side falls in love with, and makes him feel that he has really gotten himself into something groovy.

The flashing red light behind me didn't register for a second. After all, I was doing thirty in a thirty-five mile zone, my turn signals worked perfectly and I was driving my new Cadillac carefully, also not wanting to end up with minor scrapes I seemed to attract while driving my squad car on occasion.

I pulled over immediately, thinking the officer had urgent business ahead. But the police car pulled in behind me. Through his car speaker he said to keep my hands where he could see them. The officer exited his car with his duty weapon drawn. I kept my hands on the steering wheel.

He approached the driver side of my car. His hands were shaking so badly, I was afraid he was going to shoot me. "Driver's license.?"

"I'm a police officer and my badge and license are in the glove compartment."

He laughed, "Sure, you're a cop. Just shut the f--- up and get out of the f---ing car!"

"Yes sir, I'm going to remove my left hand from the steering wheel to open the door." I opened the door slowly and stepped out, faced my car, put my hands on the hood, and spread my legs.

As he patted me down the patrolman pressed his gun into my right side. I could feel his hands shaking. I thought, Oh God, I'm going to be killed.

The officer asked for my ID, and I again told him it was in the glove compartment.

"When you open the glove compartment, you will also find several bags of money and my duty weapon."

266

That really did it to him. Now his hands were jerking uncontrollably as he went to the passenger side of the car, gun still pointed directly at me. He opened the compartment, removed my weapon, and barked, "Does this belong to you? What're you doing with it?"

"I'm a sworn officer."

He removed the money bags. "Where the f---ing hell did you get all this money?"

My hands were glued to the hood. "I own vending machines and I just emptied them to wrap and deposit the coins."

He then pulled out my identification. "Oh. You are a cop."

I relaxed and stood up. "Why did you stop me in the first place?"

Holstering his weapon, he announced, "You don't fit the car or the area."

"If that's the case, officer, why didn't you follow protocol by requesting back up for the stop, since I looked dangerous and out of place?"

He threw my paperwork onto the hood of the Cadillac. His resentment at my question was obvious, as he stomped to his squad car with a final, "Shut up! I don't have to explain shit to you."

The following day I made a verbal complaint about the incident to Sergeant Bellows, my watch commander. He peered over his heavy eyeglasses and said he would follow up and get back with me. That's the same way he looked at me in my Rookie days when he critiqued my reports and threw them back at me. After asking twice, over the next couple weeks and getting nothing, I let it drop, knowing it was fruitless to pursue.

~~*~~

My shift had ended late and I was tired. It was Tuesday, May 9th and I looked forward to two nights off from work. I had two uniforms to drop for cleaning before heading home to sleep and, later in the day pick up my now thirteen-year-old son. Fernando wanted to see the western, "Buck and the Preacher" starring Sidney Poitier and Harry Belafonte. We planned on sharing popcorn and sodas at the Orange Drive-In that night.

As I pulled into the parking lot, Mrs. Hunter, owner of the

cleaners, leaned into the driver's side window of Webb's squad car. His hand rested on her arm. In unison, they looked my way. He removed his hand. She stood and made her way to the building, where I met her, and opened the door for her.

After dropping off my cleaning, I arrived home a little after 8:00 a.m. I hugged Zeus, threw a couple balls for him to chase and retrieve before I gave him fresh water and a bowl of dry food. Within minutes the telephone rang, and before I could say hello, Fernando breathlessly shouted, "Dad! Mom said I can live with you. Is it okay? Can I?"

After almost two years, our divorce was final. I had been paying spousal and child support of $1,800 a month and had weekend visitation rights with my son.

For a few seconds I was speechless. But I smiled, "Little buddy, I would like nothing better! Let me talk to Mom for a minute."

Marie said, "Fernando has needs and interests I can no longer give him and he wants to live with you. Now that school's out for the summer, this is perfect timing."

We talked it over and we agreed that I could give him the male attention he needed. She was no longer fearful, since we both lived in Tustin, which was safer than Santa Ana. Marie wanted to return to Chicago at some point. We agreed that the spousal and child support would cease, but Fernando would spend one weekend a month with her, and I would continue to pay the mortgage on the house until she sold it.

Marie stayed in the home another three years before selling it and moving to Chicago.

~~*~~

Our agreements settled, Fernando came back on the line. I said, "Okay, son, have your things packed when I pick you up this afternoon. Later in the week we'll bring a truck for your basketball goal."

My rest was fleeting, as thoughts of being a single father raced through my mind. School. Interests. Healthy meals. Clothing and shoes. Friends. Amusement. Where he's going and what he's doing. Night-time caretaker. Thoughts of whether I would be home enough for him concerned me. Cops' kids, like preachers' kids, were known for turning out really well, or really bad. I persuaded myself that Fernando would be all right.

Later that evening, my son permanently moved into the second bedroom. I was happy that he wanted to live with me. Zeus was beside himself, his ball forgotten, as he jumped in circles and Fernando hugged him happily.

School was out for the summer, relieving me of some of my worries about providing day-time care for him since I was on graveyard shift.

I answered a knock on the door. Jacob Kramer, a good looking boy with wide gray eyes, straight black hair falling over his forehead, said with a grin, "Hi, Mr. Lambert, is Fred here?"

I recalled the first time I'd heard my son called Fred. Simple. My son had explained it was easier to say than Fernando.

At school Jacob and Fernando were best friends. Both boys enjoyed football, enjoyed learning, and brought home good grades. Jacob's family lived in the same apartment complex that we did. Months before I had met Jacob's parents when the boys were trying out for the school football team.

Bill and Connie Kramer owned a fish and pet shop on Tustin Avenue, north of 17th Street. To keep the boys busy during the summer, Kramer said he would pay them to stock supplies, organize fishing gear, feed the fish, and clean their tanks. When Jacob and Fernando weren't at the fish shop, I paid them to help water, feed, and brush the dogs at the Orange County kennels, under Ernie's supervision. The boys also spent one week in Hemet with my sister Doe, and her husband Lewis, helping them with caring for the canines.

I appreciated Bill and Connie with their well-meaning faces and friendly demeanor. Bill wore silver-rimmed glasses and, like his son, he had straight black hair that fell over his forehead. Connie had a sprinkle of freckles across her nose and snip-and-curl beauty shop hair.

My schedule was tight and it wasn't always easy, but I managed to be a dad, a cop, a part-time student, and a business owner.

Until the boys graduated from high school, they studied, worked, played, ate and slept comfortably in bunk beds, alternating between apartments—always supervised. They even enjoyed occasional summer camps in California, where they learned skills ranging from horseback riding, waterskiing, performing arts, to soccer and windsailing.

~~*~~

On June 7th hundreds of students from seven Santa Ana high schools walked out of their classes in a mass exodus. The students protested school conditions, despite threats of suspension.

Two-hundred-fifty "Mexican-American and Negro students" walked to El Salvador Park. According to the *Los Angeles Times*, their specific demands included efforts to fill administration, faculty and staff positions with persons who reflected the ethnic makeup of the community and a reevaluation of curriculum and discipline policies. They wanted an end to "mass" suspensions at Valley High School and Smedley Junior High, a "community person" installed in a position to assure injustices were not committed, and to have at each school at least one Chicano counselor and nurse who spoke Spanish.

Extra Santa Ana police patrol units followed the students from their schools to the park. Two police officers were assigned to film the demonstration at El Salvador Park to make sure all participating students would be suspended.

This was one of the reasons for the protest!

I recognized many of the students as they marched quietly shoulder-to-shoulder, ignoring the cameras. During my time in Community Relations I had visited their schools and had spoken with many of them one-on-one. I understood the value of aides at each school to implement new programs, assure students' fair treatment, and liaison with the community.

The young people began their trek across the intersection. I stopped traffic to allow them to cross safely. I was grateful Fernando and Jacob attended school in Tustin, where students were treated more equally. Better treatment of students of color across the country was important. I hoped that day would soon come.

~~*~~

Later that month, Jack Boettner, a Staff Writer for *The Los Angeles Times* came to my apartment to interview me about my 150-page manuscript that one college in Orange County had offered to include as required reading in Black studies classes. Chief Edward Allen had approved the manuscript before I had submitted it to three publishing houses with hopes it would be picked up, but it wasn't.

The article, "Black Lawman: An Open Book" was published on June 27, 1972, with a photo of my son and me.[61] I pulled no punches during the interview, and among other things, told Jack I no longer felt the necessity to hate myself in order to demonstrate I was on the job and good at it.

Jack was quiet for a few moments, and then said, "Off the record, Harlen, don't let this turn into a banana peel for you, if you know what I mean."

I presumed he knew the article would not be well received by many of my fellow officers.

~~*~~

The following night at about 11:38 p.m. I was dispatched to the east side of Santa Ana.

John Link met me at the door in obvious distress. "Somebody broke in and raped my wife."

John told me that night when his shift ended, he tiptoed into the bedroom, showered, went to the kitchen for something to eat, returned to the bedroom and proceeded to make love to his sleeping wife.

Waking abruptly, she said, "John, what's wrong with you? You just made love to me!"

John told her, "No, I didn't. I just got home."

Puzzled, she explained that earlier she had heard him take a shower and go to the kitchen, that although half asleep, she was used to the sounds of his evening routine.

John got up, turned on lights and searched the house. When he saw the broken glass in the entry, he called the police to report a break-in and rape crime.

Now John and I faced each other and he said, "Officer, I have no idea who could have raped my wife." Then jerking his head, looking perplexed, he said, "The odd thing is the routine." Then it dawned on him. "Oh, shit! Mike Stone and I talk about our sex life. It was Mike!"

271

John Link and Mike Stone had been friends since boyhood, and each had been the best man at the other's wedding. Both worked at the same company for ten years. And they shared stories about their most intimate bedroom activities with each other.

Working second shift, John and Mike began swapping details about their daily routine when they got home from work. John told Mike that when he got home, his wife was asleep. "I do the same thing every night, man. Take a shower, eat, go to bed and immediately make love to my lady. Man, she never wakes up, but I still put it to her." Shaking his head and chuckling, he continued, "Sometimes I go to the living room and watch TV after."

When I contacted Mike Stone, he denied the allegations. However, further investigation and prints raised from the point of entry into the Link home identified Stone as the intruder. He was later found guilty of rape and burglary.

That was one of my most unusual calls.

CHAPTER TWENTY - FOUR
July - December 1972

July 4th was a week away, and I had received numerous requests for additional guard dogs. Chief Allen granted me vacation time from the police force through July 5th.

On Saturday July 1st, a makeshift fireworks stand was assembled in the Montgomery Ward parking lot at 1700 North Bristol Street. A bold fourteen-foot banner advertising "Fireworks" could be seen from the four corners at Bristol and 17th streets.

Customers elbowed each other to be first in line, and clamored to be heard as they pointed to the assortment of sparklers, ground spinners, pyro packs, fountains, and novelties. "How loud are the TNT poppers?" "How high do the bottle rockets go?" "That cardboard chicken spits out fireball eggs?"

Business had been brisk. At 10 p.m. the back door of the fireworks stand, and the drop windows were all closed and locked.

At mid-afternoon the following day Officer Larry Nemelka contacted me with a request that I place a dog in the fireworks stand overnight. "I responded to a 911 this morning that someone burglarized the stand sometime last night. The owner wants a deterrent, and I thought of you."

Arrangements were made to place Atlas, a one-hundred-twenty pound German Shepherd, in the stand at closing time. I put down a bowl of water and commanded him to "watch and wander" as the owner locked the door behind us.

The next morning Officer Nemelka and the pyrotechnics owner waited for me at the rear of the stand. I pulled my truck near the rear door and noted the damage—the lock had been pried off and the door stood ajar. I stepped inside. A ray of early sunlight drew my attention to the northwest corner where a man stood in semi-darkness, arms outstretched as if to ward off evil. My German Shepherd sat unmoving, focused on the intruder.

The man saw me, and cried out, "Get this dog away from me!" Atlas stood there and growled.

I called Atlas to me and leashed him with a "Good boy." Officer Nemelka holstered his weapon, cuffed the intruder, and took him to the Orange County Jail where he was booked with Code 459, Burglary.

The following two nights were without incident. Atlas was on guard.

~~*~~

That same Saturday evening a Winnebago recreational vehicle (RV) dealer, wanted a dog on premise for a long holiday weekend. The property was on a fenced five-acre site in the semi-rural farming community of Costa Mesa adjacent to the Orange County fairgrounds.

The lot of new and used motorhomes, travel trailers and fifth wheelers that surrounded the paint and body shops, the off-white concrete office, and the parts and accessories store would be closed Saturday through Tuesday to celebrate Independence Day.

After closing time on Saturday night, I walked the lot with Rex, a one-hundred-thirty-pound black German Shepherd. We located a "spot" where he was to relieve himself, and I placed a large military style kennel and a stainless-steel bowl of water at the entrance to the customer lounge and service cashier. After a "watch and wander" command, I chained and locked the main gate behind me.

The job would require morning checks to make sure Rex had abundant fresh water. He would also be fed in the morning, before resting in his kennel for several hours during the day.

On Sunday morning, Rex greeted Ernie and me with a wag, his eyes trained on the container of dry food Ernie had hoisted on his shoulder. I refreshed his water from the hose in front of the parts store. Rex watched, ears up, head slightly cocked as Ernie placed the food inside the kennel before giving the dog the "okay" to eat.

Ernie drove the truck around the lot, while I did a visual check of the buildings and vehicles. All was quiet and nothing appeared out of the ordinary before we left Rex slowly eating his chicken and rice dry food.

On Monday morning Ernie and I returned to the lot, a container of dry food hoisted on Ernie's shoulder, as I unlocked the gate. Rex was not in sight. I whistled for him. We stood still, listening for a sound. Nothing. We checked all building doors and windows. All clear. Ernie jumped in the truck to drive the perimeter, while I made my way through the rows of vehicles.

"Here. Up here!" I turned to see a vagrant sitting on top of a 1970 Minnie Winnie, brandishing a windshield wiper.

Rex calmly sat several feet away, head raised, eyes fixed on the man. I gave Rex the signal to relax. He yawned and flopped down, head on his front paws.

Just then, Ernie drove alongside. He jerked his head toward the trespasser, and said, "I found a part of the fence jerked out of the ground and mangled. Must be how he got in."

I shaded my eyes from the bright, hot sun and asked, "How long have you up been up there?"

The man stood. He had urinated on himself. "Yesterday morning," he complained. "Scrambled up on this here ladder 'fore the dog came around the corner!"

Ernie left the lot to call the police, while I commanded Rex to go to his kennel. The encroacher clambered down the ladder, where I waited to escort him—at arms length from the smell—to the front of the lot to wait for the police. The man drank greedily from the water hose as we waited.

In minutes the police arrived to take the vagrant to jail, still holding onto the broken windshield wiper. He was booked for trespassing, property damage, and petty theft.

"Good dog! A job well done." Ernie crooned, as he fed a thirsty and very sleepy German Shepherd.

My dog guard business was successful, earning me extra money, a real service to people, and a nice change from my policing.

~~*~~

The holiday was over and I was back on the job a week later. My shift was over at 11:00 p.m.

At 10:50 p.m. Dispatch broadcast a robbery in progress at a liquor store in the 1200 block of First Street. The three male blacks were described as each being 5'8" to 6' tall, wearing blue jeans and gray shirts. Each wore blue knit caps pulled over their heads with holes cut out for eyes and nose.

At 10:55 p.m. Dispatch contacted me to report to the station Watch Commander, immediately. Damn. Now what? I knew an order was coming—it wasn't unusual on Chrockran's shift. He did not respect me, or my abilities enough to request that I assist in investigating calls. He used me as a token "Nigger spy," and I made every effort when given the choice of shifts, not to be assigned to work with him.

At 11:08 p.m. I arrived at the station to make contact with Lt. Chrockran. His tall frame stood in his office doorway. As soon as he saw me, he lisped in agitation, "Lambert, did you hear the robbery broadcast that occurred in the Black district of the city?"

"Yes, sir, I heard the message."

With a scowl, he asked, "You know any of them or have any ideas who the suspects might be?"

Returning the same kind of scowl, I responded, "No, I don't know who the suspects might be, with the amount of information broadcast, plus I'm off duty now." Since I had opened Orange County Kennels, I had no longer made myself available for overtime.

We stood eyeball-to-eyeball. Without preamble, the lieutenant ordered, "Change into civilian clothes, take an unmarked car into the neighborhood, nose around and find out what you can about who the suspects are."

"Sir, with all due respect, I'm off duty and need to get home to my son."

His lisp was pronounced as he said, "I'm off duty, too, Lambert! But I gave you an order. Now do it!" Putting his hand on the door, "You know your people. Find out who they are, and furthermore, you live in the damn neighborhood!" With that, he turned into his office, and slammed the door behind him. But not before I saw the photo of his wife and two boys that sat precariously on the corner of his desk. And he'll be on his way home soon. I wondered if he checked in on his boys and covered them up before heading upstairs to sleep.

The direct order was offensive, for two reasons: one, he didn't know I no longer lived in Santa Ana, and two, I knew how he felt about anyone who wasn't White.

I left the station in plain clothes and picked up an unmarked to go into the area as ordered, watchful for three masked men, or movement of any kind. Nothing. I made the decision to speak with the liquor store manager, to see what details he could provide that might help with identifying the robbers.

The parking lot of the all night liquor store was vacant, except for the police car leaving onto First Street at the same time I entered. The bulky, muscular store manager met me at the door. He gave the same brief description of the men that had been broadcast earlier. "Punks didn't get away with anything. I pulled my .357 Magnum and they scattered like rats. They ran up toward Grand Avenue. Officer just left with the details."

I had continued to patrol, looking for the suspects, without success. At 3:18 a.m. I called Dispatch that I would be "10-97" (write report) at the station.

I settled in at a metal desk to prepare a written report on what I had—not—learned of the suspects, while the lieutenant was home in bed. I wondered if "House Mouse" Bellows would return the report for rewrite, and Chrockran would lisp that, "It's part of the training exercise, Lambert."

At 3:45 a.m. I stood and stretched, placing the completed report in Bellow's tray. It had been a long night. In less than twelve hours, I would be back on the streets.

I was used to the abuse, used to never reacting, but my guts felt it in my soul.

But I wanted to be a good example for Fernando and all the men of my kind.

~~*~~

The following night, my shift over, I was on my way to the police station. At 11:10 p.m., one block away from the unit parking lot, I was dispatched to the Shell Station at the corner of Sullivan and McFadden Streets on a Code 925 (unknown suspicious). The station attendant rushed to my car, as I came to a stop. "Officer, there's a guy in the men's bathroom unconscious. I don't know if he's hurt or not. I called the police right away."

I stepped out of my unit and put on latex gloves before entering the tiny, dirty restroom. My senses were assaulted with the smells of blood and vomit and the sight of a teenage boy, his knees tucked under him and his head face down in the filthy commode. The syringe stuck in his right arm dangled above the inside of his bruised elbow. I carefully felt for a pulse and found none. He wasn't unconscious—he was dead.

From all appearances, this was yet another "gas station overdose." I backed out of the washroom and contacted my field sergeant with the situation. As the first officer on the scene, it was my duty to note the time and as many elements of the crime scene as possible without touching anything.

While I waited for my follow-up, I tied yellow crime scene tape around the outside area, sketched the crime scene and made notes that included odors, the amount of light present, whether the door was open or shut on my arrival, and made sure nothing was disturbed.

"P. Lee" Johnson arrived in an unmarked car. As the follow-up officer it was his duty to perform the crime scene investigation. After briefing Johnson on what he would find inside, I watched him put on latex gloves and remove his 35mm camera from the trunk of his vehicle. I held up the crime scene tape for him to move under.

Not expecting a reply, Johnson turned to me, shook his head, and said, "Jesus. How many more will we see like this?" He photographed and measured. He would not take samples from the victim because the syringe was still in the body. He asked me to request the coroner.

I entered my unit, contacted communications, and requested they call the Orange County Coroner to the Shell Station to take possession of the body. At 1:40 a.m. I made my way to the police station, completed my report, and called it another night, or in this case, another morning.

~~*~~

After roll call two days later, Lieutenant Doug Garrison called me into his office. Sergeant Webb was coming out of the lieutenant's office as I entered. I stood aside to let Webb pass.

The lieutenant asked me to sit. Out of left field, he began a litany of complaints—he had been informed that my CSI (Crime Scene Investigation) procedures were "deplorable," that new officers needed the opportunity to do CSI, that I was moody, my driving required attention, and that my report writing and log details were a concern.

The lieutenant continued, "Harlen, I know you're constantly busy on the watch, making car stops, handling calls, and following up on situations. Just be aware of the talk."

I asked, "Do you care to tell me who's complaining about me?"

Before answering, the lieutenant stood and said, "That's neither here nor there, but I'll have to do a memo, and there won't be any further action taken."[62]

There was a piece of this puzzle I needed. I just wanted to know. "Doug, what's this really about?"

He shrugged and said, "It's no big deal." I countered and told him it must have been a bit of a big deal, since I was being chewed out with a laundry list of anonymous grievances. Whatever it was, my one-time coach, friend, and frequent visitor in my home, seemed ashamed as I turned and left his office.

That was the last time we addressed each other by our first names.

As I walked to my patrol unit, I recalled one of my mother's Lifeisms: "Behind every opposition there is a lesson and a blessing". Okay, think! First, what's the lesson? Don't pay attention to everything people say, Sunny, because you'll always be upset. Okay. What's the blessing?

All thought disappeared as I reached the black-and-white to begin the preliminary checks on the beat-up piece of crap assigned to me. It had scratches, a missing hubcap, and worn-out seats. On the dashboard, somebody had scribbled in ink, "This job is rotten!" Apparently the last cop to use the car was disgruntled and didn't like the job.

I sat behind the wheel, contemplating the dashboard. Confusing impressions assailed me, tumbling one over the other, as I thought about where I'd been, where I was going, and what the hell it all meant. I wasn't sad, but I wasn't happy either. I felt—numb.

~~*~~

At 10:30 p.m. I responded to a car stalled in the intersection of First and Main Streets. Pools of yellow street-light glowed and outlined the driver, who stood at the open rear door of an older model Buick. The flashing lights of the patrol car illuminated the man as he rifled through what appeared to be a stack of clothing. He ignored me as I approached, and continued searching for—something.

The muggy August heat pressed in on us. The sweat trickled down our necks and backs like warm soup. The man's loose tee shirt clung to his back, revealing an undernourished frame.

I approached with caution, my flashlight directed at his hands. "Sir, what seems to be the problem with your car?"

The man turned. "I'm not sure. Might be out of gas. It just stopped. I'm from out of town, and I don't know where I am."

"Let me see your license, and I can call for a tow truck to help you out."

He turned back to the car, handed his license to me, and resumed searching the back seat of his car. Glancing at the license, I thanked Mr. Greene and told him I would be right back. I went to the patrol unit to contact communications with a request to run records on the identification, and to send a tow truck.

While I waited for a response from dispatch, I watched Mr. Greene continue searching. His actions became frantic, and items of clothing started littering the street. The radio crackled with a response. "Greene is wanted on a 459 burglary in Iowa. Detain for out-of-state authorities. Tow truck on the way."

As I walked back to the Buick to arrest Greene, he turned suddenly and fell to his knees, sobbing and pointing to a bag of white rocks and broken needles that lay on the ground, among his soiled clothing. "Man, I need my stuff!"

After I scooped him up, advised him of the warrant and that he was going to jail, I secured the heroin and needles. He wept as I told him he would also be charged with possession of drugs and littering.

~~*~~

A week later, the hot August air remained stifling. My uniform felt damp from the humidity. At 6:30 p.m. I observed a green Volkswagen speed through the stop sign at North Flower and West 3rd Streets. I hit the siren, and the car cruised to a stop in front of a small home on North Shelton Street.

Two teens bailed out of the small vehicle, one holding a six-pack of soda. The driver, looking anxious, started talking before I could say a word. "Officer, we're in the middle of a game of Monopoly™ and ran out of drinks. I'm sorry, I wasn't thinking. I know I ran the sign back there."

With a sheepish look, the boy fished a card from his back pocket.

"Look! I have a get out of jail free card!" He looked at me imploringly.

After a check on his identification, I gave a verbal warning and said, "This one is on me. Please drive carefully and considerately. The next one is on you." I had maintained a serious police officer demeanor until I got into the patrol unit, where I could no longer control the laughter that bubbled up from my gut.

A cop sees life in all its ups and downs. "Get out of jail free card," I muttered.

I burst into laughter again.

~~*~~

Later in the month, daylight had become noticeably shorter, and the temperature had cooled a few degrees. Autumn was my favorite time of year. Late afternoon patrol was a kaleidoscope of colors ranging from golden yellow and glossy green shrubbery to brilliant red and deep purple leaves scattered on trees throughout the city.

As the sun began its descent due west, a red Ford Pinto sped north on South Fairview Street and through the red light at West Edinger Avenue. I hit the patrol unit siren, turned on the red and blue lights, and gave chase.

The driver came to a stop at a home on West Lingan Lane inside Windsor Park. As I approached her car, she yelled out the window, "Now what!" Her fists hit the steering wheel in anger.

Before asking for her license, I politely said, "Miss, I stopped you for speeding and running through a red light." She had driven into the driveway of her home. From the corner of my eyes, I saw headlights from a second car approach and stop across the street.

In a huff, Karen DeMone replied, "I wish you people would get your act together." With another strike to the steering wheel, Karen argued, "Just yesterday that cop over there took away my license and then today you expect me to show it to you!"

She pointed across the street to a black-and-white sitting under a Jacaranda tree, its leaves fading into the evening shadows. And in the shadows, Sergeant Webb sat, as was his custom, just watching me.

The soft click of a door was heard as I said to Miss DeMone, "I'm giving you a ticket for speeding, running a light, and driving without a valid driver's license." As she signed the citation, I bid Karen a good night, and cautioned her not to drive until she had a legal license in her possession.

I glanced at The Vulture, who now leaned against his patrol car, his arms spread wide in a "horaltic pose." A mental picture of Grandpa Day and me in the woods hunting rabbits flashed behind my eyes. We hunted first thing in the morning, when buzzards stood on the ground, their wings spread wide. It was a warm-up pose from overnight temperature drops. Vultures often sat with their wings spread wide, increasing the surface area of their bodies so that the sun could more easily warm them—before they took flight in search of prey.

Hesitating briefly before turning the ignition of the patrol unit, I remembered the grievances meeting with Lieutenant Garrison back in July. I had stepped aside to allow Sergeant Webb to leave the lieutenant's office before I had entered.

~~*~~

Patrol was an unpredictable animal, and the patrol officer did not control his destiny. The dispatcher did.

The first week of October I was pulled out of roll call to respond to a trouble call at a small family-owned carniceria (butcher shop) on West 1st Street near South Pacific Avenue. As I walked to my assigned unit, I recalled that almost to the day two years earlier I had been dispatched out of roll call, and in my hurry to respond to a lewd and lascivious, I failed to precheck the squad car. That failure had cost me 14 vacation days and a reduction in pay grade. The gangster with a neck tattoo and wearing a black hoodie fighting with a bespectacled college student wearing a sweatshirt that said "Cal-State Fullerton" would have to wait until my inspection was completed. By the time I reached the carniceria, the two men had disappeared.

I recognized Emiliano Flores, arms crossed over his head, as he bolted from the carniceria. His wife Catalina, on his heels, cursed him as she smacked his back with a bag of groceries. Emiliano saw me, and raced to the car, "She try to kill me! We no casado anymore!"

As I stepped out of the black-and-white Catalina joined us. Out of breath, she wheezed in broken English, "Bastardo spend our money on cerveza and pool. And we still married, fool!"

Officer Earl "Wooly" Wooldridge pulled alongside. The last time I saw Earl was on an off-duty day, and we had arrested a wannabe officer. "I got a call about these two. Same thing, different day. Moved from Fullerton less than a month ago, and I've been out to their place three times in the last two weeks. Emiliano still bitching about not being married. I'll take it from here."

I recalled a conversation I overheard at the end of my Rookie year. I had been loaned to the Fullerton Police Department on special assignment. While waiting to enter the Valencia Street location to purchase narcotics, two Fullerton detectives laughed and talked about their answer to minorities who couldn't afford a divorce. Watching for activity at the house, Detective O'Brien remarked, "Yeah, before the minorities got marriage counselors and lawyers free from the taxpayers, we had to come up with a solution for the repeat domestic problems."

My ears perked up, as he continued, "After three times, we'd ask the couple if they could get along and still live together in the same house if they were divorced. They'd tell us they couldn't afford a lawyer. And we'd tell them that the police had the power to perform a divorce, and if they could stop fighting and live peacefully together I'd give 'em one."

The sound of cars approaching silenced the narrative for a few seconds. The vehicles continued west, away from the target residence. O'Brien resumed, "The couple promised to quit fighting or a divorce would be cancelled out. And our deal was that they couldn't tell anyone about it, either. Then I'd have them stand in front of me and we'd all join hands. She had to put a free hand over my badge, and he put his free hand over hers."

O'Brien lowered his voice, looking at each of us one at a time, as we listened intently. "I then asked them to swear never to fight again and agree to dissolve their marriage here and now. They would agree, and I pronounced them divorced. But then I told them that if either of 'em violated the sacred vows and picked a fight with the other, the ceremony was automatically cancelled and they'd still be married to each other."

He went silent. I waited for a couple minutes, before asking, "Then what? Was it really that simple?"

"Yeah. I'd tell 'em to shake hands to consummate the divorce and I didn't expect to get called back out there again. Of course, living together the odds of them fighting sooner or later was high, but I assured them that the ceremony was a one-time deal and not to bother calling back for another one."

I wondered if Catalina and Emiliano Flores had had a divorce performed by a Fullerton police officer.

~~*~~

It rained most of the day on Tuesday, November 7th. The skies were dominated by tumbling grays, water droplets falling intermittently as if they had nothing better to do.

Before Fred left for school that morning, I suggested he wear a rain jacket, take the umbrella from the hall closet, and not jump in any puddles. My teenaged son rolled his eyes and groaned as if in great pain, "Dad. I'm not afraid of a little rain. Jeez!" The door slammed as he rushed out, where his best friend waited to walk to school with him in the softly falling rain.

Later that day, shortly after the start of my shift, I was on patrol on West Santa Ana Boulevard, approaching North Ross Street. A 1970 Camaro, driving south, slowly weaved back and forth across the divider line of Ross, into the red traffic light, and stopped in the middle of the intersection. Traffic waited in all directions as I turned on my siren and lights.

The Camaro shot forward, tires hissing on the blackened street. The pursuit was on. The driver abruptly slowed to a near crawl as it continued to weave south, before coming to a stop along the curb at the West 3rd Street side of Birch Park. I pulled the black-and-white alongside the parked vehicle. The light rain had stopped. The air was now made hazy by a mist.

The driver crawled to the passenger side of the car, flung open the door, and met me on the sidewalk. The brunette was unsteady, swaying back and forth. I asked to see the woman's license and registration. "Miss Iver…" She interrupted before I could tell her why I stopped her.

She giggled and said, "It's Amanda, and I know I've been a bad girl, sir." She opened her arms suggestively and moved closer, waggled her fingers, and sang, "But I can be a good girl!"

She stumbled clumsily. I could smell alcohol. I asked her to sit on the curb while I called communications to request backup and to advise that I had a female in custody. As I gave dispatch information on the stop,

Amanda pronounced her name loudly, "Uh-man-duh. It's Uh-man-duh!" She began to dry heave before she upchucked in the gutter.

The backup officer arrived, assisted me in putting on the bracelets, and placed her under arrest for driving while intoxicated. I read her the Miranda warning, helped her into the back seat of my patrol car, and contacted communications with the unit's current mileage, before transporting Uh-man-duh to jail for booking.

~~*~~

Back on patrol, the mist swallowed the landscape, leaching out all color. The thin mist turned everything the same stony gray as the street, as if it knew of the hardships both behind and ahead. Driving westbound on Civic Center Drive, I had the impression there was more to come before the skies cleared. Of that I was sure.

My musings were interrupted by a vehicle driving eastbound, abruptly crossing in front of me to make a left turn onto Louise Street. I applied the brakes hard, and the patrol unit made a 180 degree turn and slid backwards into the eastbound traffic lane, striking an oncoming vehicle. Damn! I immediately got out of the car to check on the driver, apologetic for the whole incident, and the inconvenience it would cause the citizen. At the same time I was thankful that there were no injuries— but there was minor damage to both vehicles. The resident that made the left turn came back to the accident scene, remorseful for his last minute decision to turn in front of the patrol unit.

The citizen and I drove our cars out of the traffic lane and waited for an accident investigating officer to arrive. The silvery mist had licked at every surface. I raised a hand to check for my glasses. They were there, and through the unfocused lens the investigating officer arrived. Detective Vulture. Great.

Sergeant Webb spoke with me, the citizen of the vehicle I hit, and the man who made the turn onto Louise Street. Ultimately, I caused the accident, resulting in damage to the vehicles. Webb made notes and took photos. Before dismissing me, he said, "Lambert, my findings will go to the safety committee. You'll hear from them."

I learned later that Webb asserted he interviewed three witnesses who claimed I was speeding at approximately 45-50 miles per hour. The Sergeant reported it was a wet, slippery day, but under the prevailing conditions I was driving too fast and guilty of negligent operation of the police car.

Later that night, tiptoeing into the house, I first peeked into Fernando's room. He was bundled under a pile of blankets, hands clasped across his chest, feet exposed. I then checked my son's homework, left on the kitchen table for me to review, before I went to the back patio to talk with Zeus. He stretched and lazily made his way to me, and sat next to me on the steps. Zeus put his head in my lap and nuzzled my palm, letting me know he was ready to listen.

Absently scratching his ears, I said, "I screwed up, buddy. Not intentionally. But a screw-up just the same. I suspect if my Mom were here, she'd tell me to live on the sunrise side of the mountain, not the sunset side." I contemplated the little nugget she had shared with me when we had discussed my letdown at losing the USC scholarship. "Sunny, you're young and tough. Sometimes a setback makes you stronger!" I visualized Mom's sweet, concerned smile. My embarrassment over the accident was briefly forgotten, and calm returned for the night. And that mountain? The one time I had told my mother I felt I was staring into a dark precipice, she said cheerfully, "Well then. When it's dark enough, you can see the stars."

~~*~~

The next two weeks were uneventful, but did provide me with a couple of amusing incidents.

At 5:42 p.m. I was dispatched to a residence on West Elder Avenue on a "sleeping burglar in home" call. The homeowner, fifty-two-year-old May Stevens, opened the door as I stepped onto a porch lined with small black pots filled with Jade plant starters. She had posted a sign "Jade plants for sale." Officer Katiz, the affable and friendly early ride-along mentor and guide, pulled behind my unit and joined the homeowner and me.

Miss Stevens waved us inside and indicated we should follow her. She began explaining why she called, as she led us through a narrow hallway to her bedroom. "I returned home from work. I knew something was wrong, because my jewelry box was open, and I never leave it open. Then I found this guy asleep under my bed," she exclaimed. "I shook him a few times, thinking he was a drunk that wandered into the wrong house, but I couldn't get him up, so I called the police."

As soon as we entered the room, it was obvious that with open dresser drawers, an open jewelry box, and clothing spilling out of a closet the house had been ransacked.

"Ma'am, please wait at the door." We heard snoring, and made our way to the far side of the bed. We saw the male, passed out in a fetal position, clutching gold earrings and a matching bracelet. We shouted. We shook him. He didn't wake up. We finally dragged the still sleeping man out of the house and into Officer Katiz's unit to be carted off to jail.

Katiz later told me the man was Doug Smyth, a twenty-four year old unemployed draftsman, who decided to drink some vodka and pop a few pills before robbing a house. He grabbed the jewelry, and it seemed the looting left him feeling a little tuckered out, so Smyth decided to sleep a few minutes.

We laughed together, as Katiz observed, "Guess he didn't know that like any other job, they're rules and a code of conduct. Whether you're a burglar or office worker, it's bad form to consume drugs or alcohol during work hours!"

Four days later I was dispatched on a 925 (unknown trouble call) to a disturbance in the public lot at Windsor Park, off West La Verne Avenue. Officer Paul Nugent pulled his patrol car alongside mine, which faced three females standing next to a gold Chevrolet Vega.

The last time Paul and I had been on a disturbance call together was in 1967, where the children had physically attacked Paul and me in defense of their disputing parents. His handsome face broke into a smile and, as we shook hands, he said, "Hope this isn't another night we go home raggedy and bruised!" I agreed with him as we turned to join the group of ladies.

The petite brunette began to explain why they had called for help. "This is my car. Look at the window and the door! My boyfriend did that!" The driver side window was smashed and the door had a dent in the shape of a V. After being asked how it happened, she went on, "We were at the club and we had a fight, and my friend here hit him over the head with a beer bottle."

Her friend, another brunette, not so petite, chimed in, "The jerk deserved it! He's a lot bigger, and mean, and spiteful."

Concerned about a possible serious head injury, I asked where the boyfriend was now, and ladylove said he lived two blocks over at the corner of West Borchard Avenue and South Nakoma Drive. Paul stayed with the women to continue with details of the evening from the accuser, while I drove down the street the boyfriend lived on. As I approached the corner, the patrol car headlights shined on a male wearing dark clothing. When he saw the black-and-white, he darted to the back door of the house and gained entry.

I stopped the car, walked up the short walkway, and knocked on the front door. I heard someone falling down, and knocked even harder. A few seconds later a man came to the door barefoot, wearing jeans and a white tee shirt. It was the male I had seen enter through the rear of the house.

In an effort to appear calm, the man inquired, "Yes, may I help you, officer?"

"Yes," I said. "I would like to talk with the man who just ran into the house."

The suspect groused, "I don't understand what you're talking about. I just woke up with your pounding."

I looked at him and pointed out that he had blood seeping from his hairline and across his forehead. "Did you fall on the way to the door?" I asked.

"Okay, okay!" His hands went into the air and he finally told the truth about what had happened earlier in the evening, and that he had damaged his girlfriend's vehicle. After declining a call for medical attention, the suspect was arrested and charged with willful vandalism to a vehicle.

~~*~~

On November 27th, I was invited to Chief Allen's office, where he presented me with a Resolution from the State Senate and a representative presented me with the American Legion's Medal of Valor for my part in saving the children from a house fire in May of 1970. Bob Gievet, a staff writer from the *Independent Press-Telegram* interviewed me and took photos.[63]

After the congratulations and photos were taken, Chief Allen and I were alone. He invited me to sit, and I asked him if rumors of his retirement the following month were true. "Yes, it's been a good eighteen years, but I'm ready to spend more time with the family and pursue other interests."

There was a knock on his door. We both stood. He came around the desk, hand extended, and said, "Harlen, be proud of your accomplishments. I know well how rough it's been, but you've weathered it all with decency, and no one can take that from you."

The Chief's comment was deeply and personally felt. I thought about what I knew of him. Chief Allen was the first to be appointed, after sixty-six years of elected chiefs. He came from a family of law enforcement officers from Erie, Pennsylvania. The chief had been an officer in Erie, assigned on loan to the FBI to assist agents in World War II investigations, and later graduated from the FBI National Academy. The following year, in 1948, he was named Chief of Police in Youngstown, Ohio, a city corrupted by Mafia influence. In 1954 Allen was appointed chief for the Ohio Liquor Control Department, and in 1955 he was hired as police chief in Santa Ana because of his nationwide reputation as a Mafia-fighting police chief while at Youngstown.

In 1962 Chief Allen's book, "Merchants of Menace: The Mafia" was published and was described as an authoritative effort to explain organized crime. Meanwhile, he concentrated his efforts on reshaping the Santa Ana Police Department, where internal controversy brewed and exploded in 1965 with charges, including Allen's, that some officers within the police department itself, known as the "John Birch Conspiracy," were attempting to force his resignation.

Chief Allen's background was a testament of his character and resilience to stand strong in the face of adversity.

I struggled every day, since being hired, for acceptance within the department from a handful of men I had referred to as the "BGs." I didn't know then my final test was coming—would I have the character, endurance and dignity that the Chief had many times displayed?

~~*~~

Bob Geivet, Staff Writer for the *Independent Press-Telegram*, published an article titled "Black policeman's story etched in bigotry-pride" with a photo of me holding the Medal of Valor, on December 3, 1972.[64]

The prior three articles written about me, also addressed the book I had started writing. Recently retired Chief Allen had understood and approved the manuscript outline, which revolved around proving that black officers given a baton, uniform, and a badge were not trouble.

Chief Allen confirmed that "...how well he (Harlen) succeeded has been entered in his police file many times." The article continued "... that Edward J. Allen, chief of Santa Ana police who hired Lambert, said before his retirement last Friday that he always wished the department had 20 men like him."

It would be 40-plus years before I learned my police file was not what it should have been.

~~*~~

While the search was on for a new police chief, Captains Tracey and Johnson were in charge of handling major departmental decisions. I guess I was a major issue to be dealt with.

On Monday, December 18, Captain Tracey stopped me in the hallway. His favorite meeting place with me, I thought. He had the smug look of the cat that swallowed the canary. Waving the Safety Committee report in the air, he said, "You're being referred to take Driver Training School as a result of your November 7 vehicle accident. You've become a liability, so consider yourself lucky that you're not being terminated at this time. You will suffer suspension time, but I haven't decided how much or when. You'll get that later. Now carry on."

As he turned his back to slip into his office, I asked, "May I have a copy of the Safety Report for my records?"

The captain's Cheshire grin instantly turned sour. "If I'd wanted you to have it, I would've given it to you. Again, carry on." He stepped into his office and closed the door.

During shift change that evening, comments floated between officers across the locker room. "Yeah, I heard we have a new chief coming in." "Heard it was from outside the department. Too bad. Some of our own tried for the spot and were passed over." "Word is the guy's the chief in Walnut Creek now. Wonder why he's coming here."

Later that night, I picked up the *Santa Ana Register* from my driveway. Fred had forgotten to bring it into the apartment and place it next to his homework—and a short list of what he would like to find under the Christmas tree. School would be out in a few days for the year, and we would celebrate together before he went east with Marie through the New Year.

There it was. Rumors put to rest—"Raymond Davis New Santa Ana Chief of Police." City Manager Bruce Spragg announced that forty-year-old Davis, who headed the Walnut Creek police force would assume command in Santa Ana on February 5, 1973. His eighteen year career included ten years with the Fullerton police force, where he had risen from patrolman to captain.

~~*~~

Fred was on his way to Chicago with his mother. I returned from the airport and took a run with Zeus through Tustin Centennial Park. We were tired and hungry when we returned home. I made a chicken sandwich for myself and set it aside. Zeus stood at my feet as I mixed cooked chicken in his dry food. I picked up my plate and his bowl, and moved to the patio. He stayed close at my heels in anticipation of his monthly treat. While Zeus ate, I checked my watch. I had been reassigned to the 11:00 p.m. to 8:00 a.m. shift—I had five hours to sleep before it was time to go back on patrol.

The line of patrol units each had a festive green sheet of paper with a tiny red bow tucked under the windshield. As we reached our assigned black-and-white, we removed the paper and soon we all chuckled in unison as we read:

"on the 12th day of Christmas my dispatcher gave to me…
    12 Traffic stops
    11 False alarms
    10 "Repeat your traffic"
     9 Drunks-a-driving
     8 Spouses yelling
     7 Dogs-a-barking
     6 Fresh baked donuts
     5 Sto-len rings
     4 Status checks
     3 Full arrests
     2 Car fires
    And a cat stuck high in a tree."

I thought about the officers and what we all had in common. We knew we faced the unknown every time we put on our uniform, pinned on a badge, and strapped on a gun. I sent up a silent prayer, as I turned the ignition to drive another night. I knew the hours of the shift might crawl in monotony—or zip by with lights and sirens from one emergency to the next. But there were always certainties: anguish, ruthlessness, and death are constant companions during the career of the cop. So were humor, irony, and valor. And at the end of the day, there were stories to tell— some amusing, some touching, some gripping tales of sorrow and loss, and some were wildly comical. But they were all a part of life on the beat.

There was some respect for Christmas Day even among criminals, and an unofficial cease-fire seemed to exist, at least until midnight, when the break was over and the suspension of unlawful activities was forgotten. Predators prowled the streets looking for easy marks, burglars scouted dark buildings for easy access, and dull-eyed hookers resumed their places on the street corners.

The first hour of my shift was slow and uneventful. At 12:11 a.m. I was dispatched to the intersection of Main and East Bishop Streets, where a drunk wearing a bright red Santa suit lay in a traffic lane, waving a cheap bottle of wine while singing "God rest ye merry gentlemen…"

An hour later I was waved down in front of a popular hangout at Santa Ana Boulevard and South Bristol Street. The woman, obviously tanked, complained the bouncer wouldn't let her back in.

I observed medical practitioners in blue scrubs dash out of the double emergency doors of St. Joseph's Hospital to meet an incoming ambulance. A bus driver rubbed tired eyes while he waited for a traffic light to change. A convenience store worker yawned as she attached a "closed" sign to a window, and a utility truck sped to fix a ruptured gas line. I reflected on the many others who deserved a tip of the red-tassled hat for laboring while most of the community took a holiday. First responders generally head the list of those who work on Christmas Day because crises don't take a holiday. Hospital and nursing home staff don't leave patients to fend for themselves. Air traffic controllers, bus drivers and cabbies on the job assuring revelers safe passage to their destinations. The communication business was at work for those who turned on the radio for some seasonal music, or gathered around the television for an NBA game while sipping spiked eggnog.

Ticket-takers, projectionists and popcorn-makers were at work in the movie theaters. Hotel cleaning crews, chefs, porters and desk clerks, correctional officers, airline and bus staff, newspaper reporters, radio and TV announcers, and more would be working over the holidays, as they did every day.

The car radio crackled loudly, interrupting my thoughts. I was dispatched on a Code 459 (burglary). At 4:00 a.m. I gave chase on foot after a man wearing a red Christmas vest and a white shirt—and nothing else. A neighbor called police after the half-nude man had broken into his vehicle. This criminal mastermind might have lost the red Christmas vest and put on pants, if he hadn't wanted to stand out and be caught.

And to end my shift, as I drove through Jerome Park, I spotted a woman wearing a Santa hat, red sweater and jeans urinating outside of the community center. And in the spirit of the holidays, a man was urinating next to her.

What a way to end 1972!

CHAPTER TWENTY - FIVE
January - April 1973

On New Years Eve I was dispatched to follow up on an attempted robbery at the Albertsons store in the 2000 block of 17th Street. I pulled my patrol car behind two responding officers' units. The squad car lights twirled and flashed, and a handful of people milled about, looking on as the officers handcuffed two men, one bleeding from a superficial shoulder wound.

As he held a towel full of ice to his swollen and bruised face, I overheard the store manager say, "There were two guys wearing ski masks and dark overcoats. One had a sawed-off shotgun under his coat. The other guy had a handgun of some kind. My customers and employees were forced onto the floor and the men stole money from the cash registers and pistol-whipped me. The one with the shotgun fired a shot into the ceiling and told us to stay down or they'd shoot us all."

The store manager gagged as he coughed. Officer Michael Mitchell, wire rimmed reading glasses sitting on top of his head, assured the man medical assistance was on the way. The manager pointed to Officer Brown, his normal bulldog expression relaxed, spoke quietly with a witness, before the manager continued, "Luckily, you and that officer got here before the shitheads could get away."

Officer Billy "Bumper" Brown turned to speak with another witness. At 6'2" Bumper Brown, muscular and slow speaking, notepad ready, was a commanding figure. He asked the young man what he had observed.

"I saw nothing. When I got to the parking lot, I heard gunshots, and scrambled under a parked car. But I heard what the cop said when those two guys came running outta the store waving their guns."

Bumper, a former Marine, countered gruffly, "You mean you heard the officers yell "Freeze! Police!""

"No, not exactly," said the witness. "It was more like, Happy New Year, assholes!" Boom! Boom! Boom!

Bumper later confided to me that, following an investigation, the shooting was deemed justifiable and was presented to a grand jury.

~~*~~

The following week I was dispatched to a home on South Shelley and Willits Streets. The woman called police to report a man peeping into her windows. I arrived without sirens or lights and parked a block away. I approached the house quietly, and stood silent in the dark, looking for movement and listening for unusual sounds. Nothing. I turned my flashlight on and made my way around the building in search of the perpetrator.

I walked through high foxtail grass. Thick, bristly spikes and seeds attached themselves, like Velcro, to the fabric of my uniform pants. *I hope this homeowner doesn't have a pet.* I had heard horror stories about the damage the weed had done to dogs. The peeping Tom was gone—surely he must be full of foxtail spikes, too. I hoped the peeper was miserable with thorns.

Embarrassed with the needle-like bristles poking through my pants, scratching my legs and ankles, I returned to the front of the house, climbed the narrow steps and knocked on the door. A porch light switched on at the same time the caller, a 350-pound woman squeezed into a leopard-print dominatrix outfit, opened the door. My brain stuttered for a moment as my eyes took in the lady of the house. Every part of me went on pause for a few moments, while my thoughts caught up. After assuring the caller that the trespasser was no longer on the premises, I returned to the patrol car, picking a few stickers out of my clothing. Tomorrow I would take them to the cleaners.

This wasn't the first time I had responded to a call where people sometimes showed up at the door in interesting attire and demonstrating varying levels of hospitality. Sometimes they were not even wearing pants. Or there was hard-core porn noisily playing in the background.

I recalled, as a civilian observer, commenting to Officer Katiz, "One might think citizens would adopt a standard of propriety when they know the police are coming."

"You'll learn, kid. They can open the door wearing nothing but a headband and tennis shoes and you still have to render police service with due vigilance."

I had the following day off, and I picked Fred and Jacob up after school to treat them to dinner. It would be a good time to hear about their first week in high school. On the way to the diner on 17th Street, we stopped at the cleaners.

Mrs. Hunter, folding a quilt on the counter, looked up as I entered, the boys trailing behind. She looked at the three of us questioningly. I explained we were on a boys' night out. I held up the uniform pants with the foxtail seeds attached to the hem, "I was able to pull out the tails. Will you be able to remove these seeds?"

Lifting her heavy blonde hair, Mrs. Hunter wiped perspiration from her neck before taking the pants from me. She inspected each leg closely, and said, "I'll do the best I can, Officer Lambert. These are tough little guys to get out. It might cost you a little more."

I turned to usher the boys out in front of me, "Anything you can do will be appreciated, Mrs. Hunter. Have a good evening."

Before the door closed behind me, she called out in an animated voice, "Enjoy your dinner, boys!"

On the way to the car, Fred observed, "She seems like a nice lady, Dad."

~~*~~

On January 29, 1973 I arrived to begin the two-day Los Angeles Police Defensive Driving School in San Pedro. As I waited behind two LAPD officers to sign in, I looked around the room, wondering if other officers from Santa Ana would be in attendance: the officer who recently totaled a vehicle during a pursuit, the officer who had a fender bender while drinking on the job, or the apathetic officer marking the days before his retirement.

I thought back on Captain Tracey's December 18th hallway remarks as he waved the Safety Committee report in the air. This was the first of two disciplinary actions I would receive as a result of my November 7th "negligent operation of a vehicle" accident.

Now, officers from different police departments sat in a semi-circle and waited for the instructor to arrive. I wondered what their stories were, and how many of them felt as I did.

It had been a mere two weeks after receiving the State Resolution and a Medal of Valor for saving children from a fire, that Captain Tracey ignored my contributions to the department in favor of putting the screws to me for a non-injury accident on a wet, slippery day. There's no quicker way to crush morale. It was this kind of thing that made me want to resign on the spot, feed my uniform through a shredder, and change careers. Aerospace, maybe. I'd heard there were promising opportunities at Hughes Aircraft and Northrop Grumman. Or Honeywell, perhaps.

The training officer arrived and the lecture began. He stressed the most important points of the handling and driving of a police vehicle were attitude and common sense.

The second day, the class of fifteen was taken to the driving course for hands-on training. I quickly learned that one half of all accidents were at or near intersections, how to accelerate or brake in emergencies, make quick stops and defensive turns, down shift and make other misdemeanor pursuits. On February 6, 1973 I outlined the experience in a memorandum to the Training Division, Staff Services.[65]

As a result of the training I never had another accident—nor suffered lost time nor wages. Stands to reason, since I didn't know my time was running out like sand in an hourglass.

~~*~~

On Monday, February 5th I had my first glimpse of the new chief, surrounded by captains, lieutenants, and sergeants I recognized as part of the BGs. Chief Davis was heavy set and hard-eyed. He looked as if he might have spent his younger years as a part of the defensive line for the Los Angeles Rams. In his short-sleeve shirt and vest, tattoos showed on his forearms. I overhead pieces of conversation, "Department needs upgrading." "We're underfunded and undermanned." "We need better training." It was obvious that Chief Davis had a couple big days since taking the reins on Saturday. I stood quietly against a wall with three other officers to allow the chattering group to trail behind the new chief into the conference room. We were ignored as they passed by us, but I assumed that at some point the rank-and-file would all have a chance to meet our new police chief. I knew better than to assume, but assume I did.

~~*~~

On February 11th *The Sun-Telegram* (San Bernardino) published the article, "How Minorities Faring in Police" with the subtitle, 'We're Having One Hell of a Time.'[66] The reporter had surveyed a number of police departments on their efforts to recruit Blacks and members of other minorities, how they were doing, and comments from police officials. My name was mentioned with a short quote from another news article that had referenced racial pressures and a limited social life.

~~*~~

On Monday, February 12ᵗʰ Don Bott, Personnel Director of the Uniformed Work Force of SAPD, called me into his office. "Officer Lambert, I've asked you here to follow-up on Captain Tracey's recommendation for a period of fifteen working days suspension as a result of the November 7, 1972 vehicle accident, in accordance with Civil Service Rules and Regulations, Section 1008. The suspension will begin tomorrow through March 3ʳᵈ."

He shuffled some papers, and said, "I see you've already completed the driving training school. Congratulations. I think we're done here."

I could see Tracey's memorandum on Bott's desk, paper clipped to other documents.[67] "May I read the action and have a copy for my files?" I asked.

Mr. Bott handed the papers to me to read, and countered, "Copies are available for your review at any time, Officer Lambert." Attached to the disciplinary action memo were copies of recent news articles. I wondered why.

~~*~~

The following day, I began the second of my two disciplinary actions. I piled out of bed early. While Fred got ready for school, I fixed a cup of hot chocolate and French toast topped with an egg over-easy for each of us. For the next two weeks, we had breakfast and conversations that developed into a new understanding and bonding experience.

My son was growing up quickly and celebrating the excitement of learning. After I made a particularly personal admission to Fred during breakfast, he gulped down some hot chocolate, pointed his fork at me and exclaimed, "Dad, don't you remember telling me that how I got somewhere was sometimes more important than actually getting there?"

Apparently my response was a blank look. With a roll of teenage eyes and a sigh, my son explained, "Okay, Dad. We were at a restaurant. It was raining. I saw a man helping a lady on crutches in the parking lot. I was holding the door, and you told me to shut it and wait inside, because if the man saw me waiting, he might try to hurry and they could slip and get hurt. I did what you said, and they were careful and made it to the open door without falling."

Squeezing dish soap into the sink of hot water, I absently-mindedly washed our breakfast dishes. No, I didn't remember the incident Fred related a few minutes before dashing out the door, not happy it was only Tuesday. But the episode triggered a near-forgotten memory.

Long ago my two old friends and mentors, already seated, had waved to me as I entered the Brolly Hut in Inglewood, and slid into a booth across from the two off-duty cops. During one of our many talks, LAPD Officer "Hoagie" Wilkey had many times shared his thoughts on the black police officer's journey being more important than his destination. "It's not until you're faced with challenges and obstacles that you'll discover your real purpose, and why you're on the journey." Hoagie raised his hand for the waitress to replenish his coffee, before continuing. "Those inevitable challenges will test your attitude and resolve, but that's what keeps you focused on your journey."

Cheeseburgers and chili cheese fries were placed in front of me, as Long Beach Police Officer Tooey Loflun chimed in, "Yep, stuff is always going to happen, and sometimes it'll be out of your control. But as long as you take responsibility for your actions and ultimately everything that happens to you, you'll retain personal power over how you respond. That's how you maintain control of your own destiny, each and every day."

~~*~~

The Staple Singers' June 1972 release "I'll Take You There" penetrated my brain. I turned up the volume on the radio. I had met Mavis Staple, the lead singer, when we were teens in Chicago. In my mind's eye I could see her beautiful, dimpled smile as she sang. I sang along:

> *Oh mmm I know a place*
> *Ain't nobody cryin'*
> *Ain't nobody worried*
> *Ain't no smilin' faces*
> *Mmm, no no*
> *Lyin' to the races*
> *Somebody, help me now*
> *I'll take you there.*

I left the house, ready to begin my fifteen-day suspension. Over the next three weeks I checked in with my sister Doe and her husband, Lewis. They had increased night-time canine security from ten to twenty-eight sites throughout Riverside and San Bernardino Counties. Under

Ernie's supervision, the Orange County Kennel teams in Costa Mesa had increased business three-fold, covering Orange, San Diego, and parts of Los Angeles Counties. Healthy dogs, quality training, efficient labor and schedules, operable vehicles, detailed paperwork, and client confidence were running like a well-oiled machine. I continued to collect and deposit money from the food and snack vending machine business I had started in November of 1971. Since that time I had installed machines in another seven locations. Business was good.

On Sunday, March 4th I was back on the job. I would miss the extra time spent with my son, but my suspension was over. I had been reassigned to Day Watch, so I checked into roll call at 7:00 a.m.

As I took a seat, I wondered if the disciplinary action for the accident would have been different had Captain Tracey and his gang known what a successful break it was for me.

~~*~~

It was now 2:00 pm and after thirty minutes of instruction and watching a stream of people go in and out of the house, I had been given the signal to approach. Only the red entry door identified it as different from the surrounding homes. Assigned to Special Detail, Vice Squad Unit, my job was to place a bet from a black-operated, horse racing bookie joint at Fourth and Bristol. The Vice Squad remained outside housed in a nondescript camper.

Trailing behind two men, I made my way toward the red door. I felt an electric charge that started in my stomach and ended somewhere in my chest. It was a kind of queasy excitement born from both expectation and resolve. I had first felt it in 1967 when I had assisted Fullerton Police in an attempt to purchase narcotics from a known seller. As I neared the door, I felt an adrenaline rush. I was about to enter a place where the occupants could be high or armed. Anything could go wrong. I didn't know what was on the other side of that red door. One suspect? Two? A baker's dozen?

Unobserved, I released the safety tab to my holster. Sweat salted the corners of my mouth. The door opened and our trio was welcomed in by a short, stocky man in a pin-stripe suit. He smelled of cigar smoke. The stub of a cigar was tucked in the band of his center creased, soft brimmed hat. The nerve center of the bookmaker was a bank of rotary telephones scattered on two large desks, with two men and a woman talking into them, and scribbling furiously. I recognized her as a former Santa Ana neighbor. Oh crap, don't look up, I thought, as I stared at Nahla's fingernails. They were long and curled under her fingertips. It was a mystery to me how she could hold onto a pencil and write legibly.

Money was scattered on a third desk. No words were necessary. I glanced at the men next to me, who filled out racing forms. I copied theirs. Like them, I slapped a hundred in twenty-dollar bills into the open palm of the bookmaker. The transaction with pin-stripe was quick.

Once I made the buy and opened the door to exit, the Squad rushed the house while tickets, racing forms and money were still visible, and arrested the three men and Nahla. I saw her glance at me as I walked away—not knowing then she was part owner of the bookie joint.

My former wife and I had wondered about Nahla on the few occasions we ran into one another—at the park, in the grocery, picking our sons up from school. Nahla had a nonsensical way of talking, and expressed her inane comments with a flourish of fingernails uncomfortably close to our faces. When she saw me, she greeted me with a wide smile, "Friends are baskets and hats, Lampus." When Marie and I saw Nahla, we thought of her as a little nutty.

~~*~~

Five weeks later, after being released, the foursome opened another bookie joint in the predominantly Hispanic neighborhood in Fullerton, on East Valencia Avenue near Harbor Boulevard.

Vice Squad officers from Santa Ana and Fullerton had gotten a search warrant and had teamed up to organize a raid on the bookmaker. The Full Pink Moon, mossy pink like wild ground phlox, was playing peek-a-boo, weaving in and out of ribbons of gray clouds scudding across the night sky, as we stealthily made our way toward the two-story house.

The house had iron bars on the windows, along with a peep-hole in the door to identify their visitors before opening any access to them. The door was scratched and dented with chipped brown varnish. In nosing around, we discovered a smaller, almost hidden door behind the house. It had the clawed, slightly bubbly look of wood that's starting to rot at the joints. They must have used it as a fast exit.

The squad positioned themselves around the house, covering windows and doors to back me up. My gun drawn, search warrant in my pocket, I kicked the door as hard as I could. The weathered door, splintered on the edges and scuffed on the bottom from years of use, gave away quickly.

And the first person I saw as I entered was my neighbor, whose head had jerked up at the commotion. Her arms shot up. "Oh, shit, it's Lampus!" She proceeded to pee on herself. Officers burst into the room behind me, with an explosion of commands to the bewildered numbers runners.

"Look," Nahla pleaded, "I'll do anything for you, just don't take me to jail. Cold is with the monkey's ears and toes." Same old daffy Nahla, I thought, as the Fullerton officers escorted her to a waiting black-and-white.

~~*~~

On Saturday, April 21st I followed a vehicle traveling north on Bristol Street for several blocks. A number of times I observed the vehicle dart between lanes in the heavy traffic, causing drivers behind it to swerve or jam on their brakes. Although the vehicle was under the speed limit, weaving between lanes was not only a violation, but a safety issue.

I approached his car. The Santa Ana resident identified himself as Jack Tidwell. Before I could tell him why I had stopped him, he became enraged. "I've never had a ticket before! The police department started going south when they let you people in!"

Mr. Tidwell got out of his car. "Giving me a ticket your way of showing resentment for your personal shortcomings? A chance to get back at your oppressors? I'm not signing a goddamn ticket."

"Then, sir, you'll be under arrest for refusing to sign the citation." I opened the rear door of the patrol vehicle, and he angrily slid onto the seat.

He slammed his fist, "I told you before, I've never had a ticket. I want to speak to a sergeant!"

Sergeant Webb heard my call to Communications requesting that they stamp a TI (traffic incident) for a subject who refused to sign a traffic citation and that I was enroute to the jail with a prisoner. Webb contacted me on the radio and said, "I didn't hear you call for a field sergeant to get clearance for the arrest. I'll meet you before the subject is booked."

Tidwell's attitude, when he met the sergeant, was instantly contrite. He answered The Vultures' questions in a soft, controlled manner. His demeanor was perplexed, but adamant, that he had not committed any violation and couldn't understand why the black officer had cited him.

Sergeant Webb, his smirk showing a row of small teeth, glanced at me, and voided the citation before releasing Mr. Tidwell. Webb then directed me to meet him in Acting Watch Commander Morrissey's office to relate the incident, where I was orally reprimanded for poor judgment. I would learn later that Sergeant Webb wrote a lengthy report and forwarded it to Chief Davis.[68]

On April 24th I responded with a two-page memo regarding the incident. I believed the oral reprimand would have been in order for not calling a field sergeant to the scene prior to arresting a man, but not for poor judgment. I believed that the safety of other drivers in heavy traffic should not be put aside for one unsafe driver.[69]

~~*~~

Reassigned to the 3:00-11:00 p.m. watch on Sunday, April 29th, a feeling of foreboding had been with me as the evening deepened to darkness. The crescent moon was barely visible when the short, clipped voice of a female police dispatcher interrupted the background chatter of the car radio. "Unit 3620, Code 3, follow up on reported Code 245." Distorted by static, she continued, "Make contact with a Mr. Mouton on North Sullivan, who has reported an assault with a deadly weapon at his home."

The Code 3 was an emergency call that sent cops speeding through traffic with the squad car's lights flashing, and sirens blaring. I sped to the apartment complex on North Sullivan Street.

A lean, muscular man with a butch haircut moved from under the light at the bottom of a set of stairs and met me halfway up the walk. He stood rigid, shoulders back, and began speaking in terse sentences, "I'm a Marine out of El Toro. I've been on field exercises for the past several weeks. My group returned home early. We were ahead of our training schedule. Thought I would surprise my wife. Come with me, officer."

As we climbed the stairs to his second-floor rental, he continued, "My wife doesn't work, see, so I expected her home. No problem. I walked into the bedroom and this dumb punk is hunking her. They didn't see me. They didn't hear me."

Mouton paused at the top of the stairs. His shoulders sagged as he turned and told me in a lowered and rough voice, "I backed out of the room and went to my car, where I keep my military sword. I took it out of the car, went upstairs, and put it through them both. Do you want to handcuff me now?"

I did. He turned, putting his hands behind his back for cuffing, and I led him to the black-and-white. I put him in the back seat of the patrol unit before calling in a Code 10-54 (possible dead body) and a request for backup.

Officer Wooldridge, with a police trainee in the passenger seat, arrived within minutes. As they got out of their unit, "Woolly" laughingly said, "Not a feud over cerveza and beer, I hope?" He was referring to the bickering Catalina and Emiliano, who had had a "badge divorce" performed by the Fullerton police.

After briefing Wooldridge that Mouton reported he had just killed his wife and her lover, the trainee was instructed to keep watch on the suspect before we entered the apartment.

We made our way to the bedroom, and stood at the door. The scene was as Mouton had described it. I choked back the nausea as I looked at the bed. A nude man lay face down over a woman, her face visible, eyes open and glazed over with horror. The bladed weapon was impaled in the back of the man up to the brass handguard—Mouton had forced the blade through his back and stomach and on through Mrs. Mouton and into the mattress, where the blade stuck and held. Blood had begun to seep and pool from the bed, and onto the floor. I subconsciously thought that there should be more blood. I noted clothing trailing across the room, two empty wine glasses sitting on the single night stand, the soft glow of a frosted bulb shining from the open door of the adjacent bathroom.

The paramedics had arrived just behind us and were starting through the front door when I stepped away from the bedroom door and stopped them. "Woolly" told me to make the necessary calls while he stayed to make sure the crime scene was not contaminated by the EMTs walking around and picking up or touching things that could unintentionally destroy evidence. The paramedics' job was to save lives, and in this case their lifesaving efforts would be of no use.

I couldn't wait to get out of the room and the apartment. It took me a few moments of deep breathing before I could make radio contact for a field supervisor, homicide detectives, the coroner, and other necessary officials. Mr. Mouton had heard me on the radio and he gave way to convulsive sobs as arriving officers read him his Miranda rights.

The apartment was sealed off and the bodies weren't going anywhere. There were no witnesses to the offense. We had the suspect identified, arrested and handcuffed. Mr. Mouton had established a motive for the crime. He had identified his wife. It was now up to the officer in charge of the investigation to discover clues that would lead to the identification of the man, and find evidence to be used in court. Because Mouton was active military, the case would be referred to the U.S. Marine Corp Military Police, Criminal Investigations Division; since the crime occurred in Orange County jurisdiction the agencies would work together.

Later, Wooldridge and I were told the two appeared to have died instantly, and because the homicide had been committed in the heat of passion with sudden and sufficient provocation, no charges were brought against Mr. Mouton by the Orange County District Attorney's office, who called it excusable homicide. We then learned the military convicted Mouton with a voluntary manslaughter charge, which was over-turned due to the circumstances.

CHAPTER TWENTY - SIX
May 1973 Target - Manic May

On May 8th, I received written communication from Chief Raymond Davis – whom I had yet to meet – that I was being suspended from the SAPD for a period of eight hours, as recommended by Webb for the April 21st traffic incident.[70]

It would be forty-plus years and a first look into a copy of my police jacket, that a footnote on the memo reads: "Before disciplinary action was taken on the above, Officer Lambert resigned."

Interestingly, I didn't know I was going to resign at that time – how was it the chief and his John Birch devotees knew what I did not?

Could it be what happened next?

~~*~~

May 14, 1973. The watch commander, (no longer lieutenant) Sergeant Webb, called me to his office. Now what! He wanted to question me about a complaint received the previous day. The same Joyce Hunter that had been altering and cleaning my uniforms over the past several years alleged I asked her for a date the day before and that, according to Webb, "I wanted one chance with her."

My brain stuttered for a moment. Every part of me went on pause while my thoughts caught up.

Webb knew I had been frequenting the cleaners for years, as had he. We passed one another on occasion coming in or out as we picked up or dropped our laundry. More often than not when Webb had arrived before me, he and Mrs. Hunter were in deep, cozied conversation. I told him I had the day before picked up my cleaning. Mrs. Hunter was emotional and had been crying. Her eyes were watery, her nose red. I asked her what was wrong. Running nail-bitten fingers through her hair, she told me she and her husband had been trying to have a baby, without success.

"Try to cheer up. You know, it only takes one time, Mrs. Hunter." And with that, I paid for my cleaning, took my uniform shirt and slacks off the rack where she had placed them, and left. Was Webb at the cleaners yesterday? Did we pass one another, and I didn't see him?

Sarcastically, I said, "But you would know how she feels about things, with the amount of time the two of you spend together, wouldn't you?"

He studied me for a moment. His face turned as negative and dark as a demon on a toad stool. Our eyes locked in a stare, neither of us willing to back down. After a few moments, with confident authority Webb gestured towards the door, an unspoken invitation to leave his office.

My heart was hammering, but I kept my gait casual with no hint of hesitation, as I made my way to the shift briefing. I thought about Webb, wondering once again how this man, or men like him, could represent our police department. He was an entrepreneur, for lack of a better word. He owned apartments on Sullivan and was a true slum lord, as we envision them. He would go in uniform to collect rents. He ran a pyramid scheme from the watch commander's office on the graveyard shift, and would bring in a rack full of clothes he had purchased from the local weekend swap meets to sell to the office personnel and other officers. The rumors that floated maintained that it was a combination of these reasons he had been demoted several months before from the rank of lieutenant.

Two days later Webb called me back to schedule a polygraph test, "To get the truth out of you."

I agreed to take a polygraph test, *after* a full investigation into the matter, and a meeting with both supervision and the accuser.

Were conversations I had witnessed between him and Mrs. Hunter more than cozy – even conspiratorial? Could Webb have put Mrs. Hunter up to the complaint? Could he have painted a picture of me that would take statements made between her and me out of context, and somehow convince her to go along with his plans? She was in an emotional state, and it's possible she believed she was somehow helping him with a police matter?

I never spoke with Mrs. Hunter personally, was never presented with a written statement from her or a formal complaint from the police department. No other superior or peer approached me about it, or indicated there was an investigation into the matter. As far as I knew, Webb and I were the only ones having "conversation" regarding the matter, and the entire situation was verbal between the two of us.

Again, Webb called me into his office to take the polygraph—without an investigation. He flatly denied the request that I meet face-to-face with my accuser. He moved from behind his desk, his hand casually resting on his weapon, with a look of daring and defiance. The office air was somehow frigid, keeping us locked in the moment.

It was the straw that broke the camel's back. I stood mute, staring at The Vulture.

One time, as a nine-year-old, I swung from a tree on a makeshift rope over the river bank. I waited too long on the return swing and fell ten feet to the ground, landing on my back. It was as if the impact had knocked every wisp of air from my lungs, and I lay there struggling to inhale, to exhale, to do anything. That's how I felt now, trying to remember how to breathe, unable to speak, totally stunned and feeling powerless.

I made a sudden decision. Realistically, it could have been anything at that point—something as simple as tripping over my own feet could have triggered my decision.

"Sir, with all due respect to you, I don't like the way this has been handled, your unjustified remarks and your treatment of me. I've had enough. I quit. This is my last day. I'll have it in writing and on appropriate desks before noon tomorrow."

I didn't look back as I left him staring after me.

At that moment, my feelings were deeper than frustration. I believed my efforts to this point were in vain. My problems too many. The war not winnable. Doubts overwhelmed me. This force I'd believed in, this ironclad protector of the people, had time and again revealed itself to be like any human institution with its share of corruption and incompetence, indifference and stupidity, fueled by greed, political ambition, and bias.

A handful of people like Webb, can make hate translate into cruel and unjust actions.

~~*~~

That same night, I dreamed. *I'm flying from something. I don't know what. I'm not fearful. I launch myself with a short run; arms spread wide, face down, head moving from side to side. I fly high in the air over fields, urban areas, and tall buildings. Sometimes I stop on top of a building. I come to a body of water where my altitude drops just above the water. I have to see what's down there and then get to the other side.*

As I land on my feet, I wake up.

The Dates Don't Match.

"Our lives begin to end the day we become silent about things that matter."

I recalled Martin Luther King's words.

Since May 17th I vowed to be silent no longer.

I wrote a two and a quarter page resignation with my last day worked May 16, and requested it be attached to the formal Resignation Form.[71]

May 17th. Webb wrote a confusing (to me) memo to Chief Davis, claiming I was twenty minutes late for a 1 p.m. appointment with him – and therefore in violation of a direct order. He said my shift had been rescheduled to begin at 1 p.m., and I was also on unauthorized absence from duty. Huh?[72]

He concluded this page two (where was page one?) would accompany my resignation form, which had been turned in to Captain Tracey.

May 22nd. Chief Raymond C. Davis wrote a memo stating a polygraph test was given to Mrs. Hunter by SAPD investigator R.T. Lindley, who found her truthful. He stated I refused to take a polygraph test – which I did refuse after being denied an investigation into the allegations made against me.[73] But that part had been left out of the memorandum.

And how was it that a man (Chief Davis) I had never met, could state "facts" about what happened – but from the same person (Sgt Webb) who initiated the matter?

PART FIVE
CONCLUSION

We're like flowers that God made in different colors.
That's why the world is so pretty!
We're just like the flowers.
One day, son, all the flowers will be in one field, I promise.

ANNER DAY LAMBERT

EPILOGUE

Six months after leaving the force I heard Sergeant Webb had been turned in by some office personnel for his schemes, and demoted to patrolman. He couldn't take the demotion, so he quit. I thought I would feel good about his problems, thought vengeance would be sweet.

But I didn't.

Mr. Hunter filed for divorce, and Mrs. Hunter relocated to Oakland, California.

I simply felt sad…for them…for my family…and, yes…for myself.

I now view that period of my life as a whisper in time.

Little did I know, over the next forty-plus years, that I would be subjected to more of the same old "black and white thing." That my "whispers" would become almost endless…that my prayers would feel useless. Laws could and would change, at least on paper, but not the hearts of man, I feared.

Affirmative Action was later implemented, and sensitivity training became a model in law enforcement and in the corporate world. New technology has helped officers in the field both in safety and knowledge.

My gratification, however, has come from meeting occasionally the young black man or woman who went into law enforcement as a result of my efforts.

I've learned that much of my documented evidence and sacrifices have paved the way for others to become strong leaders in Orange County, not only as police officers, but as attorneys and even judges.

But that's another story.

A Matter of Research: An Inconvenient Truth
by Sharron Lambert

It should have been a time of triumph for the Santa Ana Police Department, not an occasion when profound hatred, bigotry, and power drove a man's career and life - like a giant eraser - into obliteration.

I unlocked the mailbox and opened the envelope containing the 2005 stamped copyright title change for my husband's manuscript, "Tough To Be a Hero When You're a 'Nigger Cop,'" quoted from the June 7, 1970 *Orange County Evening News* front page headline. I placed the document in a manila folder and walked to the guest bedroom.

Several boxes were stored on the closet floor. The carton of colorful Christmas wrappings and ribbons shifted as I pulled a heavy box out from under it. With some difficulty, I dragged the box to the center of the room. Sitting cross-legged on the floor, I began unpacking the box of news clippings, framed awards, black and white photographs, the medal of valor encased in its gold-leaf frame, police department memos, and letters from community residents about my husband, Harlen "Lamb" Lambert.

Picking up the dog-eared manuscript from the bottom of the box, I brushed away a dried silver fish. The 1972 copyright date of "'Nigger Pig'" was a testament to the many years the 156 pages of typewritten memories had lain dormant.

As I leafed through the manuscript, I wondered if finally Lamb and I would settle down and dig in. We had just retired for the fourth time in 2005.

Our dining room table soon became cluttered as we organized the materials to begin structuring and rewriting the story, which at this point, read like a narrative. The bones of the story were solid, but it was necessary to add the meat. We needed to establish timelines for crucial events, build Lambs' character from childhood, develop primary themes, talk with people he worked and played with. We needed to research, among other things, the history of Santa Ana, the John Birch Society and their role within the police department, and the hurts of race and segregation Lamb experienced.

The toughest job, for me, would be to get my ever-in-motion Lamb to sit still long enough to answer questions that I would attempt to translate into word pictures.

We drove to the Santa Ana Library to meet with Cheryl Eberly, the History Room Librarian. I showed her the numerous news clippings I had with me, and told her we were looking for information regarding Lambs' tenure on the police force, and to find dates that had been torn off a couple of the articles. She explained that newspaper articles were not scanned prior to 1985; we would have to go to Cal-State Fullerton periodicals and search the micro-fische.

After ushering us to a table, Cheryl said she would search the history room computer databases for information while we reviewed a manila folder that contained police clippings, and a hard-bound book she pulled from the shelves.

Inside the folder was the *Orange County Register* article dated December 12, 1966, with the headline: "Santa Ana Police Hire First Negro." Lamb's home address was published there. Lamb had told me that the following day was the beginning of threatening phone calls and vandalism to his home for weeks to come.

Next I opened the photo book of Santa Ana police officers, put together by Investigator Chuck Magdalena and Officer Al Sawyer. In April 1979 Raymond C. Davis, Chief of Police, presented the photo book to the Santa Ana Library's History Room. The volume was produced by First American Title Insurance Company, which allowed reproductions of Santa Ana historical photos.

The pictures were arranged in alphabetical order. Lambert should have been on page 29, between officers he worked with – but his photo wasn't there. I checked under the letter H, in case he was accidentally posted under Harlen, his first name. It was not there. I scanned each page, looking for his name with the tag, photo not available. I didn't find that either.

Cheryl returned, "I'm sorry, but I can't find anything in our archives, Mr.

Lambert. What I would like you to do is to make an appointment with our archivist, Manuel Escamilla. He can scan the articles and photos you have, and make sure they get into our computer system." She gave us his direct number, and the days he would be in the library.

We returned the following week with our folder of documents and photos.

"Please, call me Manny." Soft spoken and easy going, he spent the next three hours scanning and downloading our documents into the library's history database. Then he photocopied the articles, stamped them property of Santa Ana Public Library, and placed them in the manila police folder.

"Did you bring a blank CD with you?" he asked. I had indeed – I also brought my Canon camera with me. And while Manny copied the scanned files onto the CD for our personal use, I snapped photos of the pages from the illustrated police book titled History of Santa Ana Police Department 1869-1978. Lamb had worked there from January 1967 until May 1973.

Curiosity got the better of us. Two weeks later, we returned to the History Room. Each of our documents in the manila police folder was missing. Manny tried for over an hour to find the documents he had downloaded into the computer. "Unbelievable! Everything is buried so deep it's impossible to find."

Manny would be the first –but not the last- to tell us that certain news articles had a way of disappearing. He recommended we purchase a humidity gauge or a dehumidifier, to protect the news clippings.

We did, but we also got sidetracked. Lamb started a new business that would be another first in the life and career of Harlen "Lamb" Lambert, bringing positive recognition to him both at home and abroad.

In January 2016 we completed end-of-business arrangements and formally retired for the fifth time.

In March 2016 it had been eleven years since we'd worked on Lamb's book. My son-in-law carried the box out from the guest bedroom closet.

He helped me unpack and organize its contents on the dining room table.

Within an hour, folder and CD in hand I made another trip to the Santa Ana Library. I checked the police folder and requested the library archivist review the history database. Nothing had changed – there was no information, with the exception of the original hire notice and one line in the library's Raitt Street Chronicles parroting the same information.

We had held on to the contents of the manila folder Harlen had picked up from the Santa Ana Police reception desk on February 19, 2009. Reviewing the contents once again was the last affront – we were now eager to complete this memoir about one man's experience as the first black police officer in Orange County, in the city of Santa Ana, California. His words, his story, his sorrows and successes are typically American - but unique to him.

It's time to break the silence - without stories like his, people might forget that life in these United States was regrettably once really like this. Is it still?

SAPD File Jacket
March 16, 2009

It had started with a request to renew my Carry Concealed Weapon (CCW) license September 16, 2008. The new sheriff-coroner in town, Sandra Hutchens, questioned the number of CCW licensees. I had held my license for seven years and it was time to renew.

Lieutenant Rojas, head of the SAPD personnel department, said, "Somebody really hated your guts. It's protocol that all files are purged after five years. I'll call OCSD (Orange County Sheriff Department) with a referral and personally see to it your file is purged." I thanked him.

At home I put the phone in its cradle deliberately, gently. I knew if I wasn't deliberate, I would smash something. Once again I picked up the offending manila envelope.

The envelope that, on February 19, 2009, the front desk SAPD officer had slid across the counter. I signed the release form. The envelope that contained information that, unknowing to me until this date had, for the last 40-plus years, affected my life in ways I would never have imagined.

It immediately brought back Sergeant "The Vulture" Webb's final indignity directed toward me: hate translated into action.

I removed the papers for the umpteenth time, holding them in my hands as I leaned back into the headrest of my office chair, and closed my eyes. Microfiche handwritten notes on stenographer notepaper with no signatures, incidents I had never heard of, reports without supporting documentation, statements without dates, reports written by a second officer with "unfounded" buried in the text, exaggerated data, and half-truths.

Was I perfect? No. Did I have vehicle accidents? Yes. Was I occasionally moody? Yes. Did my superiors ever ask me about what might be behind my different moods as I came on shift? No. Were fair investigations conducted and reported? No. I can go on and on, but nothing will change history.

Did I note that each and every piece of paper in the jacket was dated after I was hailed a hero by the *The Orange County Evening News*, *The Los Angeles Times*, and the *Long Beach Independent* newspapers? You bet.

Where were the accolades? The news articles? Mention of the medal of valor award? The Officer of the Year and Officer of the Month awards? The State Senate Resolution plaque? Thank you letters from citizens I served as an officer of the law? Roll-call statistics as leader in traffic stops and citations?

And last but not least, the policy of the SAPD files are supposedly purged of all information except date of hire and date of leaving the department. Yet over the years, and recently, after my renewal request to Paul Walters, the Chief of Police, his Assistant, the Human Resources Department, the Civilian Personnel Investigator, and the District Attorney's Office – all had reviewed this information and nobody ever questioned why this information was still in my jacket.

Of course, I could do as my retired SAPD SWAT officer friend suggested, "Sue the bastards."

The remembered incidents and conversations were like a slide show that raced across my closed eyelids. Over the years different departments approached me to think about joining them – full time, part time, voluntary or in a reserve capacity. I interviewed with 22 departments from Northern to Southern California, and in-between, off and on over a period of twenty-five years.

I passed physical, psychological, polygraph tests, and oral boards. Newport Beach claimed I had the highest rating of an oral interview conducted in their department. I had welcoming comments from Buena Park, Placentia, Oceanside, Fullerton and Yorba Linda, among others – until the background check.

Suddenly the departments lost interest, and gave me no reason, with the exception of Fullerton (where I have resided since 1980). The officer,

over the telephone, just said I didn't pass the polygraph.
I'm now retired and writing my story.

I recalled Martin Luther King's words: "Our lives begin to end the day we become silent about things that matter."

The contents of the manila folder lit the flame to complete my memoir. The micro-fiche contents released to the departments I interviewed with was the complete snapshot of my police career with the SAPD.

But then, as documented in an article "A Matter of Research – An Inconvenient Truth," I was erased into obliteration. Now, the Santa Ana Police Department can't have it both ways.

I refuse to be silent any longer.

Harlen "Lamb" Lambert

END NOTES

Documents reproduced here in thumbnail form are available in full at lambtheauthor.com.

1. December 8, 1966: *The Orange County Register*, "Santa Ana Police Hire First Negro."

2. January 1, 1967 through May 25, 1969: Police Applicant Success Scale for the period.

3. April 26, 1967: Memorandum: Commendation for Volunteers for Stakeout Duty.

4. May 26, 1967: Memorandum: Crime Clearances Due To On-Sight Arrests By Patrol Division.

5. June 10, 1967: Police Science Department, Fullerton Junior College, Civil Disorder Control Institute Certificate.

6. July 24, 1967: Letter addressed to Police Chief Allen from citizen, Bruce W. Albert.

7. August 9, 1967: Letter of acknowledgement from Director of Lincoln School Headstart Staff.

8. September 10, 1967: *The Independent Press-Telegram of Long Beach*, "Orange County Racial Tensions Become Apparent," Part I.

9. September 17, 1967: *The Independent Press-Telegram of Long Beach*, "The Ghetto Is Like a Bad Ache," Part II.

10. September 19, 1967: Letter addressed to Police Chief Allen from P.N.Perak, Bristol Drug Company, Inc.

11. October 12-13, 1967: Certificate of Participation, 1ˢᵗ Annual California Police Olympics, San Diego.

12. October 25, 1967: Letter from L.E. Romaine, Youth Director, The First Methodist Church.

13. November 13, 1967: Memorandum: Personnel Commendations referencing line-up.

14. November 8, 1967: Letter from Wayne H. Bornhoft, Chief of Police, City of Fullerton.

15. January 15, 1968: *Independent*, "Freeway Pursuit Jails 2."

16. April 13, 1968: Memorandum: Commendation for assistance.

17. April, 18, 1968: Memorandum: Elected to represent SAPD at Insurance Agents of Orange County dinner meeting.

18. April 25, 1968 Letter from James L. Prager, P.A. Prager & Son.

19. July 15, 1968: Memorandum: Citizen Commendation from Ruth M Gallo.

20. July 28, 1968: Memorandum: Citizen commendation from Ellen Swearingen.

21. October 6, 1968, *The Los Angeles Times,* "Negro Policeman: Minority Within a Minority" page 1; "Negro Policeman" page 2.

22. November 20, 1968: Letter addressed to Police Chief Allen from Mr. and Mrs. James Johnson (3 pages).

23. December 13, 1968: P.B.A. (Police Benevolent Association) Meritorious Service Award.

24. January 28, 1969: Letter to Police Chief Allen from Orange Coast College Police Science Program staff.

25. January 29, 1969: Letter to Police Chief Allen from Donald G. Tibbetts, Principal, Roosevelt School.

26. February 21-June 23, 1969: Letters of appreciation and thanks ranging from February 21 (Orange Coast College Faculty Committee for Confrontation '69), March 17 (Parent Involvement Council, Inc.), March 25 (Santa Ana Unified and Junior College Districts Commendation), April 1 (Jay E. Hynds, County of Orange), April 2 (St. Barbara's School), June 23, 1969 (Patricia Sinkey & Karen Howard, Santa AnaHigh School students).

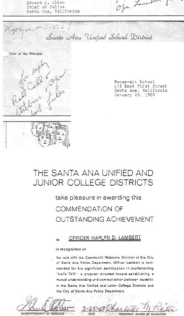

27. June 5, 1969: Article from Santa Ana Police Dept., Santa Ana Public Library, *Santa Ana Register*, "SA Policeman Slain On Street"; June 6, 1969: *The Los Angeles Times*, "Slain Officer Hailed by Fellow Patrolmen."

28. December 4, 1969: Letter addressed to Chief of Police from James D. Hewitt, Chandler Research.

29. January 19, 1970: Memorandum:
Police Community Relations
Commendation.

30. March 12, 1970: Memorandum:
Commendation for alertness.

31. April 17, 1970: Crime Scene
Investigation School Certificate.

32. April 25, 1970: Pre-Sergeants
Supervisory Institute Certificate.

33. April 29, 1970: Handwritten letter
of recognition on behalf of Teenage
Christian Doctrine Class.

34. May 26, 1970: Santa Ana Complaint
Incident Report at 2064 S. Evergreen,
Santa Ana (3 pages).

35. May 26, 1970: Memorandum:
Officer commendation.

36. May 26, 1970: Meritorious Service Award.

37. May 28, 1970: Chief Allen pens nomination letter to IACP (2 pages).

38. May 30, 1970: Letter of commendation to Chief Allen from citizens with signatures.

39. June 6, 1970: Citizen letters of appreciation and signatures to Chief Allen, forwarded to Lambert (3 pages).

40. June 7, 1970: *The Orange County Evening News*, "Tough to Be Hero When You're a 'Nigger Cop!'" (two page one's); "Cop Tells Hardships" page two.

41. June 8, 1970: Memorandum:
Information regarding threats.

42. June 16, 1970: *The Register*, article
with photo, 'S.A. "Officer of the
Year"; Policeman of the Year
Award; June Policeman of the
Month Award (3 documents).

43. June 16, 1970: *The Santa Ana*
ews, citing The Santa Ana Rotary
$50.00 check presented to the Jerome
Park Center basketball team.

44. June 25, 1970: Memorandum in
File Jacket – Citizen's Complaint.

45. August 19, 1970: Letter from
Don Regan.

46. September 16, 1970:
Chemical Agent Training
certificate.

47. November 2, 1970:
Memorandum: Complaints of
Police Conduct.

48. December 6, 1970:
Memorandum: Commendation.

49. January 22, 1971: Letter
from Bruce A. Hand, Golden
West College.

50. April 23, 1971:
Memorandum: Commendation.

51. June 28, 1971: Letter of
appreciation to Chief Allen from
Captain Goodwin, CHP.

52. November 10, 1971:
Memorandum in File Jacket -
Possible misconduct.

53. November 17, 1971:
Memorandum in File Jacket -
Involved in accident.

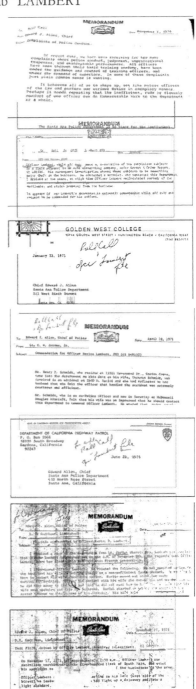

54. January 14, 1972: Advanced Officer Training certificates.

55. January 22, 1972: Memorandum in File Jacket – Laginess complaint.

56. February 20, 1972: Memorandum in File Jacket – Beasock complaint (3 pages).

57. February 26, 1972: Memorandum in File Jacket – Beasock complaint unfounded.

58. March 16, 1972: Memorandum in File Jacket – Misuse of Department Key (2 pages – see 3/20/72, pg 2).

59. April 19, 1972: *Pacific Clippings*, article with photo," Image of St. Bernard" (2 photos).

60. April 28, 1972: *The Orange County Register*, article with photo, "SA Policeman pens Racial View of OC" (2 pages).

61. June 27, 1972: *The Los Angeles Times*, article "Black Lawman: An Open Book with photo.

62. July 1972: Note in File Jacket to Captain Johnson with a litany of anonymous grievances.

63. November 27, 1972: Photo with Chief Allen presenting Senate Resolution and Medal of Valor.

64. December 3, 1972: *The Independent Press-Telegram*, article "Black policeman's story etched in bigotry—pride."

65. February 6, 1973: Memorandum re: LAPD Defensive Driving School lessons learned.

66. February 11, 1973: *The Sun-Telegram*, article "How Minorities Faring in Police."

67. February 12, 1973: Memorandum in File Jacket: Disciplinary action.

68. April 21, 1973: Memorandum in File Jacket: Judgement & Violation by Departmental Order (2 pages).

69. April 24, 1973: Memorandum in File Jacket: Traffic Incident – missing page one of the document.

70. May 8, 1973: Memorandum in File Jacket: Disciplinary Action.

71. May 17, 1973: Formal Resignation and Separation Forms in File Jacket (2 documents) – three page resignation memorandum missing from file.

72. May 17, 1973: Page two – page one missing from file – violation of a direct order in File Jacket.

73. May 22, 1973: Memorandum in File Jacket: Polygraph Examination.

HARLEN "Lamb" LAMBERT

Rainbow Protector
by Isabella Beltran

The colors that make America can not roam and be free,
trapped in a box of white with a lock and key.

Many colors have fought, many colors have been lost
but the fight will never stop, no matter the cost

With souls like his, a death is in sight,
of an idea and culture that has been policed
since the beginning of our life,
the source of colors fright.

Going into the belly of the beast,
he decided to be the first black
of Orange County police.
To be the voice and protector
of the colors, a justice of the peace.

It was not easy, from racism and being
thrown out by a fellow into the streets,
to his own colors seeing him as a traitor.
He knew that the colors would
understand later.

Being "the ugly duckling"
in a pond of swans,
he knew that he was only as
powerful as a pawn.
But it is still a step towards good change,
to make life as we all know start to rearrange.

With souls like his, a death is in sight,
of an idea and culture that has been policed
since the beginning of our life,
the source of colors fright.

The surrounding fire and adrenaline
at its peak.
With no distinction of color,
he saved 2 children who were too weak.
The children were white, seeing black carrying
them to safety,
a sight many thought was crazy.

HARLEN "Lamb" LAMBERT

That day he showed that colors and whites
can care for each other and live as one,
a step for Orange County to realize
that the shade of a person
shouldn't matter to anyone.

With souls like his, a death is in sight,
of an idea and culture that has been policed
since the beginning of our life,
the source of colors fright.

A basketball star, he seemed to do it all.
Leaving the police in '73 was his call.
He now trains dogs for the police,
writes poetry, and lives his life in no hurry.
He also shares his story to many,
since the main media thinks people
like him are as irrelevant as a penny.

Wasting websites on the best jean trends
and the best butt exercises,
it seems that it is all of what
our society idolizes.
He does not want fame,
he just wants to be heard.

For stories like his remind us to fight
for those who are forced into a box,
to be unheard.
The fight for freedom will never stop,
people like him will stop it
from being a backdrop.

With souls like Harlen's, a death is in sight,
of an idea and culture that has been policed
since the beginning of our life,
the source of colors fright.

Isabella Beltran is a writer living in Southern California.

ACKNOWLEDGEMENTS

This wasn't an easy book to write. But with the help of hovering angels who researched, supported, empowered, challenged, kicked me in the butt, and patiently listened to my rants and raves, publication of my fifty-year writing journey is now a reality.

Individuals and staffs of institutions who have given generous support and countless hours of research and public events to validate my place in Santa Ana's history are: Cheryl Eberly, Santa Ana Library History Room; Kevin Cabrera, Heritage Museum of Orange County; Doctor Sandra Perez, Honors Program, California State University-Fullerton; and Sharon Sekhon, Director of the Studio of Southern California History. Thank you for your belief in me.

Long before I knew which direction to take my writer's wings, there were the encouraging words from Barbara French and her weekly writers groups—along with her tough-love red pencil on the pages. Joan Horrigan and Barbara French, thank you for your countless hours of editing and for making my words stronger. The book would have been the poorer without your meticulous attention and gracious input. Thank you to Brenda Valencia for her care in reading the next to final draft of this manuscript. A special thank you to Isabella Beltran for allowing the use of her poem "Rainbow Protector." Any remaining errors are wholly mine.

The book's godmother, Sharon Sekhon, has been relentless and gentle as she pushed and applauded the delivery—from creative cover to a lasting format of words and images— always calm in the face of my panic. Sharon, thank you for that shove off the fence. It worked!

Finally, I reserve the greatest measure of gratitude for my wife, Sharron, who has given so much of herself and with unfailing faith in this work carried me through when I doubted what was possible.

HARLEN "LAMB" LAMBERT

has a varied career in basketball, is an Army veteran, was the first black police officer hired for the Santa Ana Police Department in Orange County, CA, is an entrepreneur, a world-renown K-9 trainer, radio and television personality, and published author.

Harlen writes in Southern California, where he lives with his wife, Sharron and their family of four-legged companions.

Also by Harlen "Lamb" Lambert

AFFAIRS OF THE HEART Vol. 1

Published 2016

A beautifully full-color illustrated collection of honest, and often painful free verse about love, faith, distance, being lonely, betrayal, loss, longing, relationships, neglect, abuse, longing, survival, regret, bad decisions, possibilities, protection, acceptance, change, celebration, and more. All familiar themes that vary in emotions and is something to which readers are sure to relate to. Lambert took up the pen during a tough-and lonely- time thousands of miles away (out of the country) from home and family in the 1990's; he copyrighted 400 free verse poems on his return to the U.S. Writing became his therapy during those two years. Lambert wrote of experiences that left him both surprised, entangled in emotions, and painful to acknowledge. This is his first book of poetry - the good, the painful, the confusing.

AFFAIRS OF THE HEART Vol. 2

Published 2017

Black and white illustrated free verse poetry covering emotions of love, faith, friendship, joy, loss, trust, and much more that people can identify with. The author completed Affairs of the Heart, Volume 1 in 2016. The 288 page color-illustrated free verse poetry was well received and reviewed, prompting him to complete and publish Volume 2, the remaining poetry he wrote while out of the country in the 1990s.

Made in the USA
San Bernardino, CA
17 March 2020